DARING
TO WIN
Special Forces at War

DARING TO WIN

Special Forces at War

David Eshel

ARMS AND
ARMOUR

Arms and Armour Press
An imprint of the Cassell Group
Wellington House, 125 Strand, London WC2R 0BB

Distributed in the USA by Sterling Publishing Co. Inc.,
387 Park Avenue South, New York, NY 10016-8810

Distributed in Australia by Capricorn Link (Australia) Pty. Ltd.,
2/13 Carrington Road, Castle Hill, NSW 2154

British Library Cataloguing-in-Publication Data: a catalogue record
for this book is available from the British Library

ISBN 1-85409-283-9

Cartography by Peter Burton

Designed and edited by DAG Publications Ltd. Designed by David Gibbons;
edited by Michael Boxall; indexed by Peter Burton;
typeset by Ronset Typesetters, Darwen, Lancashire; camerawork by
M&E Reproductions, North Fambridge, Essex; printed and bound
in Great Britain by Hartnolls Limited, Bodmin, Cornwall.

Contents

Introduction

T he élite fighting unit is a vital component in most world armies today, even the smallest developing nation having a cadre of superior soldiers often charged with presidential protection but who display the same motivation as their counterparts worldwide. The history of Special Forces can be traced back to Biblical days, proving the validity of the need for the highly trained 'super warrior', and history records the existence and deployment of what we now call the élite unit in wars from Ancient Rome and the Crusades. Consider the reputation Genghis Khan and the Mongols created with their sweeping victories over Europe from China. At the vanguard of his forces were outstanding mounted warriors who attacked enemy weak points with speed and surprise, clearly anticipating the tenet of the Blitzkrieg strategy by centuries. Essentially the special force is created to perform similar tasks today, although the covert element of operations is more important than the dashing breakthrough of defences.

If the tools of his trade are now numerous, varied, and often at the leading edge of technology, in temperament today's élite soldier is still similar to his predecessors in the Old Testament. Trained to the highest levels the personal qualities required are more than mere fitness alone. Dedication is the fundamental criteria for these men: volunteering to fight outside normal conventions of warfare demands loyalty to cause and comrade for it is only working as a team that accomplishes a mission and ensures safe return afterward. Special purpose troops have always performed at the sharp end of warfare with raids behind enemy lines, isolated unit actions, rapid deployment to global trouble spots, daring rearguard stands and a readiness to use the unorthodox to achieve the impossible. Selected, trained and deployed apart from the main structure of their national forces, they are the *crème de la crème*. Their skills are extraordinary, their means irregular and their action daring and exciting.

This book is in no way intended as the definitive work on all special force teams and actions for, by the very nature of their secrecy, there are as many untold stories as there are those we know about. Rather the accounts which follow relate the most famous élite team deployments on land, at sea and in the air, limiting technical detail to highlight the drama inherent in this thrilling mode of warfare and hence give a flavour of the nature of the special force action. If you find it difficult to believe that you are not reading fiction, this book will have served to indicate just how awesome have been the nature of many of the tasks these men have undertaken, where risk is an accepted aspect of life. Background to the action has been given only to the degree that the reader can better understand the scope of the operation and overall perspective, but mostly the text is concentrated on the operations themselves. From stormtroopers in shell-torn France, the invasion beaches of Commando and Ranger fame, the flak-ridden skies of low-level bombing raids to the deserts of Kuwait and Iraq of recent drama; this is a story of dedication and valour unsurpassed.

PART ONE
Great Commando Actions

1. STORM TROOPERS ON THE WESTERN FRONT

In 1917 – the third year of the First World War – the German and Allied forces stood facing each other across the muddy wastes of Belgium and France like two huge wounded animals.

Both sides had lost enormous numbers of men during the months of trench warfare. The shell bombardment from both sides, together with double the average rainfall for that year, had wrecked the system of streams and dykes which normally drained the Flanders countryside; the entire area was one gigantic quagmire. Many men who slipped from the duckboards which criss-crossed the ground drowned in the sea of mud. The fear created by the almost incessant noise of the bombardments, together with the months spent living in the stinking, soaking wet trenches, could – and did – drive men mad.

The fighting was at an impasse – neither side could gain any ground and, if one did, it was at disproportionate cost in men. Field Marshal Haig, speaking from the British HQ, spoke of 'successful operations by our troops', only to admit later that the actual ground gained was only a few hundred yards.

This static warfare caused great concern to military commanders on both sides; they needed a way out of the dead end; they looked for, and found, new tools of war.

On 15 September 1916, the British had sent 49 rhomboid-shaped steel monsters across the German lines at Flers on the River Somme – the first tanks ever used in action. Many of them suffered mechanical failure even before they started to move into action, but the very nature of their appearance, together with the fact that they withstood the vicious automatic fire of the machine-guns which had previously dominated the battleground, made a strong impression on the Germans. One year later the British tank attack at Cambrai placed the tank in the position which henceforth it never lost – that of the most effective means of restoring mobility on a static battlefield.

With less manpower available than the Allies, the Germans looked to other tactics in an endeavour to reduce losses. Accordingly some German commanders, using their own initiative, found a method of carrying out infantry attacks in a more cost-effective manner, and with improved results. Thus were born the storm troop battalions – some of which first saw action in the great offensive of March 1918.

Actually, the concept had already been demonstrated some six months earlier, in the Baltic region, where German assault battalions used the indirect approach to rout a large, entrenched enemy force. The action took place in September 1917, at Riga, near the Baltic coast, where the 12th Russian Army held a bridgehead along the River Dvina. The commander of the German troops was General Oskar von Hutier, an unconventional and open-minded soldier. He realized that the Russian position inside the bridgehead was heavily defended in depth, with the best troops deployed forward to meet the imminent attack. His plan, therefore, was to force a crossing over the river on the enemy's flank, and then to turn northwards toward the coast, thus surrounding the Russians within their own brigehead. To spearhead his main body he used specially trained assault troops who could infiltrate the enemy lines and, using speed and individual firepower, quickly overcome local resistance while the remainder worked themselves around the enemy's main line of defence.

On 1 September 1917 the attack went in, after a relatively short preparatory bombardment by the artillery, including chemical shells which temporarily blinded the defenders, allowing the outflanking attack to go in unnoticed. Once across the river, the German assault troops quickly gained ground. They advanced past the Russian defenders, who were completely surprised by the unconventional nature of the attack. Within hours the Russian front was in chaos, thousands of troops streaming eastwards in an attempt to escape the trap. Of course, the Russian defeat could have been excused on the grounds that most of them no longer cared who won this particular war. Their Tsar had abdicated the previous March, and the entire nation was in a state of flux.

No such excuse could be used, however, for the next exercise of the new German tactics, which took place one month later on the Isonzo-Caporetto sector of the Italian front. In the course of a major offensive, German assault infantry again bypassed the main centres of resistance along the front line and, despite the Italians' attempt to stop them, the Germans were soon in hot pursuit of the defenders, who broke and ran in total disorder as far as the River Piave. One of the officers who took part in this action was a 25-year-old German officer named Erwin Rommel, who had already distinguished himself in front-line combat.

Rommel commanded an attack force of the newly formed Württemberg Mountain Battalion of the Alpine Corps, which was ordered to capture Monte Matajur, south-west of Caporetto. An Austrain regiment had suffered badly from the Italians and was calling desperately for help. Rommel's unit was given permission to attack the Italian flank independently and, leading two companies across the Italian front line before dawn, Rommel managed to penetrate the enemy position at first light, and soon captured an important artillery position.

Once that position had been secured, Rommel left a small force to hold it while he pushed on in to the enemy's rear zone with the rest of his force. As he started to deploy, one of his runners rushed up to report that his other force was being attacked by an entire Italian battalion. Not losing a moment, Rommel gathered his men and took the Italians by surprise in the rear. They surrendered in droves as soon as he opened fire. When he sent back scores of prisoners, his battalion HQ were happy to send him four more companies to continue the attack, which he then led as a composite force back into the enemy's rear zone.

The Italians were still occupied with their own front lines, so Rommel's force was undetected. On the mountain slopes, the Germans captured about 2,000 men of the 4th Bersaglieri Brigade, which was on its way up. Then, cutting straight across country towards the key enemy position, Rommel drove his almost exhausted troops throughout the night in a gruelling forced march. At dawn they came unexpectedly down the mountain to assault the enemy in the rear. Rommel had been on the move continuously for more than fifty hours, had covered some 20 kilometres of enemy territory and climbed a mountain of about 3,000 metres. Finally he was able to fire his success rocket on the summit, having captured it, together with thousands of prisoners and a large amount of booty. It was a remarkable operation, carried out with great dash and courage, for which he was awarded Germany's highest decoration, the Pour le Merite, very rarely conferred on such a junior officer.

On the Western front the continuing stagnation called for new techniques, and the Germans soon formed assault troops into special battalions to spearhead their divisions. The storm troopers were chosen from the best men available. Many of them were young volunteers, quite rare in the war-weary armies of later 1917 and early 1918. These willing youngsters were led by young officers who, hating the boredom of the trenches, were quite ready for any new activity, however dangerous it might be.

This tactical unit evolved into a squad of 14 to 18 men. Each squad had its own fire-base – a light machine-gun and a light mortar. Assault rifles, newly introduced, were also used by the storm troopers for the first time, substantially increasing the amount of fire. The method of attack involved the storm troopers advancing behind a rolling artillery barrage, probing for weak spots in the enemy defence. Centres of strong resistance, if known in advance, or encountered during the attack, would be bypassed, thus increasing the speed of infiltration into the enemy rear zone. The guiding principle was to maintain the momentum of the offensive and to push forward, catching the enemy unprepared, at which point the breakthrough would be forced.

As the assault units pushed through at full speed, the main body of the attack would follow and exploit the breakthrough, while the storm troopers raised havoc in the enemy command and supply centres in the rear.

Although this method was not a dramatic innovation, it nevertheless attained considerable success when practised by the Germans, due to the element of surprise. The main reason for their success, however, was the German élite troops' determination, which overwhelmed the war-weary Allied troops who, immobile in their trenches, were unprepared for the sheer audacity of the German onslaughts.

On 21 March 1918, for example, the storm troopers infiltrated the British positions, quickly bypassing isolated strongpoints. The front of British Fifth Army was soon ripped apart and the German tide poured through. It was a spectacular success. Making skilful use of assault rifles, light maching-guns and grenades, the German élite units also used man-pack flame-throwers to reduce enemy machine-gun positions and bunkers. Jumping over trenches without stopping to deal with the men defending them – as dictated by their new assault tactics – the storm troopers fought their way forward as far as the British artillery zone, and destroyed the guns. Then they pressed on to the command centres, which were attacked before the British could organize a defence.

Continual movement was the very essence of their tactics, and it paid off handsomely. Behind the storm troops came specially trained battle groups to reduce strongpoints which had been left unconquered. Then, while the British commanders were rallying their men, the mass of the German infantry divisions came on, mopping up the last resistance, and securing the captured ground. German battle flights flew overhead, strafing the retreating enemy troops and creating more confusion.

The new offensive spirit demonstrated by the German storm troopers came too late in the war to enable the German High Command to win. The fighting spirit of the assault troops was superb but the main body of the army was extremely war weary and, after two days of non-stop fighting, the German attack – without sufficient reinforcements – started to peter out. The battleground was the site of the old battles of the Somme, where the mud hampered the German advance considerably, leading to the failure of their strategic objectives.

Another factor in the Germans' final lack of success was that fresh American troops were being fed into the front line to bolster the Allied front. Their appearance caused a significant loss of morale in the German ranks, their advance was halted, and an Allied counter-offensive soon struck the final blow, bringing four years of warfare to an end.

2. COMMANDO RAID INTO POLAND

According to the history books, Hitler's *Wehrmacht* invaded Poland at dawn on 1 September 1939, but combat operations had actually started four days earlier, when a small group of German commandos fought a sharp battle near the railway station at Mosty – just inside the triangle formed by the borders of Germany, Poland and Slovakia. They fought very well. It was just that – due to a misunderstanding – they had started a little early!

Thursday, 24 August 1939: An unending stream of German military traffic made its way over the dusty roads toward the Polish border. Tension was high all over the world. At noon on that day, Lieutenant-Colonel Adolf Heusinger, senior duty officer at the German GHQ, made an important telephone call to the chief of intelligence, informing him that Adolf Hitler had decided that 'H' Hour – the code-name for the invasion of Poland – was to be at 0415 hours on Saturday, 26 August. Eight hours after that call, a special order went out over the wire to a secret unit, consisting of 26 highly trained men, commanded by Lieutenant Dr Hans Herzner, a reserve officer experienced in covert operations.

Among his more recent exploits was a plot to eliminate Hitler himself, which was due to have been carried out by a special team under his orders in Berlin, but had been called off at the last moment by someone high up in the *Wehrmacht*. Luckily for him, Herzner's plan was not discovered by the Gestapo, so he was able to return to his unit at Breslau unscathed.

On Friday, 25 August Italy's leader, Mussolini, decided to call off his promised support for Germany and remain neutral – at least for the present. At the same time, intelligence reports indicated that Great Britain had just signed a defence pact with Poland, which France was about to join. Hitler, fearing to start a war without Italy's support and against a united front, hesitated, and ordered his general staff to stop all military preparations.

This last-minute order caused turmoil in the German GHQ, where plans were already in high gear. Staff officers frantically telephoned divisional commands, telling them to stop their forces, some of which were already poised to strike at dawn. Only a well-oiled military machine like the *Wehrmacht* could have achieved the feat of stopping the proceedings, as they did, at the very last moment. It was too late, however, to stop Herzner.

Early in the evening of 24 August, Herzner, dressed in civilian clothes, entered his private car and drove through the night, crossed the Slovakian border, and arrived at the HQ of the German 7th Infantry Division at Cadca on the Polish border. The Germans were based in wooded positions on the mountain slopes, camouflaged, and poised for action. Unaware that the invasion had been postponed, the staff briefed Herzner on his mission: He was to infiltrate Polish territory after midnight on 26 August, make for the Mosty railway station, where he would link up with special agents already in place, then take the station in a *coup de main*. With the station in German hands, immediate measures were to be taken to prevent the demolition of the adjacent railway tunnel leading to the border by removing the explosive charges placed there by the Poles. The operation had to be completed by 0200, to allow time for the capture of the entire area by dawn.

Herzner organized his small force into two assault teams. One was commanded by himself and included twelve men, some of whom knew the terrain well; the second team was commanded by his deputy, with fourteen men. That evening the men set out on foot towards the border, crossing it near Dejuwka, at point 627, a prominent feature which was easily identifiable even in darkness. Despite their familiarity with the terrain the scouts frequently went wrong, and it took both the teams much longer than planned to reach their objectives. At 2.30 a.m., however, Herzner and his men were in place, undetected, overlooking the station at Mosty. En route they had passed several machine-gun positions, totally unmanned, but – to their surprise – there were several Polish soldiers on guard near the tunnel. Soon after their arrival rifle fire was heard from that direction: the second assault team had clashed with the Poles, losing one man in the process, but the encounter caused no reaction at Mosty.

Herzner decided not to wait any longer for his second group, and ordered his men to begin the attack. Shortly before 4 a.m. the small team stormed the station, meeting only very light opposition from a few guards, and the station was soon captured. Leutnant Herzner disconnected the telephone and interrogated the German-speaking Polish commander, who informed him that the charges had been removed from the tunnel the previous day. Apparently the Poles had already done Herzner's work for him. However, his mission was not over yet.

Soon after he had finished talking to the Polish commander, Herzner heard renewed firing from the direction of the tunnel: the Polish guards had courageously mounted a counter-attack on the German team, which was hiding nearby in the dark. Ignoring German fire, the Poles approached Mosty station along the railway line. Firing also began from the other direction. Herzner's situation had become extremely dangerous, as he had no contact with his other group, nor with the German division on the border.

In order to test the situation in the tunnel, and regain contact with the German troops at Cadca, he sent two men in a steam locomotive along the tracks to the German border. At the same time he herded the captured Poles into the station master's room, and organized the rest of his team into all-round defensive positions.

After an eventful ride, Herzner's two 'engine-drivers' made it unscathed to Cadca, where they arrived shortly after 6 a.m., to be met by a surprised 7th Division intelligence officer. The division, which had by then received the postponement orders, had been trying to raise Herzner's force throughout the night, hoping to get through to them in time to prevent them making contact with the Poles at Mosty. When Herzner's messengers arrived at Cadca, they were turned round and sent straight back to Herzner with instructions to break off all contact with the Poles and get back to the border immediately, in order to prevent an embarrassing situation for the Führer. However, just as his men started on their return journey, Herzner finally managed to get through to the 7th Division HQ by telephone, and he was given his orders verbally.

Herzner did his best to comply with them, but he was in a tight spot. An attempt to leave by train failed when the Poles blew up the track just as the locomotive left the station, forcing the Germans to return to their lines on foot. As the small force left the railway station, heading for the high ground, it was pounded by the enemy, compelling Herzner and his men to make a detour.

Meanwhile Corporal Kulik, returning to Mosty by locomotive, had no idea that Herzner's force had already left. As he entered the tunnel, his team was fired upon by Polish guards. Returning the fire, Kulik increased speed and passed through the tunnel. Suddenly he saw cables which led to explosive charges. Kulik leapt from the still-moving engine, and cut the cables with an axe. But as he left the tunnel he realized that the Poles were once again in charge of the station.

Outside the station, he noticed some men hiding in the brush above the tunnel. Taking a chance, he shouted to them in German – and was answered in the same language! It was the second team, which was still holding its position, unaware of the changed orders from Divisional HQ. Kulik immediately ordered the leader to assemble his men and make for the border by the fastest possible route.

As the Germans began their trek on foot, they were again engaged by the Poles, but succeeded in evading them, and entered a wood which gave them cover. From there it was only a short distance to safety.

The last of Herzner's group reached the Slovakian border, after having been in Polish territory for twelve hours. Herzner's private war was over – and was totally ignored by the Polish high command, much to the relief of the German staff officers, who had been in a state of high anxiety!

Herzner received a well-earned decoration, the first any German officer received in the Second World War. However, his career was cut short when, after some hair-raising exploits in Russia, he was eliminated by the Gestapo, who apparently had found out by then about his involvement in the plot to kill Hitler.

3. DAWN ATTACK ON EBEN EMAEL

T he small, water-logged country of Belgium was always a tempting target for the Germans as part of their strategies against northern France. At the beginning of The First World War, masses of German infantry stormed the forts blocking the way across the River Meuse, which were finally reduced by tremendous firepower from German siege guns.

When Hitler's juggernaut once more made ready for its attack on the west, at the beginning of the Second World War, Belgium stood in the way again, while the Germans stood poised to attack. However, before the German panzers could strike at the Dutch – Belgian water obstacles along the border, they planned a series of commando operations in order to seize key objectives, thus ensuring that all such obstacles would be in German hands before their armour started to move westwards.

The Belgians were aware of these 'secret' plans, and decided to focus on fixed border fortresses, designed to delay German progress, even if they could not entirely halt it. Although the seemingly impregnable forts had been battered into submission in 1914, the Belgians still placed great faith in such defensive measures and, with their topographical advantages and heavy armament in modern fortifications, they believed that they could withstand or delay a German ground attack, at least until Anglo-French reinforcements arrived.

One of these forts was Eben Emael, constructed during the 1930s, and one of the most modern, well-constructed fortifications ever built. The fort, located in excellent topographical conditions, had been built in the space of three years – ironically, using the expertise of two German construction companies, Hochtief AG Essen and Dycherhoff and Widmann of Wiesbaden. Although this has never been officially revealed, one must assume that some information was made available to the German military from records kept by these two companies, since the German assault forces underwent extremely thorough training on an almost identical model prior to the attack.

The German command – although convinced of the efficacy of its *Blitzkrieg* tactics, which had already proved themselves in Poland and, recently, in Scandinavia – were not completely certain about being able to breach the formidable line of forts guarding the Belgian frontier. It was Hitler who came up with an unconventional – and unprecedented – solution: an airborne attack, using gliders to transport a highly trained *coup de main* force to reduce the Belgian fortress. Thus, in this impromptu manner, was conceived one of the most brilliant military operations the world had ever known.

Commanding the 7th German Airborne Division was General Kurt Student, a former First World War fighter ace and a close friend of Reichsmarschall Herman Goering, commander of the *Luftwaffe*. At noon on 27 October 1939, with the war barely two months old, Student was alerted to fly to Berlin immediately and present himself at Hitler's chancellery. He wasted no time, flying his Fieseler Storch light aeroplane straight to Tempelhof airfield, where he was whisked off by limousine to meet the Führer. Hitler led the general to a map and some aerial photographs and pointed at Eben Emael. Indicating that he knew that Student had made many test flights with gliders, he asked if a glider-borne assault could be mounted to reduce the Belgian fort. At first this daring idea seemed incredible to Student; on second thoughts, though, it didn't sound so bad, so he asked for time to consider.

A day later, having studied the problem thoroughly, Student gave an affirmative reply, on condition that any landing had to be made during daylight, so that pilots could identify their exact landing positions on the fortification grounds, enabling the combat teams to seize their objectives without too much exposure to enemy fire. The German high command would have preferred to work in darkness, for the sake of surprise, but Student got his way and was given the green light to start a detailed planning and training programme. His orders were to seize the fort and three major bridges in the neighbourhood, over which the German assault planned to pass into Belgium.

The fortress of Eben Emael was poised 60 metres above the Albert Canal, and measured some 900 metres from north to south, shaped like a menacing arrowhead pointing north towards Maastricht. Anti-tank ditches had been constructed to blend in with water-filled moats. The defences included a series of casemates or cupolas with revolving guns, machine-guns set in concrete and anti-aircraft gun cupolas. In the southern part of the fort were three triple and two twin 75mm gun batteries, and one heavy twin 120mm long-range battery. Another battery, situated in the centre, served as ground defence for the fort itself, and consisted of anti-tank guns in blockhouses. There were also some gun positions in the outer defences. The gun batteries and outer positions were linked by seven kilometres of underground tunnels, where the troop accommodation, ammunition chambers and control centres were situated.

The Belgian garrison totalled some 1,200 men, but at the time of the German attack about half of the men were in their billets nearby. The commander of the fort was Major Jean Jottrand, a veteran regular who knew his trade well.

As commander of his attack team General Student chose a young captain named Koch – a sensitive, highly talented officer with sufficient imagination to carry out such a daring feat of arms. The choice of Koch emphasized that, even at this early stage of the war, senior commanders of high quality were choosing relatively junior commanders even for important strategic missions which might determine the outcome of entire operations, whereas – in other armies – more senior officers would probably have been chosen. To lead the attack on the fort itself, Koch selected Leutnant Rudolf Witzig, a quick-witted paratrooper, always ready for a fight.

Having selected their men from the cream of the crop in 7th Flieger Division, the commanders instituted a thorough training schedule, which included precise battle drills on a specially constructed model, the objective itself remaining a well-guarded secret until the very last moment. Secrecy, indeed, was the name of the game during the whole operation. The men trained for six months in an enclosed camp at Hildesheim under conditions of total secrecy and under threat of death if security were breached.

The German military command had been experimenting with para-chutes and gliders ever since the Treaty of Versailles of 1919 had prohibited Germany from engaging in any military activities. They realized the advantages of glider operations over dropping men by parachute. A glider could carry a squad of heavily armed soldiers straight into battle, whereas paradrops could only scatter lightly armed men over large areas, making it extremely difficult to assemble them into combat groups in time to gain their objective. Hence, during the early 1930s, when the Germans were reconsidering their offensive options, new military gliders were constructed, among them the DFS 230 – an aircraft capable of carrying about one and a half tons of combat load. The DFS 230 was produced in quantities prior to the start of the war. It was towed by the tri-motor Ju 52, one of the best transport aircraft ever made.

Assault Force Granite, slated to storm the fort, was commanded by Leutnant Rudolf Witzig, and originally numbered 85 men. They were heavily armed, carrying – in addition to automatic assault rifles and grenades – the main demolition loads, aimed at reducing the gun batteries. These demolition loads contained hollow-charge explosives, never before tried in action. Invented in the late 19th century by an American scientist, the hollow-charge was a hitherto untried concept: When exploded, a powerful detonation produced a shock wave, creating ultra-high pressures and temperatures. The hollow cavity over which the charge was shaped then drove inward, producing a thin, powerful jet of molten steel, which burned through the steel or concrete target, causing devastation unprecedented in warfare up to that time. The Germans had developed two hollow-charge explosive devices: one a two-piece 110-pounder, and the second, a bell-shaped 25-pounder for smaller targets, which would be carried by one man.

As the time for the operation drew nearer, Force Granite arrived at Ostheim airfield, just outside Cologne. The gliders had been transported in furniture vans late at night in order to safeguard the secrecy of the operation, and were hidden in specially constructed hangars at Ostheim and another airfield near Cologne, Butzweiler.

On the evening of 9 May the men gathered at the airfields to receive last minute instructions. Take-off was planned for 0430 the next morning, to coincide with first daylight over the target area. The men were more than ready for action. They had trained on their model for months without knowing the actual target. Each man knew his personal mission thoroughly, and could operate his weapons and demolition charges with his eyes closed.

The darkened airfields were alive with activity – most of it silent – as the ground crews manhandled gliders towards their tow planes and connected cables by the light of their torches. Then the silence was broken by the roar of dozens of heavy aero engines starting, their pilots opening their throttles to test the power. The assault teams went aboard their gliders and silently settled into the cramped tandem seats, taking care that their weapons would not damage the thin fuselage. Leutnant Witzig's force, 85 men in all, were ready for action.

The men started singing their battle songs to relieve their tension as the planes picked up speed, and soon the noise of the roller-coaster wheels stopped as the gliders became airborne. The great armada was on course,

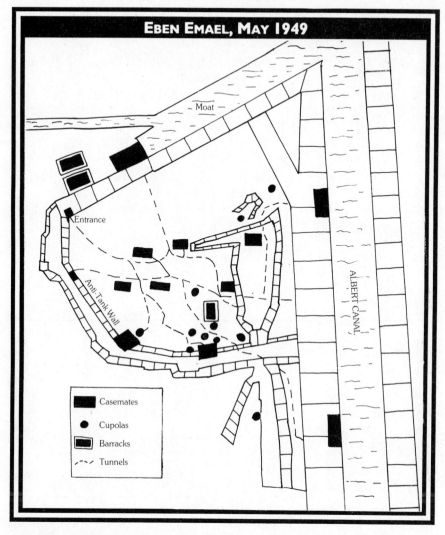

EBEN EMAEL, MAY 1949

- Moat -

Entrance

Anti-Tank Wall

ALBERT CANAL

Casemates

Cupolas

Barracks

Tunnels

navigating by a series of pre-placed beacons lighting the way from the Rhine to the Belgian border.

At 0335, precisely on schedule, the last glider took off. In it were Leutnant Witzig and his reserve team. Corporal Pilz, a seasoned glider pilot, was at the controls. The countryside was totally blacked out, making identification of the beacons easy. The pilot had just passed one when suddenly the glider was jerked roughly downward. Everyone inside stiffened in shock, but Pilz kept his head and wrestled with the controls. There was no communication with the tow plane pilot, but Pilz realized what had caused the disturbance: Another plane had crossed their flight path and he had to take immediate evasive action in order to avoid collision. He dived, and the tow rope broke under the pressure, whipping against the fuselage. There was no chance of making the target, and the pilot landed in a field west of the Rhine.

Once safely down, the officer ordered his men to clear the field for eventual take-off, and set off to find a telephone.

Unaware of the misfortune which had befallen their leader, Force Granite was on its way to the Belgian border, which it crossed at 2,500 metres altitude at 0430 German time – 0330 Belgian time. Shortly before, another glider had had to turn back, reducing the force to nine gliders and their combat teams.

In the fort at Eben Emael, the duty officer was awakened from his sleep by an urgent telephone call from his HQ at Liège, ordering him to alert the fort for immediate action as German troop movements had been observed near the border. There had been many such calls, all of them up to now false alarms. Major Jottrand, however, decided not to take any chances, and ordered immediate action. Although half his men were not immediately available – billeted in the nearby village – soon the giant fort came to life as sleepy gun crews raced for their cupolas, some of them still buttoning their tunics. By the time the men from the village were assembled it was already three in the morning, just as Force Granite crossed the border.

Soon after, while making his rounds, Jottrand heard artillery fire from the direction of Maastricht, and he alerted his anti-aircraft crews to be ready for action. Then reports came in of enemy paratroops landing near the bridges of Canne, Vroenhoven and Veldwezelt. Machine-guns started chattering from the direction of the bridges. Suddenly, in the haze of dawn, unfamiliar silhouettes came swooping down over the fort. The sergeant in charge of the air defence battery hesitated, as he could not identify the aircraft insignia, but Jottrand ordered him to open fire. Then he contacted the officer in charge of the Canne bridge and ordered him to explode the demolition charges. When the first German glider troops landed, the bridge blew up in their faces, but it was the only one – the rest were captured intact by the German assault teams.

At 0425 the frightening shapes came to rest on Fort Eben Emael. None of the defenders had yet realized that they had become the target of the world's first airborne attack from gliders. Private Remy was at his anti-aircraft gun when he saw strange forms in the sky above. Before he had time to shout, a great dark object swooped overhead, barely missing his head. The gun crew just stared as the aircraft landed straight in front of them, too low to shoot at. But soon there were other targets, as more gliders came into view, manoeuvring for landing positions. Before Remy had time to fire, however, he was killed by a grenade lobbed into his position by the German paratroopers who had landed nearby.

One of the German assault teams was tasked with taking out the anti-aircraft guns which were firing yellow tracer, making their positions easy to identify. Bullets tore through the glider's fabric, but the pilot coolly made a perfect landing a few metres from the gun position. As the glider came to a halt, a wing was torn off, but no one was hurt, and soon the team leader was outside, lobbing grenades into the gun position where four terrified Belgians were staring at the Germans, their hands up high in surrender.

German gliders were now landing all over the fort. There was some resistance, but most of the fire was badly aimed, as the gun control crews were confused by the Germans coming at them from all directions. The assault teams were now racing to place the hollow-charge explosives in strategic positions, setting the fuzes and then speeding on to the next target. There were tremendous explosions as gun tubes were hurled from their trunnions and men were flung headlong to the ground. Inside the fort men were thrown from their seats and blown on to the walls. Those who were not killed outright were in shock and unable to act. Even those who remained on their feet were prevented from acting by the smoke and dust which covered everything. Wounded men were dragged into the corridors; some of the survivors staggered groggily down to the lower parts of the fort, where they met confused officers trying to get some order into the chaos.

By now, however, the Germans were already inside the fort, having jumped through the holes blown by demolition charges. The gliders had landed so close to the target that the German assault teams were able to reach their goals in seconds. They were so well trained that they fought individually, without central control, so that Witzig's absence was hardly noticed. Only when team leaders had completed their missions did they find out that their commander was missing. Master Sergeant Wenzel, the senior NCO, took over command and was directing the battle when suddenly, in the heat of the fighting, a lone glider came in to land on the fort in broad daylight. It was Lieutenant Witzig who, having commandeered a tow plane, managed to take off and join his men just in time to direct the critical aftermath of the action inside the fort.

Meanwhile, on the river below, two major bridges were captured intact, enabling the German armoured spearheads to cross. Only the bridge at Canne had been demolished. Later in the morning a German sapper battalion managed to force a crossing of the canal and blew their way through a heavily fortified blockhouse to enter the fortress, in time to beat off a hastily ordered Belgian counter-attack.

While the sappers were still fighting on the far side of the fort, however, Witzig's units were facing heavy fire from Belgian artilley above the fort; many of the Germans took cover inside the damaged cupolas. Witzig realized that he was in trouble, as his small force was much too weak to withstand a major counter-attack. But the Belgians, too, had trouble mounting their counter-attack. Due to lack of communications, they had no information as to which part of the fort was actually in German hands. Jottrand's men therefore charged only single casemates. During the day several local counter-attacks were tried, but they were mostly sporadic and half-hearted, especially when Witzig managed to call in Stukas for support. Despite the Belgians' low morale, however, they managed to hold out during the night – a fairly pointless operation, since the German panzers had bypassed the fort and were already on their way into Belgium.

The next morning, after a terrific explosion shook the Belgian command post, the battle, to all intents, was over, although the Belgians still held out for another 36 hours. The Belgians lost 23 dead and 59 wounded, the Germans six dead and fifteen wounded. In all only 55 men from Witzig's Force Granite fought at Eben Emael. They had carried out their task with superb courage, and great success. Because of them, Eben Emael never became a threat to the German ground attack forces, as its guns were silenced long before the first German tank neared the banks of the river over which the fort was poised.

Lieutenant Witzig survived the war and became a colonel in the new Bundeswehr. Captain Koch was killed during the war in a road accident, driving a fast sports car. Eben Emael was used by the Germans as a machine shop after its capture; its guns – those that remained intact – were used in the Atlantic Wall defences. Towards the end of the war, as the US Army neared the German frontier, the Americans assumed that the Germans would put up a stiff fight in the fort, but their intelligence was wrong: It had already been evacuated when the Americans attacked.

4. THE COMMANDO ATTACK ON VAAGSO

I n the bitter aftermath of France's conquest by Germany and the forced evacuation of the British forces from Dunkirk, Britain in 1940 was isolated and in urgent need of an offensive victory. It was in this atmosphere that the Commandos were founded, and shortly after Dunkirk the first reconnaissance raid was made against the coast of France, while they were still a motley force of volunteers, assembled from all branches and units of the British Army.

However, the first period of the Commandos' existence was a fairly frustrating one and, in order to maintain the enthusiasm of the men, a successful morale-raising operation was needed. The right man for the job was thought to be Commodore Lord Louis Mountbatten, chief of the newly created Combined Operations Force. Mountbatten, then only 41 years old, was quick-witted and imaginative, possessed first-class leadership qualities and – just as important – had a fine sense of inter-service relationships.

Vaagso, in the fiords of Norway, was the site chosen for the operation. It would be a first attempt to attack a well-defended target using the element of surprise, and would also serve as a trial run for future attacks. The thinking behind the choice of Vaagso was that it would pin the Germans down in that remote region, forcing them to keep troops there instead of sending them to Europe or Africa. The objectives were to destroy German-held installations, mainly at the garrison in South Vaagso, where some 150 infantry and one tank were thought to be stationed.

The area was strongly fortified with a battery of captured Belgian 75mm guns which was mounted on the Island of Maaloy, only a few hundred metres from the mainland in the middle of the Ulvesund, blocking access into the fiord. There were four more guns on Rugsundo Island in the southern Vaagso fiord. The northern entrance into Ulvesund was protected by a mobile battery of the 105mm howitzers at Halsor. However, no German warships had been reported in the area up to the time of the raid, although there were three Luftwaffe airfields within range, two at Stavanger and Herdla to the south, and one at Trondheim to the north.

The British forces aiming to land at Vaagso were made up of five assault parties from No. 3 Commando, under Lieutenant-Colonel J. Durnford Slater, a former artilleryman who volunteered for the Commandos in 1940. Slater, a man full of energy, had extremely high standards both for himself and for his men, but he never expected his men to do anything he would not do himself – a trait which earned him the unstinting loyalty of all his soldiers.

No. 3 Commando formed the main body of the assault force, with two platoons added from No. 2 Commando, together with a detachment of Royal Engineers and some Norwegians – in all, 51 officers and 525 men. The attacking force was given strong air support, with Hampden bombers to drop bombs and smoke canisters and blind the defenders during the landing stage. Twin-engined Blenheims and Beaufighters would keep the Luftwaffe busy over their airfields.

The British naval force was made up of the light cruiser HMS *Kenya*, in which the naval and ground commanders would sail, four destroyers, a submarine, and two infantry assault ships. Commanding the force were Rear-Admiral Burrough and Brigadier Haydon.

In mid-December 1941, the raiding force assembled at Scapa Flow where final exercises were held and the men were thoroughly briefed. Scale models and recent aerial photographs helped to make each member of the combat team familiar with the objectives over which he was to fight.

On Christmas Eve 1941, the force sailed for the Shetlands, head on into a Force 8 gale. The lighter vessels, especially the landing ships, suffered most severely and many of the men were seasick. When the ships struggled into Sullom Voe at lunchtime on Christmas Day, the admiral was compelled to postpone the raid for 24 hours in order to repair the damaged ships and let the men recover. So at least they had their Christmas dinner on dry land.

The force sailed again on the afternoon of 26 December with a forecast of better weather – a relief to soldiers and sailors alike. However, it was still bitterly cold. As they neared the Norwegian coast, dawn was approaching; the sea was calm and visibility excellent. During the winter months in Norway, darkness prevails for most of the day, with only a few hours of twilight. Thus most of the attack would be made during night conditions, with only the moon lighting up the snow-covered surroundings – a near perfect setting for a combined operation.

As the line of ships steamed quietly into the sound, the men's attention was caught by a single light shining out like a beacon from the window of a hut on the hillside. The flotilla entered the Vaagso fiord and started to turn north and the commander ordered the battle ensign hoisted, lowering the landing craft into the water at the same time. It was 0842 but still dark.

Almost immediately, precisely on time, No. 50 Squadron's Hampdens appeared and began to attack the Rugsundo gun battery, while tracer bullets from the now-alerted German anti-aircraft guns pierced the dark sky. The arrival of the naval flotilla had not gone unnoticed: the German lookout on Husevaago Island had – very efficiently – phoned through to the battery on Maaloy, informing them that enemy ships were entering the sound. The German commander was in a Christmassy mood, however, and paid little attention to the warning.

While the guns remained strangely silent, an alert signaller on Maaloy did his best to raise the alarm. Having received a message by signal lamp, he ran to the beach, leaped into a boat and hastily rowed to the mainland where he ran straight to German naval HQ to deliver his warning. But the Germans, being sticklers for the rules, failed to inform the Army gun battery – since it was a different Service!

This delay allowed the first British Commando force to land almost unopposed on the shore at Hollevic, on the southern tip of the Vaagso fiord, where they dealt with the small German guard post without a shot being fired. Minutes later, the cruiser *Kenya* fired a salvo of starshells which illuminated the sky over Maaloy. During the next nine minutes the cruiser put down 450 6-inch shells on the island. Colonel Durnford Slater in the leading landing craft then fired a pre-arranged signal – ten Very light shells – calling for an end to the naval bombardment.

There then followed, according to plan, a smokescreen, placed by the RAF bombers, and a brief calm descended over the area. In the dark, the eerie sound of bagpipes could be heard as Major Jack Churchill, leading his two troops, encouraged his men with traditional Scottish 'tunes of glory'.

Advancing through the smokescreen in perfect battle order, the Commando quickly occupied Maaloy, encountering little opposition. However, while searching a building for documents, Major Churchill was badly wounded by an exploding demolition charge which went off nearby.

Meanwhile, on the mainland, Colonel Durnford Slater was the first man to step ashore at South Vaagso, leading 200 men into battle. As he stepped ashore, three RAF Hampden bombers made a low level attack, placing smoke and phosphorus bombs, one of which fell so close that it scorched the Colonel's tunic. One bomber, hit by German ground fire, went out of control and, before crashing into the sound, released a fire bomb which unfortunately fell into a landing craft, causing many casualties among the men. Ammunition and grenades exploded like a display of lethal fireworks which lit up the entire area and created some confusion.

The colonel's party landed at the base of some sheer, snow-covered rocks overlooking South Vaagso which was relatively clear of enemy machine-guns, since the defenders did not expect that a landing could be made in such rough terrain. Once on land, the Commandos set off along the single main road, prepared to fight their way into the town. Vicious street fighting followed, with the Germans defending every house. Having silenced two machine-gun posts barring the way, the Commandos moved rapidly up the main street, tossing grenades into houses, which started burning fiercely.

The vanguard was held up, however, by a determined group of Germans in the Ulvesund Hotel. The British troop commander, Captain Algy Forester, pulled the pin from his grenade and led the frontal attack. He reached the front door of the hotel, but was hit by a German bullet, and fell forward on his own grenade, which exploded, killing him outright. A Norwegian officer took command and led the charge, only to die in the doorway, but the defence caved in when a Commando sergeant fired a mortar shell from the hip, setting the building on fire. As the Germans tried to escape, they were taken on by the Commandos with tommy guns and grenades.

While this stiff fighting was going on in South Vaagao, the force in Maaloy was completing its mission there and, led by Captain Peter Young,

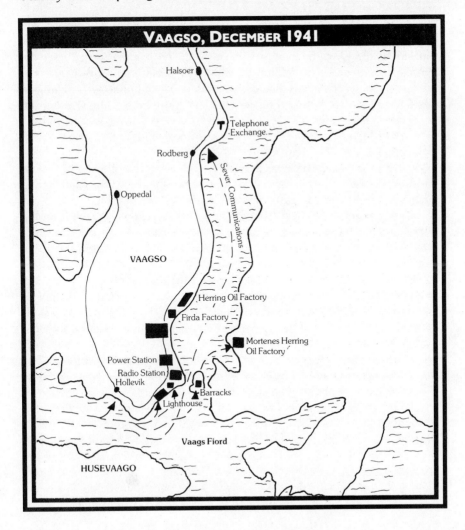

VAAGSO, DECEMBER 1941

moved off to the mainland to bolster the attack. First they rushed a warehouse, but were pinned down by heavy fire, the source of which could not be immediately defined. Young decided to move to another warehouse which was blocking his view. As they rushed across the open space, they were confronted by a solitary German who began to lob grenades at them, but, shooting from the hip, Young's Commandos reached the warehouse unscathed and threw their own Mills bombs into the building. They rushed in through the doorway, exchanging fire with some Germans defending the upper floor. Realizing the difficulty of taking the warehouse, Young decided to burn it down, but as he started organizing the action he suddenly saw Lieutenant O'Flaherty and one of his men kick down the front door and race into the building. Both men were hit by fire and fell in the middle of the room. Young rushed in, firing his tommy gun, and killed the two Germans who had fired. Then he dragged his two wounded men to safety and set the warehouse ablaze with fire bombs.

As his radios had malfunctioned, the colonel was totally out of touch with his combat teams which were fighting individual battles in the town; so, walking boldly forward down the main road, the colonel went to see for himself how things were getting on. His signals officer, followed by some runners, went with him. As the colonel passed one of the houses, a grenade was thrown and fell between his feet but, by some miracle, he was unhurt, apart from a few splinters. One of his runners, however, was badly wounded.

At noon, having joined up with his men and fought some sharp engagements with German snipers, the colonel decided to order a with-drawal: the short Arctic day was drawing to a close and most of the objectives had been achieved. The men started to make their way through blazing buildings, smoke and flames, toward the rendezvous on the shore.

The rearguard deployed to resist any German counter-attack from the north, but the operation was now completed, with virtually every military establishment destroyed. More than 100 Germans had been killed and about the same number taken prisoner, but despite the savage hand-to-hand fighting which had gone on for four hours, only one Norwegian was dead. The Navy, which had been operating in the fiord against German shipping, had sunk several merchant ships, totalling 16,000 tons. Some 77 Norwegians decided to join the withdrawing British Commandos and continue the fight against the Axis forces from Britain.

Vaagso had been a bruising fight for everyone concerned. The Rugsundo battery had managed to score a hit on the cruiser *Kenya* while it was directing operations. The RAF lost eight aircraft, but it succeeded in attacking the airfields and keeping the German fighters away from the operational area. The Commandos had lost 20 men killed in action and 57 wounded, most of these due to the tragedy of the fire bomb on the landing craft. But the raiders returned to base feeling that they had done well. For the first time since Dunkirk they had hit the Germans in their bases and given them a bloody nose. More than that, their conduct in battle fighting a determined enemy had demonstrated that their training and motivation was sound. Mountbatten's combined operations force was now ready to take on even more ambitious challenges.

5. THE BRUNEVAL RAID

When the Second World War started in 1939, British scientists had little or no knowledge of radar, and certainly had no access to any hardware used by the Germans. Actually German scientists had already begun radar research and development in 1934 and some of their equipment was deployed in early warning systems, mainly on ships, by the outbreak of the war. The RAF's attempts to carry the air offensive to the German mainland were frustrated by the German air defences, which were becoming more and more efficient as experience grew and more sophisticated tools became available. One of these tools was radar.

The first encounter with German radar was extremely lethal to the RAF: they lost several medium bombers over Wilhelmshaven in daylight during a raid in September 1939, the British raiders being detected by radar long before they reached their target.

Some hints of enemy activities in this field did reach British Intelligence in November 1939 in the report of a secret agent based in Oslo, Norway, describing two separate systems; another indication as to the deployment of radar was shown on a photograph taken by a journalist of the German raider *Graf Spee*, scuttled after the Battle of the River Plate on 18 December 1939. This photograph showed a gun ranging radar mounted topmast. An indistinct photograph of an apparatus mounted on a tower in the Berlin Tiergarten reached the RAF delegation in Washington in September 1941 via some Chinese scientists who had actually seen the device and described it as some six metres in diameter – much larger than anything hitherto known.

Two German radars, therefore, were known to exist. One – code-named Freya – was identified by the Enigma code-breakers in July 1940 and the other – known as Würzburg – remained shrouded in mystery.

At the end of November 1941, British Intelligence was intent on tracking the German radars. The English physicist Dr. Charles Frank was examining an aerial photograph of the German radar station near Bruneval on Cap d'Antifer, not far from Le Havre, when he noticed something strange: the radar position was situated on the high cliffs which rose steeply from the sea. He identified a foot track leading to an isolated house which Dr. Frank believed to be a command post, but on closer inspection he saw that the track also led to another structure, halfway to the house and to its right, which he could not identify.

Dr. Frank, an experienced man, sought assistance from Major Charles Wavell of the Photographic Intelligence Section at Medmenham, Berkshire, where some of the best interpreters were working. Frank and Wavell put their heads together and decided to request a low-level reconnaissance sortie to bring home a good photograph of the radar position.

On 3 December 1941 Flight Lieutenant Tony Hill went to Medmenham to be briefed by Major Wavell. They discussed the best way to fly in and photograph the site, and Wavell also mentioned the unidentified structure which Frank had seen. The following day Tony Hill flew his PR Spitfire to the French coast to see the thing for himself. As he approached the French coast he dived to zero height and raced over the cliffs, straight over the radar station. He identified a bowl-shaped object, which he estimated to be some three metres across, but when he returned to his base at RAF Benson, the photographic development section discovered to their dismay that the camera had not worked!

Next day Tony Hill went to Bruneval again, although, strictly speaking, it was against the rules to fly the same sortie two days in succession. This time the camera worked perfectly and the result was one of the best low-level photographs of the war. The close-ups were taken from such a low level that the pilot could actually see through the ground floor windows of the building near the radar installation.

Tony Hill's excellent photograph of the radar installation at Bruneval conveyed for the first time some indication of a Würzburg radar installation and, understandably, the British 'boffins' were very excited as they peered at the photograph in their workshop at Swanage on the south coast of England. A sharp-eyed scientist and an enthusiastic pilot had together launched one of the most famous – and most skilfully performed – combined operations of the war.

The idea of pilfering the Bruneval radar first took shape in the minds of Combined Operations HQ staff, headed by then Commodore Lord Louis Mountbatten, in January 1942. After an examination of the photographic data, it was suggested that a parachute raid be mounted instead of the more usual Commando landing from the sea – ruled out from the start by the steep cliffs overlooking the beach.

Although the German command post seemed to be located in the isolated house clearly visible in Tony Hill's photograph, it became known to the planners, through agents, that a farmhouse called the Presbytère – about 150 metres to the north – sheltered about one hundred men, part of a coastal defence company manning the outposts, as well as off-duty signallers and radar operators.

More serious was the company-sized local reserve force with armoured cars which was located at the village of Bruneval, about three kilometres to the south. A secondary macadamized road led from Bruneval to the north, about one kilometre from la Presbytère, with dirt tracks leading towards the coast. An infantry regiment serving as regional reserve was in garrison near Le Havre to the south. With such a large defensive force in the operational area, the entire success of the attack would depend on meticulous planning and ultra-rapid execution. A skilled, well-trained combined arms force was needed – a tactic which was still in its infancy in those days.

A team of British scientists headed by R. V. Jones met to consider exactly which parts of the radar would be needed for close examination. The best solution, of course, would be dismantle the entire installaion and bring it home. However, this possibility was ruled out almost immediately, as the equipment would have been much too heavy to lift, let alone haul to the beaches for transportation by sea. The 'boffins' therefore selected those parts of the system which had priority. For this job a special man was needed, a man with special expertise.

On 1 February 1942 Flight Sergeant E. Cox, an expert in radio and radar equipment, arrived at the Air Ministry in London and shortly found himself in the presence of an Air Commodore who congratulated him on having 'volunteered' for a very special mission. Cox was not given details of the nature of the job ahead, but was ordered to undergo parachute training at RAF Ringway, the paratroop training centre. Intrigued, he obeyed and soon reached the stage of being allowed to jump from a captive balloon in the middle of the night. To Cox it seemed that jumping out of the hole in the bottom of the basket was like looking out at a bottomless pit. However, he was soon jumping out of aeroplanes, and made five jumps to qualify him for the coveted blue parachute wings. Cox was no longer a 'wingless wonder'.

Meanwhile 'C' Company 2nd Parachute Regiment commenced a painstaking course of training, unaware of the task assigned to them. Commanding the company was Major John Frost, recently seconded to paratroops from the Cameronians. The six-footer was an experienced soldier who had seen action against Arab marauders in Palestine during the nineteen thirties, but he did not yet have his wings, so he hastened off to Ringway and completed a crash parachute course in only six days. Then, duly decorated, he returned to his men and took up command, training them for the difficult task which he knew lay ahead.

As training proceeded, the officers were briefed on their mission and viewed their objective for the first time at Medmenham, where RAF Intelligence had prepared a precise model of the Bruneval site – an exact reproduction of Tony Hill's photograph made by a soldier who was a sculptor in peacetime and whose skills were now being put to a different use. On this model, and with the aid of aerial photographs, Frost and his officers now worked out their plans and tactics.

In all 119 officers and men were to take part in the action, divided into three assault parties, each code-named after a famous sailor. This was partly in tribute to the Navy and partly in what was hoped would be the Navy's role in picking up survivors from the beach after completion of the mission. Designated to fly the assault teams in to their objective was No. 51 Squadron, flying Armstrong-Witworth Whitley bombers, by now almost obsolete for night flying, but still excellent troop carriers. The squadron was commanded by Wing Commander Charles Pickard, already well-known, and later to gain almost legendary fame flying a daring low-level raid against Amiens prison in which he and his Mosquito navigator were both killed.

The Bruneval mission became more urgent when the German battle cruisers *Scharnhorst* and *Gneisenau* weighed anchor from their moorings at Brest harbour and, heading out to sea, defied both the RAF and the Royal Navy, dashing in broad daylight through the English Channel and jamming British radar stations as close as 40 kilometres offshore. Prime Minister Winston Churchill, worried about the blow to British morale, urged prompt action. On 15 February Frost's force made its final parachute jump over Salisbury plain, and a week later all was ready.

The three parties of the raiding force aimed to land together on a designated drop zone far enough inland to avoid immediate detection, but close enough to prevent too much time being wasted. Well-defined ground markers, visible in darkness, would clearly identify the approach route to the objective. Commanding the main party would be the CO, with Lieutenant Peter Young, a journalist in peacetime, commanding the assault team under him. After securing the radar station, Frost would bring in the team of experts, including sappers from 1st Field Squadron Royal Engineers under Captain Denis Vernon, whose task was to dismantle the radar sections indicated by Sergeant Cox. The sappers had been specially trained on a British artillery radar set which was as close in appearance to the German one as the British scientist could get. Leading the second party, with 40 men, was paratroop Lieutenant Charteris of the King's Own Scottish Borderers, whose task it was to secure the defended beach area and cover the retreat. The last party, headed by Lieutenant John Timothy of the Royal West Kent Regiment, with 30 men, was to act as a blocking force sealing off the combat area from German reinforcements.

After several postponements due to bad weather, conditions on Thursday 27 February were perfect, with a full moon and high tide, the target itself covered in snow. Twelve twin-engined Whitleys lined up on the tarmac at RAF Thruxton in Wiltshire and Frost's paratroopers emplaned with their cumbersome gear. One by one the heavily laden aircraft gathered speed and took off, Major Frost in the lead flying in Pickard's Whitley.

As the formation roared over the airfield heading for France, the naval task force of landing craft and motor gunboats, under the command of Captain E. N. Cook of the Australian Navy, were already well on their way out to sea toward the rendezvous off the Bruneval beach. To distract enemy attention, Bomber Command had mounted several diversionary raids north and south of the target area so that aircraft noise would not attract too much attention.

The force arrived safely at their drop zone, although some flak was encountered near Le Havre, causing some damage but no losses in men. However, just before the drop zone was reached, two Whitleys with Lieutenant Charteris's party aboard were forced to take evasive action and thus went slightly off course, dropping the men further inland than planned.

Major Frost jumped first, quickly followed by all his party, and everyone fell safely to the soft snow-covered ground, the entire drop unnoticed by the sleeping Germans, who by now were accustomed to the nightly noise of aircraft. Operation 'Biting' was on its way.

As the sound of engines faded into the night, Frost whispered his final instructions to his party leaders and all set off to their assigned objectives. Moving quickly, four men at his heels, the major burst into the isolated command post, killing a German soldier with his Sten gun. Outside, sounds of battle could be heard as Lieutenant Young and his men raced into the radar post. When Frost joined him there, having left two men guarding the house, he found the position already secure; some Germans were dead and one terrified German radar operator sat in shocked silence, watching Captain Vernon and Sergeant Cox examining his set. Soon the sappers were at work, dismantling the vital parts selected by Cox. This included the receiver, amplifier, the pulse generator unit and the transmitter. Finally Cox selected parts of the antennae elements. The whole operation was carried out by flashlight. This started to draw fire from the enemy who had been awakened by the sounds of shooting.

Time was running short now. Noises of motors could be heard coming from the east as German reinforcements started to arrive. They were fired on by Lieutenant Timothy's road-block party, hiding near the road. Major Frost and his men were now forming a defensive perimeter round the position, but Frost urged Cox, Vernon and the sappers to hurry as the fire grew in intensity. One man was killed and two bullets struck a part of the apparatus which Cox was hauling out of the radar station, but fortunately he was unhurt.

Meanwhile, Charteris and his party, who had been dropped further inland, were making their way towards the sound of guns in an effort to join Frost. They finally caught up with him near the largest pillbox overlooking the beach. By now the work inside the radar station was nearing completion, with the last units being ripped from their consoles, manhandled with crowbars by the sappers. Then, hauling their precious prizes on their backs, they began their withdrawal over the winding track down the cliffs to the beach which was, however, still heavily defended by Germans.

Charteris and his men, yelling their war cry. 'Caber Feigh', and supported by Timothy's unit, rushed the German positions on the beach with machine-gun and grenade attacks, storming the cliffs just as Frost and his party were withdrawing with their heavy load. Just after two in the morning, the beach secure, all parties assembled on the beach, waiting for the boats to arrive.

Several attempts to raise the naval commander by radio failed to produce results, but finally the dark shapes of the landing craft glided across the water, and beached. A covering party was landed and took up positions to ward off any last-minute attempt by the Germans to interrupt the embarkation. British gunboats started to fire at the clifftop positions still manned by the Germans, while Major Frost directed the embarkation. Soon most of his force was safely aboard the landing craft, which immediately put out to sea beyond the range of the German fire, which had been intensifying as reinforcements arrived on the clifftop.

Once out at sea, the raiders were taken off the landing craft on to fast gunboats which made for the shores of England, landing craft in tow. On its way across the Channel, the naval flotilla was met by a Squadron of RAF Spitfires, who covered it through the final passage. On board one of the boats was Dr. R. V. Jones, impatiently waiting to examine the equipment. He was more than pleased with what he saw.

So ended the raid on Bruneval which, at the cost of two killed in action, six wounded and six missing, had fulfilled exactly its planners' intentions. Most of the radar equipment taken off contributed greatly to the improvement of Bomber Command's operational efficiency. One stroke of luck was the 'acquisition' of a German radar operator who was able to contribute greatly towards understanding the German equipment. The Bruneval Würzburg radar had far-reaching effects on British radar developments and electronic warfare countermeasures. The Germans increased their vigilance over such sites by boosting the number of men on the job – clear sign of how impressed they were with the operation. Major Frost was awarded the Military Cross for this operation, and was to participate in many more operations, the most famous being his capture of the Arnhem Bridge in 1944, an exploit which gained him almost legendary fame.

6. ST-NAZAIRE: THE GREATEST RAID OF ALL

March 1942 saw what was probably the greatest Commando raid mounted by Combined Operations during the course of the Second World War, and one which certainly had an enormous effect on the war effort.

On the west coast of France, where the River Loire joins the Atlantic, stands the port of St-Nazaire. One of its greatest advantages to the Germans, quite apart from its considerable harbour facilities, was the huge dry dock, capable of holding up to 85,000 tons of shipping or – in other words – a battleship as big as *Bismarck* or *Tirpitz*.

The *Forme Ecluse*, the dry dock, at St-Nazaire was a top priority target for the British, since they knew that without its resources *Tirpitz* would not be able to operate for prolonged periods. In addition the Germans had established at St-Nazaire a submarine base for the deadly 'wolf packs' which haunted the Atlantic convoys, causing heavy losses in shipping and vital military cargo, so any serious damage to the dry dock infrastructure would be welcome.

The Germans, however, were fully aware of the importance of their naval assets, and St-Nazaire was one of the most heavily defended targets in

Europe, with scores of coastal guns, anti-aircraft artillery and highly motivated troops in fortified positions guarding every possible approach route. There had been plans to mount a Commando raid even before March 1942, but they had been abandoned because it was thought that, with only one deep water channel leading up the River Loire, there was little chance that a force of sufficient strength to overcome the coastal batteries would be able to get through. The river's broad mud-flats had been considered impassable until a perceptive naval captain established that these shallows were exactly what was needed to get a force into the harbour. He believed that, when the spring tide was at its height, it would be possible to get lightly laden ships over the flats. There was no boom protecting the gate of the dock, nor any other defensive construction, since the Germans also believed that the approach was impassable.

Once the naval captain's ideas had been accepted, the plans for the combined operations raid on St-Nazaire were extremely ambitious. Initially, the proposal was to destroy the dry dock's lock gates, including their mechanism; this was to be achieved by the ingenious approach of ramming an explosives-laden destroyer into the gates.

The destroyer *Campbeltown*, formerly the US Navy ship *Buchanan*, which had been given to Britain under the Lend-Lease agreement, was chosen for the task. Two Hunt Class destroyers, HMS *Atherstone* and HMS *Tynedale*, were to act as escorts, while sixteen Fairmile motor launches, a motor gunboat and a motor torpedo-boat were to carry the Commando force, which consisted of 44 officers and 224 other ranks, all volunteers.

The naval force would be commanded by Commander Robert Ryder, a former Antarctic explorer, who had once survived four gruelling days aboard a raft in the Atlantic after his ship had been torpedoed. Commander of the land force was to be Lieutenant-Colonel Charles Newman of No. 2 Commando, formerly a territorial officer of the Essex Regiment. Although Newman was not a regular, being an engineer in civil life, he had extraordinary military abilities, which made him an excellent choice for the job which lay ahead.

Having received their initial briefing from Lord Mountbatten, now an admiral, the two officers worked out the details of their plan together – and what a plan it was! Surprise was the essence, with speed a vital ingredient, so that the target could be gained before the Germans could bring their entire, massive defences into action. A diversionary bombing raid might take some of the heat off, but it had to be borne in mind that this would not hold the Germans' attention for long.

One important detail in the scheme was to disguise the *Campbeltown*: two of her four funnels were removed, and the other two replaced, to give the ship a 'German' appearance. Her crew was reduced to 75 men and she was considerably lightened so that she could ride over the shallows. The bridge and wheelhouse were armoured, and the decks cleared, except for some armoured screens to protect the Commandos who would be transported on the destroyer. Her most important cargo, however, was the explosive charges, totalling almost five tons, placed forward to blow the dock gates in after she had rammed them. The plan was to scuttle the destroyer after impact, to prevent the Germans from dragging her clear before the explosives went off.

Commanding *Campbeltown* was Lieutenant-Commander Sam Beattie, an old friend of Ryder's; they had sailed together as young officers in a training ship. Beattie, then in his early thirties, had nerves of steel, and was undoubtedly the right choice to sacrifice his ship in the suicide attack ahead.

The force code-named 'Chariot' assembled at Falmouth on 25 March in conditions of the utmost secrecy. The date for the operation had actually been set for two days later, but as weather conditions were favourable – an important factor in the success or failure of the mission – Ryder obtained permission to leave on the 26th. A last-minute air reconnaissance sortie brought some updated photographs which showed that four German destroyers of the *Moewe* Class had entered harbour and were berthed near the submarine pens in the main basin.

Accordingly, at noon on 26 March, under a clear sky and escorted by Spitfires, the motor launches carrying the Commandos sailed out of Falmouth, followed an hour later by the three destroyers. In all, 611 men sailed on that day.

On the first leg of the route, Ryder took his flotilla quickly on a south-westerly course and out of sight of land until, at dawn on 27 March, they were level with St-Nazaire. Shortly after dawn, the conning tower of a submarine was sighted. *Tynedale* hurried to the scene and opened fire with her main gun, forcing the U-boat to crash-dive. Depth-charges were dropped, but the submarine did not show up again. Her captain, managing to evade the British flotilla, later surfaced and signalled home that a force of British destroyers was sailing on a westerly course; however, he did not mention the motor launches, which he had not identified in his hasty dive.

Shortly after the U-boat had dived, two French fishing trawlers came into view, and one of them was boarded in order to verify that no German radio operators were aboard. The crews were taken on board one of the destroyers and the trawlers sunk.

On the afternoon of the same day, the skies became overcast as the force moved towards the French coast. At 2000 hours it was dark, and the two escort destroyers made for their station. Commander Ryder and Colonel Newman transferred to Motor Gun Boat 314, commanded by Lieutenant Curtis, RNVR. Meanwhile *Campbeltown* hoisted the German ensign, which now fluttered from her main mast as well as from the jackstaff of every other vessel. Still five and half hours to go.

At 2200 hours, a white pinpoint of light flickered in the darkness, and shortly afterward the force slipped past the dark shape of HM submarine *Sturgeon* which lay in position at the entrance to the River Loire. At that moment the RAF bombers bound for St-Nazaire appeared overhead and heavy flak was seen as they arrived at their target. However, heavy clouds now covered the area and the bombers, not wishing to endanger the civilian population by indiscriminate blind bombing, withdrew. Some of them, though, continued to cruise, arousing the suspicions of the German commander, who alerted his troops to prepare for a possible airborne assault.

Just then the British flotilla, spearheaded by the motor gunboat, entered the Loire, shrouded by mist and cloud. *Campbeltown* sailed next, flanked on both sides by the motor launches which carried the Commandos, with the motor torpedo-boat making up the rear.

As the gunboat was passing the tower of Les Morées, a searchlight suddenly swept over *Campbeltown*. It was a tense moment, but one which had been expected. Leading Seaman Pike, who was both an expert German speaker and familiar with German Navy signals, flashed a message with his Aldis lamp, identifying the flotilla as being German, and asking permission to enter harbour as they had just been engaged at sea with a British force.

While that message was being examined by the German ground station, the British were challenged from the other bank of the river, and gunfire followed. Attempting to hoodwink the enemy, Ryder fired a recognition signal from his Very pistol, while Pike continued signalling. This worked for a while, but not for long.

The Germans, recovering from their temporary bewilderment, now opened up with every gun they had, while the British force returned fire, simultaneously taking down the German ensigns and hoisting their own battle flags. Most of the German fire was directed at *Campbeltown*. A direct hit on her forward deck wiped out the 12-pounder gun and took a heavy toll of the Commandos hiding behind the steel screens. In spite of this, however, the destroyer went on her way, guns blazing, her captain determined to carry out his job.

Campbeltown was speeding at 20 knots as Beattie, in position on the bridge, gave the order to ram. Commander Ryder, standing next to Curtis on the bridge of the MGB, ordered it to veer to starboard, giving the destroyer a free run to the lock gate. For a moment he lost sight of her in the glare of the converging searchlights, then she emerged, all her remaining guns blazing and, smashing through the anti-torpedo net, crashed into the outer gates, her bow crumbling like a tin can. Beattie, turning to Captain Montgomery, who was in charge of the demolition team, looked at his watch and observed that they were four minutes late – a tremendous feat of seamanship!

Six minutes after *Campbeltown* struck, Commander Ryder directed the MGB – under heavy fire – to dock at the old port entrance and Colonel Newman and his party went ashore. Meanwhile the Commandos who had survived the ordeal aboard the destroyer also disembarked on to the docks, under the direction of Major Copland. They were dressed in white denims for easier recognition, every second man carrying a blue-lensed pencil-beamed torch.

One party under the command of Lieutenant Roderick went straight for the gun emplacements and stormed in with grenades. Two more positions were also destroyed and most of the Germans were killed before they realized what was happening. Nearby, Captain Roy's kilted Scotsmen were attacking

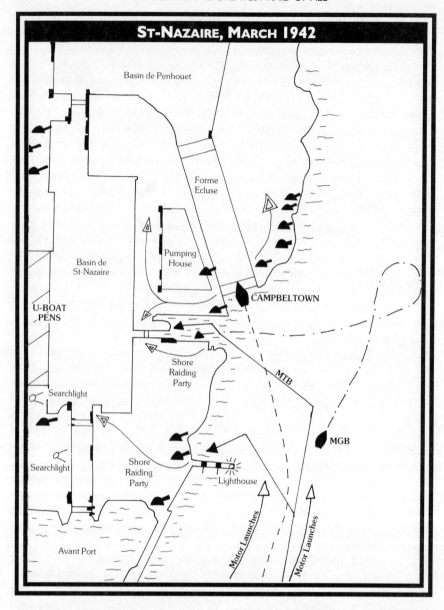

ST-NAZAIRE, MARCH 1942

Basin de Penhouet

Forme
Ecluse

Pumping
House

Basin de
St-Nazaire

U-BOAT
PENS

CAMPBELTOWN

Shore
Raiding
Party

MTB

Searchlight

MGB

Searchlight

Shore
Raiding
Party

Lighthouse

Avant Port

Motor Launches

Motor Launches

the pumphouse, scattering the German anti-aircraft gun crews who fled as the
Commandos came on them out of the darkness.

Lieutenant Stuart Chant with four sergeants went for the main pumping
station, which was a prime target. Chant and another member of his party
had been badly wounded in the destroyer but he kept going in spite of his
pain. The five men, Chant in the lead, blew in the steel door with an explosive
charge and stormed into the building firing machine-guns from the hip.
Leaving the wounded man to keep guard, the party ran down the long

stairway to the pumps, and placed demolition charges by torchlight. Once these were set, the men raced upstairs again, where they met Captain Montgomery, who had just completed his own demolition work nearby. Then the building blew up with a roar that shook the entire harbour. Nearby another shed was burning fiercely, adding to the light that illuminated the whole area.

On the way to his HQ adjacent to the dock entrance, Colonel Newman observed German storm troopers pouring into the dock area to reinforce the gun crews. He tried to raise Ryder on his portable radio, but in vain. Seeing that the Germans were now counter-attacking with determination, Newman and Major Copland took their men to edge of the dock area where they formed a small defensive perimeter, and went on to silence a German machine-gun position.

The area was now an inferno of noise and smoke. Flames from destroyed motor launches covered the waters of the harbour, while survivors clung to flotsam floating in the murky waters. Many of the searchlights had been shot out, but the battleground was now lit by flickering, intermittent fire, eerily reminiscent of a haunted house at a fairground, as sharp bursts of tommy gun fire was answered by the staccato of Schmeisser sub-machine guns.

Captain Pritchard, who was responsible for the demolition parties, went forward with a team to neutralize the southern lock of the dry dock. They placed their charges near the Old Mole and retired. As they left they heard two heavy explosions. Pritchard, however, was concerned about his other squads and returned into the old town of St-Nazaire to search for them – but ran straight into a German soldier, whose Schmeisser went off, killing Pritchard outright.

Simultaneously, other Commando parties, among them Captain Roy's Highlanders, were still fighting hard in the north of the port area. Pressed hard by advancing German storm troopers, Roy's party dropped back towards the old port entrance, where they met up with Colonel Newman, who was now attempting to assemble his forces and ascertain their situation. Captain Montgomery, who had led the Commandos from *Campbeltown*, reported that all demolition missions had been completed. However, many officers and men were missing, and Newman did not know which were still involved in isolated pockets of fighting and which had been lost. Until then Newman had been too busy directing his part of the battle to worry about how to withdraw. Now, scanning the harbour, he saw that the entire area was just an expanse of blazing oil upon which floated the wrecks of eight motor vessels. With most of his ships gone, there would be a problem in getting the survivors out to sea and back home. Two motor launches managed to get into the old entrance and take on Commandos, speeding back into the river before the Germans could concentrate their fire.

Commander Ryder, who was still out of radio contact with Newman, ordered his MGB alongside the scuttled *Campbeltown*. Ignoring the danger, he went ashore with another officer to check for himself that the destroyer was firmly jammed into the lock. Not knowing where Newman's units were, he collected some of the Commandos and took them aboard. Just as he was about to board his ship, Lieutenant Wynn, commander of the MTB, came alongside and Ryder ordered him to fire his torpedoes into the outer lock gate. Wynn was happy to comply. He launched two of his time-fuzed weapons and set off down the river, manoeuvring carefully between the floating wrecks.

Ryder, in his MGB, also moved out, attempting as he went to establish contact with Newman on the shore, but still without success. He felt very bad about leaving his comrade and the Commandos still fighting, but saw no choice but to try and get out to sea with those men he had collected.

The situation on board the few motor launches which still remained reasonably intact was appalling. Dead and wounded were crowded on the bloodstained decks, and fires were burning. Some of the launches stopped in midstream to pick up survivors, were hit again, and more fires broke out.

Even out at sea the launches were far from safe. The German destroyer *Jaguar*, investigating a shadow on her port beam, found and engaged a British launch packed with survivors. As the German searchlights picked out the launch, some of the British sailors opened up with their Lewis and Oerlikon guns, smashing the light. But the tiny vessel had no chance against the heavily armed enemy ship. The German skipper, Kapitänleutnant Paul, was a humane man and ordered his men to stop firing the main guns and only to use light weapons until the British survivors, accepting their fate, surrendered. Some launches and Ryder's gunboat did succeed in reaching safety, meeting up with the waiting British destroyers which took the men on board. But there were not many left.

Meanwhile, on the shore, Newman and his remaining men continued to fight a hopeless battle, but by daylight, as he heard the Germans begin to search the house in which he and some of his men were hiding, he accepted the inevitable, and surrendered.

A few men did manage to escape. Aided by the French underground, they reached safety in Spain. Most of the survivors sat out the remainder of the war in German prison camps. Of the eighteen naval craft which had set out from Falmouth only two reached home. The price was a heavy one: Some 169 men were killed in action and 200 taken prisoner. But the reward was great: St-Nazaire remained closed for a very long time; in fact, the dry dock did not reopen until years after the war.

There was a bloody aftermath. Many Germans, among them senior officers and female army workers, came to visit *Campbeltown* the morning after the raid. As they were laughing and talking, some looking for loot, the ship exploded in a gigantic ball of flame – almost five tons of explosives had blown. It was never established how many Germans had been killed in the explosion, but even a conservative estimate must be in the several hundreds – a strange climax to a night packed with drama. Lieutenant-Commander Beattie had been picked up by a German trawler after his own launch had been blown up, and heard the tremendous noise of the explosion. It must have given him some satisfaction to know that his part of the mission had been successful, as he sat out the rest of the war in a German POW camp.

7. OPERATION 'MERCURY' AT MALEME AIRFIELD

The island of Crete, strategically placed in the Mediterranean, was of vital importance in the German war effort. General Kurt Student, father of the German airborne forces, who had already demonstrated his abilities in Norway, Belgium, and Greece, saw it as the key to the defence of the Middle East. In a meeting with Adolf Hitler in the Führer's personal train on 21 April 1941, following the fall of Greece, the idea of Operation 'Mercury' – the airborne invasion of Crete – was born.

Confidently, Student gave his appreciation of the situation and the merits of his plan to an attentive audience. The early capture of the island would deny the RAF access to the Roumanian oilfields, and would give the Germans control over the eastern Mediterranean. From the new airfields on the island, targets in Egypt could be attacked and, most important of all, Crete could serve as a jumping-off base for further airborne attacks on Cyprus and Palestine, at that time two of the most important British-held zones in the Middle East.

Hitler was impressed by Student's presentation, and especially by his fighting spirit, which was quite unlike the normal caution of his senior commanders. Göring, too, gave his blessing and the operation was given top priority, both forces and supplies arriving in quantity in the south of Greece, from where the mission was to be launched.

The Germans assembled a massive force for 'Mercury'. Some 15,000 paratroops of 7th Airborne Division, 8,500 mountain troops and 700 motor-cyclists of 5th Armoured Division were concentrated. To fly in the airbridge, 539 three-engined Ju-52 transports assembled, as were more than 100 DS 230 gliders. Hundreds of dive-bombers, bombers and fighters were to fly support missions, and a motley collection of ships – trawlers, fishing vessels and so on – would transport the seaborne forces. 'Mercury' was the first military combined operation ever to be mounted on such a large scale.

However, there were insufficient transport aircraft to allow a single air assault, so Student's plan encompassed two separate ones: a morning lift to land about 3,000 men in the Maleme, Canea and Suda Bay area while, some hours later, a second airlift would drop at Retimo and Heraklion, bolstered by a seaborne landing to ferry in the mountain troops.

Crete is an extraordinarily difficult place to defend against attack. Its topography includes a long, thin mountain range extending some 250 kilometres in length and 40 in breadth. Extremely steep in the south and with a narrow coastal plain in the north, it had only a single paved road to connect the three gravel covered airfields at Maleme, Retimo and Heraklion. No defence in depth was possible, so the British had established their defences round the airfields and seaports, hoping to ward off any attack in its early stages and leave the Roya! Navy to destroy any incoming reinforcements by sea.

On the morning of 20 May 1941 – the eve of 'Mercury' – the garrison at Crete numbered some 32,000 men. Unknown to German Intelligence, 26,000 of them had been ferried over from Greece after it fell. Despite their large numbers, the troops were in bad condition: Most of their heavy weapons had been left behind in the evacuation, and ammunition was low. All aircraft had been flown out, as the airfields were under almost constant air attack. Commanding the British forces on the island was Major-General Bernard Freyberg, a New Zealander, who had gained fame in the First World War when he was awarded the Victoria Cross for bravery both at Gallipoli and in France. The British had received information from their intelligence services as to a possible attack on Crete but were too short of heavy weapons to be able to mount much of a defence.

On the morning of 20 May it was fairly quiet at Maleme airfield. The few RAF Hurricanes which had been guarding it for several weeks had departed for Egypt; there were some eight hundred men in defence, mainly New Zealanders of 22nd Infantry Battalion, with some ground crews from 30 and 33 Squadrons – well dug in and awaiting an attack which they knew would come. At dawn the Luftwaffe arrived and strafed the empty runway – fairly routine, so far. Messerschmitts, the sunlight flashing on their wings, came in from the sea, sweeping low over the airfield, some of them heading for the nearby hills – again, a pretty commonplace occurrence. On the ground, the morning began as usual.

Fifth New Zealand Brigade was deployed in the area from Maleme to the village of Platanias which lay to its east, held by a Maori battalion. Lieutenant-Colonel L. W. Andrew, a VC from the First World War, commanding the New Zealand 22nd Battalion, had positioned his five companies around Kavkazia Hill with his HQ on top. This incline, also known as Hill 107, dominated the airfield, and was to play an important part in the battle to come. Two Matilda infantry tanks were also in the area, but both were almost useless – in one of them the guns could not even fire. There were, however, a couple of Bofors guns – soon to prove their worth.

When the first wave of German aircraft departed, the British ground staff waited with the New Zealanders, some of them still manning the anti-aircraft machine-guns placed around the airfield. But then a new formation of German aircraft larger than the last, arrived from the north.

Lieutenant John Lorimer, in position south of the airfield, saw what he thought at first were hundreds of bright stars in the sky over the sea. Actually they were the reflections of the light shining on the plexiglass windows of the Luftwaffe transports, flying in tight formation towards the shore. It was a wonderful sight, but the British soldiers and airmen did not have much time to enjoy it.

At precisely 0650 there was an eruption of shattering noise as scores of Stuka dive-bombers, their Jericho sirens screaming, raced straight for the airfield, their bombs crashing down everywhere. The dive-bombing attack went on for twenty minutes. Then, suddenly, the gliders arrived. An airman crouching in his foxhole ducked as a silent, sinister shadow swooped overhead. Then there were cracking and crashing noises as another glider dived straight into some olive trees. It careened on, skidded into a tent only a few metres away, and stopped with one wing dug into a sandbank, showering loose soil and dust. Another glider landed right next to it. Lorimer ducked back into his foxhole in dismay as, within seconds, the door of the nearest glider opened and out jumped, or fell to be more exact, a completely dazed German soldier. Lorimer fired his rifle at him and he fell backwards, cannoning into the second glider trooper who was just emerging.

The rest of the Germans now piled out, some racing for cover in the trees under fire from the Allied soldiers. Overhead appeared some German bombers, their gunners spraying the countryside from tree-top height. Bullets sliced through the trees and flicked into the ground, and men began to fall. One airman ran through a deserted trench and picked up a submachine-gun in exchange for his rifle. On the way out he met a party of Germans and there was a rapid exchange of automatic fire.

There was much confusion, on both sides, but it soon began to seem that the best place to go was Kavkazia Hill, where at least some defence was being organized. German fighters were strafing the hill almost continuously; the noise and dust were overwhelming, but those who reached the top could see some of the Messerschmitts below, going for the airfield defences at zero level. There were other dramatic scenes being played out all over the airfield. One damaged glider thudded against a machine-gun barrel and slewed around in a spinning circle. The first man who managed to get out was killed outright by the commander of the gun post. A corporal came out next and threw two hand-grenades into the machine-gun position.

Five trucks filled with Allied soldiers raced towards the airfield perimeter. From 50 metres a German gunner fired his machine-gun and killed the driver of the leading vehicle, which turned over in a cloud of dust, while men spilled out on all sides.

It was now just five minutes since the gliders had landed. For a moment the sky was clear of attacking aircraft – but only for a moment. Soon the paratroops arrived, commanded by General Meindl, one of the first men on the ground. Assembling some of his men and his adjutant, Meindl made for the river bed, but they were hit by a machine-gun burst, which killed his adjutant and badly wounded him. Within minutes almost the entire German tactical HQ was eliminated. But worse was to befall the paratroopers. They came in in an armada of Junkers transports, which flew in impeccable formation, low over the sea, circling left as they dropped the paratroops. Soon the sky was filled with mushrooms of many colours, slowly descending into what was to be known as the hell of Maleme. A strong thermal stream made the fall too slow. In some cases, men literally hung in mid-air – perfect targets for the British, who fired until their gun barrels became red hot. It was a virtual turkey shoot. Some of the Germans tried to shoot their way clear before they landed. Each man held a quick-firing Schmeisser between his legs with which he sprayed the ground below, but the results were inaccurate due to the swaying of the parachutes. One isolated parachutist, caught by the thermal current, drifted out to sea.

The transports suffered, too. One Junkers slashed into a group of paratroopers on their way down and, out of control, plummeted to earth festooned with parachutes. Another burst into flames and men could be seen leaping out until the troop carrier hit the sea with a wing and cartwheeled with a mighty splash.

Meanwhile the battle round Maleme airfield was heating up. The German plan was quite simple: to take Kavkazia Hill, silence the Bofors guns around the landing ground and capture the iron bridge over the bed of the River Tavronitis. Without that bridge reinforcements, which had been dropped farther to the west, would not arrive quickly enough to assist the glider troops on the airfield and, without complete control of the runway and perimeter, troop carriers could not be flown in to bolster the attack.

The hill, however, was the all-important ground feature. Unless it could be held the entire plan would fall apart. The assault of Kavkazia Hill was assigned to Major Walter Koch and his assault battalion. Koch was one of the best airborne commanders in Student's force and was well known for his fine work in the Eben Emael operation at the beginning of the war. Here, however, the situation was different. There was no element of surprise; the British were waiting, guns at the ready.

Koch and his men landed on the south-west slopes of the hill, obtaining reinforcements from some of the paratroopers who managed to reach him. Together they secured a footing on the hill. Just above them was a party of airmen from 30 Squadron, who held a foxhole and directed withering fire downhill. The Germans suffered heavy casualties from this and from some New Zealanders on their flank, and before they could take up defensive positions the Allied airmen and a platoon of infantrymen tore into them from above, driving the Germans from the hill. In the savage hand-to-hand fighting which took place, Major Koch was badly wounded, but he was taken to a forward aid station which had been set up.

Some glider troops under a Leutnant Plessen did better. Landing in the river mouth with sixteen gliders, they stormed the east bank of the riverbed and overran some New Zealanders who held an inferior position. Two Bofors guns were captured but Plessen himself was killed in the fighting.

The greatest success was for Major Braun's men. They were able to seize the iron bridge and drive a wedge between New Zealand companies. A vicious close-in battle followed, in which the Kiwis bitterly contested the area north of the RAF camp. Major Braun was killed but his men doggedly hung on to their prize.

From the hillside, Squadron Leader Howell of 33 Squadron, who had chosen to remain with his ground crews, saw the gliders coming in and set off down the slope to look for those of his airmen who were still in the camp. He was accompanied by two other officers, among them the commander of the naval air squadron, Commander Beale. It soon became apparent to Howell that some of his men were cut off, but he managed to gather some of them together. Organizing them into two groups, he led them uphill and positioned them behind a stone wall which offered good protection. Nearby a line of New Zealanders was forming preparing to withstand an attack. There was a good deal of firing going on, but the RAF officer, ignoring the bullets, once again went down the hill in an attempt to collect some more of his men. Suddenly Commander Beale was hit and as the squadron leader bent over to help him he too was hit by a burst of fire which shattered both his arms. Some of the airmen dragged their CO to safety across the bullet-swept ground. Beale, although in severe pain, set about organizing the defence and led an attack which recaptured part of the camp where the glider troops had been digging in. Both Howell and Beale were eventually captured, but survived.

Back on the hill, the New Zealanders were still holding out despite determined assaults mounted by the German paratroopers. Colonel Andrew was now personally directing the defence. When darkness fell at last, he organized a counter-attack with the aim of recapturing the Tavronitis Bridge. He even attempted to use the two tanks, but both of them broke down soon after their engines were started. The counter-attack failed and, realizing that his forces were totally outnumbered, he decided to pull his men from Hill 107 – a mistake which was to give the Germans the airfield.

The next morning, the exhausted paratroopers – or what was left of them after the previous day's carnage – made their way cautiously uphill. To their utter surprise, they found the place empty. As they established themselves in the dominating position on top of the hill, they could see a Ju-52 landing on the runway, piloted by a Captain Kleye, who had been sent by General Student to obtain an updated assessment of the situation. Surprisingly, the transport landed unmolested.

Student, who had been following events closely, decided to reinforce his success. At 0800 six supply aircraft touched down on the beach west of the river bed, and an hour later two parachute companies were dropped in the same location, but a supply drop landed, in error, to the east, in the middle of the New Zealanders who were dug in there and, once again, the paras suffered heavily.

By now, however, news had come through that Maleme airfield was secure and in roared the Junkers, landing in clouds of red dust and disgorging Colonel Ramke's air landing troops. Ramke immediately set about clearing the runway, using a tank to bulldoze the tanks blocking the way. But the battle was not yet over.

As the invading seaborne force approached the shore, it was intercepted by the Royal Navy, which struck a terrible blow against the assorted collection of ships, scattering them all over the sea. Hundreds of men died, but many escaped to the neighbouring islands.

The success of the Royal Navy seemed a good omen for a renewed attack to be mounted by General Freyberg's New Zealanders. He allocated two infantry battalions, with as much support as he could muster from his meagre resources, and he was hopeful that they could dislodge the Germans from Maleme airfield or, at least, hamper further German landings there. Unfortunately, however, the Allied infantry columns bumped into the survivors of Major Scherber's 3rd Paratroop Battalion, which had been badly mauled the day before when they had dropped near the village of Pirgos. The New Zealanders' attack had to be called off.

The Allies' defence of Crete was now virtually over. Their courage was never in doubt, but it had not been enough. General Student had arrived and established his headquarters on Maleme airfield, which by now was secure enough to support the inflow of reinforcements. German losses had been severe, but he had secured the north-western area of the island, from where he could advance eastwards and roll up the other two airfields at Retimo and Heraklion.

The Luftwaffe now ruled the skies over Crete, and there was no recourse but to evacuate those survivors who could be taken off in time by the Royal Navy. About half of the original garrison were eventually taken off, and thousands more trekked over the mountains to the north where naval vessels waited to receive them.

In all the British lost almost 2,000 men killed, with the same number wounded. Eleven thousand men went into German POW camps. The Germans suffered even more severe losses. Of a total of 22,000, six thousand were final casualties. Almost half of the transport fleet was destroyed, wrecks littering the airfields and beaches. Most painful for the Germans, however, was the loss of their best airborne officers and NCOs – doing away, in one single operation, with almost the entire leadership cadre. It was for this reason that Hitler lost all faith in the airborne solution and, although paratroops were still used in small actions, they were never again used in a large one.

8. AIRFIELD RAIDS

The idea of stealth Commando raids on airfields originated with David Stirling, creator of the Special Air Service. Born in 1915, the son of Brigadier Archibald Stirling, David joined the Scots Guards in 1939, but requested transfer to the Commandos when they were formed a few months later, and became part of Colonel Laycock's special forces in the Middle East in 1941.

Stirling began to think of ways to mount Commando attacks which, until that time, had been unsuccessful in the Middle East. He contacted Lieutenant Jock Lewis of the Welsh Guards, and the two men began experimenting with parachutes on Mersa Matruh airfield in Egypt. To attack enemy airfields one needs the sort of explosives that can be placed in minimum time for maximum effect. Jock Lewis invented a small light incendiary bomb made of plastic, oil and thermite. To test the device, the SAS staged a dummy run on Heliopolis airfield near Cairo, and placed dummies on RAF aircraft after penetrating the airfield perimeter.

However, the first real raid – on a German airfield in Cyrenaica – went totally wrong. Stirling's plan was an ambitious one. He wanted to attack, simultaneously, five enemy airfields in the Gazala-Tmimi area, in Cyrenaica, the raiders to be parachuted in some 24 hours before. During daylight they would hide in the rocky escarpment, make observations of their targets and then, at nightfall, carry out their mission, using the element of surprise to overcome the enemy defence. After the raid, the parties would meet at pre-arranged rendezvous points with the Long Range Desert Group, who would pick them up.

The plan seemed simple enough on paper, but from the start everything that could possibly go wrong did. The weather deteriorated; a strong wind blew, reaching gale force proportions by the time the operation was to start on 18 November 1941, just prior to the start of Operation 'Crusader'. It was pouring with rain, and the cold was severe. A parachute descent was thus totally ruled out, as there would be no hope of collecting the men on the ground. GHQ Cairo recommended that Stirling cancel the raid but left the final decision to him. At the HQ of 216 Squadron, which was to carry his men, he consulted the officers in charge, who thought that they could made the drop, given reasonable conditions. Jock Lewis was also for it, not wishing to lose the chance of proving their concept right. Stirling, therefore, decided to go for it and that evening the SAS party boarded five RAF Bombay transports and they took off. The ride was terribly bumpy; the men were thrown all over the aircraft.

Previously, some Wellingtons had been over the coastline dropping flares to assist the pilots in identifying the drop zones. As the doors opened, letting the cold air rush in, the Commandos stood up and hooked up their static lines in preparation for the jump. Stirling went out first. He landed badly, hitting the surface with a crash, and was dragged along by the strong winds. After he extricated himself, with great difficulty, from the parachute he tried to contact his men but could find none of them nearby. Many of them had been badly hurt by their fall and it took a long time to gather them together. Worse was to come when he realized that, of ten supply cannisters, only two could be located. So far as blowing up enemy aircraft was concerned, the raid was already doomed.

Stirling decided at least to mount a ground reconnaissance operation for future reference, but the weather turned even worse, with visibility down to a few metres. The normally dry wadis became rushing torrents, ruling out any possible crossing. There was nothing for it but to turn south and make the rendezvous with the LRDG. Not all of them made it, however; of the 62 officers and men who had set out, only 22 came back. Stirling's superiors, who had in any case been sceptical about his ideas, were extremely displeased. But Stirling did not despair easily. He continued to think up new concepts for future operations. Also, the strategic war situation was deteriorating badly at this time, making the top brass willing to reconsider any idea which might erode enemy supply lines and air support.

The LRDG seemed an ideal way of getting his raiding parties to their objectives. Stirling, examining intelligence reports, found that those German airfields that were a long way from the front were inadequately guarded, surrounded by a single wire fence, if at all. These airfields would make wonderful targets for hit and run raids, with the added possible benefit of destroying aircraft on the ground, especially transports bringing urgent supplies to the German forces far up front.

The first successful raid against enemy airfields in North Africa took place in December 1941, while Rommel was in full retreat after 'Crusader'. By then Stirling had moved his SAS to Jalo, a desert oasis in southern Libya, isolated enough to shield them from the eyes of German reconnaissance aircraft. Three airfields were earmarked for the raid. Stirling, with Paddy Mayne and ten men, would go for Sirte, which lay some 700 kilometres to the west of Jalo; two days later, Jock Lewis would set out for El Agheila with his force and eight days after that Bill Fraser would drive for Agedabia.

On 8 December 1941 Stirling and his party left Jalo, transported by Gus Holliman and his Rhodesian LRDG patrol. They travelled in seven trucks, piled high with stores and equipment. The journey passed without incident apart from an encounter with an Italian aircraft which dropped some bombs but caused no damage. As they neared their designated location not far from the coastal road, Stirling went off on foot to look and listen. By then it was dark, but in the distance he could hear enemy transports driving along a road. Suddenly the sound of engines could be heard much closer, together with excited voices shouting orders. Fearing that it might be a patrol searching for them, alerted by the Italian aircraft, Stirling decided to change his plan. He sent Paddy Mayne and his party to attack the airfield at Tamet, while he himself with a small team would go for Sirte and see what could be done there. Holliman agreed to split the trucks and let them have three for both groups.

The time for the attack was set at 2300 hours for both raids simultaneously in order to prevent communication between the two airfields. Paddy Mayne's unit was lucky. Having got on to the airfield unobserved, they made their way towards a group of buildings, one of which was the officers' mess, where a noisy party was in progress. Flinging open the door, Paddy sprayed the room with his tommy gun and got away fast, his men acting as rearguard. Then his party sprinted across the field to the aircraft, 23 of them, neatly in line. The men placed their bombs but Paddy Mayne had to rip the instrument panel off the last one, as his explosives were already spent. They had hardly left the scene when the aircraft started exploding. In the distance the lights of the LRDG could already be seen and, reaching the trucks, the men leapt into them and roared away into the desert.

Stirling himself was not so fortunate. He had also reached his objective unobserved, but to his dismay was forced to watch 30 Caproni bombers taking off before his eyes and disappear, leaving the airfield empty of aircraft. To his satisfaction, however, he could hear the thundering results of Paddy Mayne's raid as he made his rendezvous with the LRDG.

Bill Fraser could boast the biggest 'catch' of all. His force destroyed 37 enemy aircraft at Agedabia. Stirling had finally achieved his goal; from now on he would not need to promote his ideas about the SAS.

Some of the SAS raids have become legend in the annals of warfare but some are less well known, having been kept on the secret list for many years. Among them is the story of the Jewish-Palestinian Commandos who served with 51 Middle East Commando and took part in some of the most noteworthy raids on enemy airfields.

51 ME Commando was formed in 1940, when a mixed company of Jews and Arabs arrived in France under the command of Major H. J. 'Kid' Cator of the Royal Scots Greys. Cator had raised the Palestinian volunteers earlier and recognized their potential, but although they were extremely keen to go into battle, Cator's 401 Palestinian Company Pioneer Corps was given only guard duties, mere bystanders in the great events occurring then in France. Before the fall of France, the company was evacuated from St-Malo and reached Britain, where they were deployed in the defences along the Dorset coast. Cator, who had personal connections with the Royal Household through his family estates near Sandringham in Norfolk, pushed to make the Palestinians into a proper fighting unit.

At this time the Commandos were being formed and his unconventional unit seemed to him ideal for the Commando framework. He finally managed to get them transferred back to the Middle East. Here Cator received word from GHG Cairo that his men, in their new address in the Canal Zone in Egypt, would form the nucleus for 51 ME Commando, which would later gain acclaim in the bitter fighting in Eritrea and Abyssinia. However, political considerations later dictated that most of the Jews, who had already distinguished themselves in combat, were sent back to the Pioneer Corps, to their dismay.

The German-speaking Jews were formed into a special unit which was to participate in a very ambitious programme. They came under the command of Captain Herbert Buck who had formerly served with the Punjabis. Fluent in German, Buck had recently been captured but had managed to escape wearing an Afrika Korps uniform and was surprised at how easily he could pass for a German soldier. This gave him the idea of forming a special unit to operate behind the German lines and cause havoc in the rear zone. There could be no better candidates for such a job than the Palestinian Jews, many of whom had actually been German citizens until expelled by the Nazis in the thirties. Most of them knew the German lifestyle intimately, for it had been their own. Moreover, they looked like Germans and spoke German dialects as only the German-born could speak them. Faced with the boring prospect of rejoining the Pioneer Corps, they rushed to volunteer for Captain Buck's special unit and underwent training with great enthusiasm.

The new unit trained in a far corner of the desert, unseen by prying eyes. Two of the instructors were Germans, Corporals Essner and Brückner, who had volunteered to work with the British and were taken from prison camps in Egypt. Formerly members of the French Foreign Legion, they professed themselves ardent anti-Nazis but the Jews who were their trainees regarded them with suspicion – unfortunately borne out later by traumatic events.

The Special Interrogation Group (SIG), as the unit was designated for secrecy, was given its first task in June 1942, when it was directed to take part in an SAS attack on German airfields in Libya. Stirling had drawn up a wide-ranging plan to raid six airfields simultaneously in a gigantic Commando operation. The six airfields were at Benghazi and in the Derna area. Since the presence of heavy German forces was expected, the SIG was enlisted to transport a French patrol and bring it into the designated airfield in captured Afrika Korps lorries.

One of the Palestinian Jews taking part was Sergeant-Major Israel Carmi, who had served with 51 Commando and was already a veteran fighter. Also participating were Captain Buck and Lieutenant Ted Russell, a former Guards officer, who was Buck's second in command. Carmi aired his concern about the loyalty of the two German instructors to Captain Buck before they set out, on 6 June 1942, but was told to keep his worries to himself and not to cause alarm. The party set out from the British lines still wearing their own uniforms, but their weapons and equipment were German, as were the trucks in which they and the French Commandos were travelling. They were heading for two airfields, Martuba and Derna, taking a southerly route to outflank the German lines. On the way they changed into their German uniforms and took their positions in the truck cabins, and the small convoy returned to the main road as darkness fell.

Somewhere along the coastal road the trucks left the highway and hid in the hills, where they laid an ambush. Soon a German convoy appeared. One of the 'Germans' signalled it to stop. There were two enemy vehicles and the first stopped. As soon as it came to a halt, the Commandos rushed it and killed the passengers, a few supply soldiers who died before they knew what hit them. Taking the equipment from the trucks, the SIG returned to the British lines and reorganized with the new uniforms and documents they had captured. By then it was time to move out and meet with the LRDG and Stirling's party and head for the airfields.

For four days the raiders travelled with the desert patrols. In their last hide-out the SIG changed into their German uniforms, with Essner and Brückner as NCOs, and Captain Buck as a private. As evening approached they came to a roadblock but were waved on by a bored Italian sentry who hardly looked at their credentials. Brückner needed no disguise as a normal German sergeant and he even yelled at the Italian to hurry up. All this time the French Commandos were hiding under tarpaulins.

The next morning the party arrived at a spot near the airfield and the officers carried out a quick reconnaissance. Then, just as they were passing through the main entrance of Derna airfield, they were stopped by a German guard. Brückner, who was driving one of the trucks loaded with half a ton of explosives, conferred with the German guard, while two Palestinians hiding in the back of the truck watched through a slit in the tarpaulin. They saw Brückner go into the guardroom. Suddenly several Germans emerged and approached the trucks, loading their rifles as they ran. The two Palestinians opened fire; one, Peter Haas, realizing that their fate was sealed, ripped the pin from his hand-grenade and blew himself and the truck up, killing the Germans at the same time. The French now came out, guns blazing, but in the mêlée that followed only one of them managed to escape; the rest were either killed or captured. Brückner, who had betrayed his comrades, was flown to Berlin where he was decorated with the German Gold Cross. The French officer who had managed to escape met Captain Buck and the other patrol at the LRDG rendezvous and they returned safely to the oasis of Siwa. At Benghazi and Berca airfields, however, the SAS were more successful and destroyed a number of aircraft on the ground.

From that same oasis, a twenty-strong party left for Berca, ten kilometres outside Benghazi, in an extremely successful raid. Led by Stirling and Paddy Mayne, they travelled more than 800 kilometres across the desert, splitting into four separate teams, each going for a different target. Mayne's team consisted of himself, Bob Bennett and Johnny Byrne. They hit the perimeter at about midnight and saw German sentries strolling along the road. Waiting until they had passed, the raiders then shot across the road into some trees where they hid. Then, still undetected, they walked towards the aircraft which were placed neatly in line, extremely conveniently for the Commandos. Lobbing Mills grenades on to the wings, they soon finished the job and withdrew into the darkness. As soon as they had left the perimeter fence they heard the aircraft exploding one after the other.

During the eighteen months in which Stirling's men operated against the enemy airfields in North Africa some 300 aircraft were destroyed on the ground, a remarkable feat if one considers how much effort would have been required to achieve the same result in air combat. Almost 50 attacks were made. Both Stirling and Mayne were eventually captured by the Germans, as were most of the others, although they made several escape attempts.

Worthy of remembrance is another exploit which took place several years later, long after the SAS raiders had stopped fighting. On a rainy night in February 1946, the Palestinian Jewish underground mounted a daring raid on three separate RAF airfields in Palestine. One attack, mounted by the ETZEL, an acronym for the *Irgun Tzvai Leumi* or National Military Organization, struck at RAF Qastina, which was a heavily guarded airbase used by 6th Airborne Division. Stationed there were two squadrons of Halifax bombers. Sixteen men crept silently into the perimeter, raced for the bombers on the tarmac and, using ladders, climbed up on the aircraft wings, placing specially prepared explosive charges on to the wing roots. When they had nearly finished their task, the guards were alerted and heavy fire was directed at the raiders, one of whom was killed. The rest withdrew safely. Within minutes twelve four-engined bombers blew up, totally destroyed, while several others were damaged.

At exactly the same time, another group broke into an airfield near Kfar Sirkin where two squadrons of Spitfires were stationed. Avoiding an armoured patrol which shone searchlights over the fences, the sappers managed to destroy an entire fighter squadron without losing a single man. The damage would have been even greater had it not been for the personal courage of the CO, Squadron Leader Sylvester who, disregarding his own safety, neutralized the explosive charges in some of his Spitfires before they blew up. In a single night the Jewish resistance destroyed almost 30 British aircraft and, bearing in mind that not a single British life was lost, it could be considered quite an achievement.

9. TARGET ROMMEL

I n the autumn of 1941 the British forces in North Africa were poised for a counter-offensive. The British Eighth Army had been chased from Cyrenaica to the Egyptian frontier by General Erwin Rommel's Afrika Korps. Tobruk, which held an entire division, was surrounded by the Germans, who were preparing to eliminate them, while the Eighth Army was also preparing to liberate the Tobruk garrison and revitalize its tired forces.

The planners were looking for a way to disorganize the German command and control network. Many schemes were mooted, but one of those finally accepted as being liable to bring about the best results, was the capture of the top German commander, Rommel himself, in a daring raid on his headquarters. He was thought by British intelligence to be at Sidi Rafaa, better known as Beda Littoria, halfway between Tobruk and Bengazhi, not far from the seashore.

Early in October 1941 six officers and 53 men from 11 Scottish Commando under Lieutenant Colonel Geoffrey Keyes, were given the mission. Keyes, an Aberdeen-born regular soldier, son of Admiral Lord Keyes, Director Combined Operations, had already distinguished himself in the early stages of the Syrian campaign. Then, during the River Litani operation, he had taken command of the Commandos during a difficult phase in the fighting and had brought the action to a successful close. Now, in the action to follow, himself in charge of a Commando, he was to exemplify the highest summit of personal courage.

Preliminary ground intelligence had been carried out by the remarkable Captain John Haselden, who had already become a legendary figure to the desert fighters. Haselden, born in Egypt of mixed English and Greek parentage, spoke fluent Arabic and knew the North African desert extremely well. Attached to the Libyan Arab Force, he had wandered there freely, disguised as a nomad Arab, spying out the land. He had recently landed on the beach at Hamma, which was earmarked for the landing, and returned to

Alexandria, where he gave all the information he had gathered to Keyes and to Colonel Robert Laycock. Laycock commanded the Middle East Commando, and was to accompany the attacking party himself as an observer.

Many of the top brass regarded the proposed capture of Rommel as a harebrained scheme, impossibly hazardous, with very little chance of survival for those taking part even if it succeeded. Colonel Keyes, however, decided to go ahead and set about training his men on a beach near Alexandria. Shortly before the landing was slated to take place, Captain Haselden set out once more for Hamma, this time parachuting in. He took cover at the house of a pro-British Arab who lived there and then, taking with him two Arab guides, he left for Hamma beach, where Keyes' Commandos were expected to land.

The same day two British submarines, HMSS *Torbay* and *Talisman*, carrying the assault parties, arrived offshore. So far all had gone well, but now the weather took a turn for the worse, the sea running a high swell. As darkness fell, *Torbay* closed the shore; the party on deck could see the signals which Haselden was making with his torch.

Conditions were by now very bad. The rubber dinghies, which were passed with great difficulty through the forward hatch, could barely be launched in the rolling sea. Some were swept overboard and others capsized. It took six hours to get seven boats ashore, their crews drenched to the bone and exhausted. Haselden greeted the shivering men as they stepped ashore, and guided them to a cave where they could dry their wet clothes and attend to their weapons.

Meanwhile, HMS *Talisman*, with Colonel Laycock and his reserve party on board, was still standing out to sea until a signal was received that Keyes and his men had arrived on shore. With only a short time left before dawn, Laycock decided to land his men in spite of the rough sea, but the submarine touched ground on its way in, sweeping overboard several boats which were just being launched. The sub commander, not wanting to risk his vessel,. decided to withdraw out to sea, so only four boats were launched, Colonel Laycock in one of them.

That morning the sun came out for a few hours and the men enjoyed some respite from the cold, but a head count showed that only half of the planned force had come ashore. Keyes had to change his plans quickly.

The raid, as originally planned, had had four objectives: (1) To attack the villa near the seashore where Rommel was thought to be staying; (2) sabotage the Italian headquarters at nearby Cyrene by cutting communications; (3) assault the Italian intelligence centre at Appolonia; (4) create as much havoc as possible to the Axis lines of communication. Now, however, with less than half his men available, Keyes conferred with Laycock and decided to abandon the other raids and concentrate all his efforts on Rommel's HQ, which would bring the biggest dividend.

Laycock, with a small party, remained in the hideout on the beach; Colonel Keyes set out with his Commandos on the first leg of the journey, marching in knee-deep mud caused by the incessant rain. They had two Senussi guides with them, who had come in with Haselden. When they reached the first escarpment, about one kilometre inland, in the evening, the guides suddenly disappeared, leaving Keyes to navigate by compass and inaccurate maps, with the clouds making starshoots almost impossible, so he let the men rest.

Just before daylight the Commandos were roused from their fitful sleep and dispersed among the scrub where they spent most of the day. During that time some Arabs approached, but they were quite friendly; Keyes conversed with them with the aid of Corporal Drori, a Palestinian Jew who spoke fluent Arabic, and one of them agreed to guide the British force. This Arab also led them to a large cave giving shelter from the ceaseless rain which had made the men extremely miserable.

Early next morning, Colonel Keyes set off with his party for the final assault. The attack had been planned to take place on the night of 17/18 November 1941, to coincide with the great CRUSADER offensive which was to open that day. Marching once again in pouring rain, soaked to the skin and ankle deep in mud, the going was terrible. Men slipped and fell over each other as they staggered in single file. At about 2230 they reached the bottom of an escarpment and rested awhile. Then there was another climb up a rock face. At the top they found a muddy track, which the guides had told them would lead them to the villa which was their objective.

Here Keyes split his party. Lieutenant Roy Cooke took one team to find the pylon from which the telephone wires ran in order to blow it up. The remaining men, led by the colonel and his second in command, Captain Robin Campbell, went on ahead. After a while, the guides refused to go on, and melted away into the darkness, leaving the raiders alone. Suddenly two figures – an Italian and an Arab – loomed out of the darkness and confronted Captain Campbell, who addressed them in passable German. Corporal Drori, who was nearby, took over, telling the Italian that they were a German patrol, but the Italian had already lost interest. He was more concerned with finding some shelter from the cold night.

The Commandos passed on and, cutting the outer wire fence, entered the garden of the villa. There was almost no one to be seen. Most of the guards, like the Italian, were looking for protection from the rain and, in any case, the place was so far behind the lines that nothing ever happened. A single sentry, however, was standing in the doorway and Colonel Keyes killed him.

The men now formed up for the assault according to their briefing. Keyes kicked in the door, but was immediately confronted by a German officer. As the colonel closed on him, the German leapt for the tommy gun and, seizing its muzzle, tried to wrest it from the colonel's hands. Before any of the others could approach the German retreated, still holding onto the gun, but Campbell shot him with his revolver.

Aroused by the shot, a man came clattering down the stairs, shouting as he sighted Sergeant Terry, who cut him down with a short burst from his submachine-gun. From the garden came a man shining a torch; he was shot by one of the men guarding the outside. Colonel Keyes went over the house throwing open doors until he found a room containing about ten Germans, scrambling for their weapons. The colonel sprayed the room with his tommy gun, slammed the door shut and waited for Campbell to arrive. Then he reopened the door and Campbell lobbed in a grenade, but before the door could be slammed shut again, Keyes was hit in the heart by a bullet fired by one of the Germans – who himself was to die seconds later, hit by Campbell's exploding grenade.

Captain Campbell dragged the colonel's body out into the front garden and went back into the house, but could hear nothing, so he ran out into the garden, where, in the half-light, he was mistaken for a German and shot by one of his own men.

Sergeant Terry now took over and began to place demolition charges while he ordered the men to assemble for the withdrawal. They offered to take Captain Campbell with them, but he refused, knowing that it would be impossible for them to make it back to the beach carrying him. The captain was later found by the Germans and taken to hospital, spending several years in a German prison camp. Colonel Geoffrey Keyes' body was also found and given a military burial in a nearby cemetery. He was posthumously awarded the Victoria Cross for his leadership and supreme courage.

The raiders, with Sergeant Terry now in charge, made their way back to the beach and found Colonel Laycock waiting in the wadi close to the shoreline. He was shocked to hear of Keyes' death, but he also had other troubles. Lieutenant Cooke's party had failed to arrive. Laycock could see the submarine *Torbay* lying offshore but she ignored his signals and did not venture inshore to pick them up.

The night wore on and it became obvious to Laycock that no evacuation would be possible under these conditions, so the Commandos went under cover, hoping to try again the following night. At first light a defensive position was formed, but later in the day they were attacked by Italians and German troops who maintained sustained fire from a distance. The Commandos were stuck and unable to move and it seemed likely that it would soon become impossible to hold the beach position. Colonel Laycock ordered his men to split up into small groups, dash across the open ground and seek cover in the hills inland, with the hope of meeting up with roving patrols of the Long Range Desert Group or returning to the beach later that night to be picked up by the submarine, if she came in again.

After the party had scattered, Colonel Laycock, in company with Sergeant Terry, crossed about a kilometre of open country, dodging enemy sniper fire. For days the two men walked in the desert, befriended by some Senussi, who helped them along. Forty-one days after having left the British lines, they managed to link up with British troops near Cyrene. They were, however, the only ones who made it out of the entire group.

General Rommel was not present at his headquarters that night; in fact, the house at Beda Littoria was used by him only infrequently. At the time of the raid, Rommel was at his forward HQ near Gazala, preparing his own attack on Tobruk. British intelligence had been totally inaccurate, and the raid was deemed a complete failure – the more so as it had cost the life of the brilliant young Keynes who was one of the best Commando officers. The raid did achieve one important result, though: The Germans became increasingly nervous about Commando raids into this rear zone, and stepped up their vigilance, thus tying up large numbers of troops away from the front line. However, the main lesson learned from this almost total fiasco was that British intelligence would have to become much more reliable before men were sent again into the unknown.

10. THE COMMANDOS AT DIEPPE

T he small French seaport of Dieppe lies at the mouth of the River D'Arques, approximately four kilometres east of centre of a 22-kilometre coastal strip bounded by the village of Berneval on its eastern and Quiberville on its western sides. In April 1942 the area was dominated by two German artillery batteries, one at Berneval and one at Quiberville.

During that month the town was selected as a suitable target for the largest combined operation yet mounted by British forces. In the words of Winston Churchill, it was to be 'a reconnaissance in force to test the enemy defences' of a strongly defended sector of occupied France. The idea was to harass the enemy, thus compelling them to maintain large forces there, and also to discover what problems would be involved in the massive landings required for any future invasion of the mainland.

The operation was more complex than any attempted so far. It would involve not only landing men and equipment on the enemy shore, but also bringing them home once the mission was completed. The plan, code-named Operation 'Jubilee', envisaged multi-pronged Commando assaults. On the left flank, No. 3 Commando was to land a strong force at Berneval and Belleville-sur-Mer, to assault and destroy the German battery there, while the Royal Regiment of Canada was assigned to wipe out a battery at Puys and a field battery farther inland. On the right flank, No. 4 Commando was to land at Vasterival, east of Quiberville at the mouth of the River Saane, move inland and demolish the coastal battery south of Varengeville-sur-Mer. The main assault would be made in the centre by a division-sized Canadian force, supported by a battalion of Churchill tanks. With the two flanking batteries already secure, it was hoped that by the time of the main landing, the Canadians would land on the Promenade at Dieppe, move into the town and raise havoc among the German defenders, who were estimated by intelligence to be at regimental strength. But first, in a *coup de main*, seven Free French chasseurs led by the Royal Navy gunboat *Locust* would attempt to rush Dieppe harbour and seize forty German invasion barges. After appropriating war documents from the German HQ, the forces were to assemble and return to England.

The 'Jubilee' assault force totalled some 6,000 men, mostly Canadians, who were in the peak of condition, trained to the hilt and itching to get into action. The Commandos, who would have the vital job of neutralizing the German guns, numbered about 1,000 officers and men from Nos. 3 and 4 Commando, together with fifty US Rangers, whose first sight of battle this would be. Major-General H. F. Roberts commanded the military side of the operation; the naval officer in charge was Captain J. Hughes-Hallett, RN.

The assault force sailed on the night of 18 August 1942, in 252 ships from four south coast ports. There were nine infantry landing ships, eight destroyers, 24 tank landing ships – carrying 28 of the new 38-ton Churchill tanks – and a motley collection of landing craft and assorted vessels. The ships sailed behind minesweepers which swept the route. The entire flotilla arrived fifteen kilometres off Dieppe at 0300 on 19 August.

The landing area between Berneval and Quiberville consists of vertical chalk cliffs, broken by river valleys and narrow, steep-sided gullies. All the exits from the beach area, as well as the gullies, were obstructed by barbed wire and mines.

No. 3 Commando approached the assigned landing area in 23 landing craft led by a gunboat in which the commander, Colonel Durnford-Slater, stood beside Commander Wyburd. At first all was quiet, but just before 0400 the group suddenly encountered a number of armed enemy trawlers some twelve kilometres from the French coast. Starshells lit up the sky and heavy gunfire was directed from enemy warships. The two escorting destroyers were only some eight kilometres distant but could not manage to come in and help, so the unarmed British flotilla, completely outgunned, had to scatter. One hour later, it was clear that the dispersion of the fleet meant that it would be impossible to land the Commandos. In fact, only five landing craft were still there.

Four ships did make the beach near Petit Berneval but by then it was daylight and the enemy fully alert. Once the men had landed, they made straight for the cliffs, breached the minefield, cut a passage through the wire and – silencing a German machine-gun position on top of the cliff – started inland. Once in the open, however, they encountered withering automatic fire and casualties began to mount. Among the first to fall was Lieutenant Loustalot of the 1st US Rangers – the first American to be killed in Europe during the Second World War. Within minutes the small party lost all its officers. One of the wounded officers unsuccessfully attempted to advance with his men, but, pinned down by heavy gunfire, decided to withdraw the survivors to the beach, carrying the wounded with them down the steep cliffs. When they got there, however, there were no boats; the entire party was later captured. Only one man managed to return to England – picked up by a naval beach party under heavy fire.

Major Young's group fared much better. They landed on the right beach – three officers and seventeen men. The party quickly crossed the beach and started to go up one of the gullies, only to find it blocked by barbed wire and mines. He called for a Bangalore torpedo, but none could be found, nor were there any wire cutters! No doubt saying many uncomplimentary things under his breath about the people who had planned this operation, Major Young decided to search for a passage around the obstacle. As he climbed ahead of his men, he lost his balance, but recovered and continued upwards.

After a difficult climb the party reached the cliff top and, led by the major, reached a small wood which gave them cover. They then advanced cautiously inland to a rise where they had a good view of the German battery which, at that moment, was being attacked by Hurricanes which were pinpointing their target with the aid of the anti-aircraft fire from the battery.

Major Young tried to set up an observation post in a nearby church tower but could not find a ladder, so his small group started to go through a cornfield adjacent to the German positions. Until then the Commandos had not been detected but as they came within range of the German battery, they started sniping at the sentries and, forming into lines, advanced on to the guns.

Now fully alerted to the danger from the rear, the Germans turned their heavy guns inland and began shooting. This was exactly what Young wanted, as it prevented the gunners from targeting the main British landing force at Dieppe. In any case, the guns were firing much too high to do any harm to the Commandos who were lying low in the corn. Every time a round came from the Germans, the Commandos returned small arms fire, aiming at the smoke from the heavy guns. But soon their ammunition ran low and, having done what they came for, the major decided that it was time to get back to the beach.

Disengaging, each man guarding another's back, they withdrew, coming under fire from German riflemen who followed them. Major Young and his men rendezvoused with the boats and were taken up safely, reaching Newhaven after an uneventful voyage. But No. 3 Commando had lost some 100 men. Some of them roamed the countryside for days until they were killed or captured by German troops. But they had done their job: the guns at Berneval were silent.

Some ten kilometres to the west, behind the village of Varengeville, was a formidable German gun battery, including six 150mm coastal guns, commanded by a Captain Scholer. The destruction of this objective was entrusted to No. 4 Commando, led by Lieutenant-Colonel the Lord Lovat, already a seasoned Commando leader at the age of 31. A Scottish peer, with a family tradition dating back to the Middle Ages, Lord Lovat was to prove his worth in battle throughout the war. In Operation 'Jubilee', his Commandos performed admirably and achieved what was perhaps the only real success of the action.

The German battery was situated in a built-up area about 100 metres from the beach, protected by steep cliffs which could only be scaled at one place. The guns were mounted on a concrete platform, protected from air attack by anti-aircraft guns, which could also be fired at ground targets if the need arose. Nearer to the cliff top, connected by telephone to the battery, was an observation post overlooking the beach and the area to the east. Lord Lovat decided to send in two groups; one he led himself; the other would be commanded by his deputy, Major Derek Mills-Roberts. The latter would land at Vasterival, where two gullies led up the cliff to a wooded area, from where it was thought that the battery could be observed and engaged with small arms fire. Lovat's group, which was somewhat larger, would land farther down the coast to the west, at the mouth of the small River Saane, where the cliffs sloped down to the beach.

Their passage across the English Channel was uneventful although as they sailed they could see the starshells and tracer indicating the naval engagement which No. 3 Commando was fighting against the enemy warships. No. 4 Commando continued towards the beach in their landing craft but, as they drew nearer, a lighthouse could be seen flashing its signal. Suddenly, without warning, the light went out and in its place several starshells shot upwards, illuminating the area.

Mills-Roberts managed to land unopposed with his group and he sent an officer with a scout section to find one of the designated gullies. When they came back, they told him that it was totally choked with barbed wire and mines, requiring a substantial breaching operation, so he decided to find a more suitable passage up the other gully, which he cleared with a Bangalore torpedo.

The party scrambled through the gap and made its way uphill, reaching the top well ahead of schedule. Just as they reached the cliff top, several RAF fighters, firing cannon, swooped low over the cliff and raked the German gun battery. It was perfect timing: the flurry caused by the air attack allowed the Commandos to advance rapidly into the nearby woods. Then they went forward through the thick undergrowth towards a barn-like structure on the edge of the wood, from where the major could scan the area through his binoculars. His men could observe the German guns and crews, but remained undetected.

As soon as they were in place, the snipers went to work and some of the Germans dropped. Unable to locate the source of the shooting, the Germans raced for cover behind sandbags. Some of their heavy guns had already stopped firing, which meant that at least part of the Commandos' mission had been carried out. But others continued to shoot and a 20mm gun started firing from a flak tower, raking the woods, with the sound of mortars following. Mills-Roberts ordered his own light mortar to start bombarding the enemy positions, and a lucky round landed in a stack of explosives which blew up with a tremendous crash. While the Germans scrambled to extinguish the blaze, the Commandos directed their automatic guns on them, another move which kept the big guns silent.

His job almost completed, Mills-Roberts tried to raise Lord Lovat by radio, but was unable to reach him. As he did not know if the other group had got ashore, he decided to wait and rush the battery with his own force if Lovat did not get there soon. Then Lovat's voice crackled over the air waves, informing him that he was in position to attack the battery perimeter. Mills-Roberts' group, still undetected by the Germans, now covered the entire battery area with smoke rounds.

While the other group had been distracting the Germans' attention, Lovat's Commandos had advanced inland along the river bank, encountering some mortar fire which caused several casualties. On the way to their designated assault point, they split into two groups and advanced along different routes. Suddenly one of the sections ran head on into a party of German assault troops armed with submachine-guns. A sharp fire fight ensued, but the Commandos, quick-witted and quick on the trigger, succeeded in wiping out the Germans without losing a single man. They reached the designated assault point just as more British fighter-bombers roared overhead to deliver their planned two-minute strike.

As soon as they had passed, Lord Lovat fired a Very light indicating that the assault was about to begin and, according to plan, Mills-Roberts' force withdrew towards the gully and mounted an all-round defence to cover Lovat's retreat.

But the Germans were now thoroughly roused and their resistance stiffened. Several men were lost to enemy fire, including two officers. A sergeant took command of one of the units, but was also killed a moment later. Then Major Porteous, an artillery liaison officer, came up and took control, leading the charge on the battery. Close hand-to-hand fighting began with Lord Lovat in the middle of the fray and, to add to the confusion, some Spitfires came in low and strafed the guns. The Commandos began to fight with their bayonets and Major Porteous, in the lead, reached one of the guns but fell, shot through the thigh. Furious, his men rushed the Germans, killing them with grenades and bayonets. Two German officers dashed out of their dugout firing their pistols, but were picked off before they could do any harm. In the end the demolition teams got to the heavy guns and blew off the breechblocks. The rest of the Germans were dispatched; the battle was over.

Their job completed, Lord Lovat assembled his men and led them down the steep gully which had been guarded meanwhile by Mills-Roberts and his men. All the wounded were got off and all survivors embarked, to reach the safety of England's shores. At the cost of two officers and ten men killed and seventeen wounded, 4 Commando had fulfilled its task admirably.

But the rest of Operation 'Jubilee' was a disaster. The attempts to seize Dieppe failed before they even began. Many of the Canadian troops who hit the shore went down in the face of terrible German fire – leaving the beaches soaked in blood. Of the 28 Churchill tanks only some fourteen managed to land, but all were destroyed or abandoned.

As for the raid on Dieppe itself, German reinforcements came in much faster than had been anticipated, and the promenade bristled with deadly weapons which British intelligence had failed to spot in low level recce sorties flown shortly before the raid. The Canadians, despite their courage and determination, could not even reach the sea wall. By the afternoon, more than a thousand men were dead and two thousand in captivity of the six thousand who had left England.

Only a single Canadian battalion succeeded in driving inland, led by Lieutenant-Colonel Merrit who, disregarding his own safety, encouraged his men onward in the face of tremendous odds. His regiment, the South Saskatchewan, were honoured by the award of a well-earned Victoria Cross for their commander.

Operation 'Jubilee' was the first full-scale raid ever mounted on enemy-held shores and, although never likely to succeed in the face of such tremendous odds, it nevertheless taught the Allied Command some important lessons, the results of which were seen two years later in the invasion of Normandy.

11. SOVIET AIRBORNE TROOPS

I t is an interesting fact that the earliest attempts to create an airborne force were made in the Leningrad Military District of the Soviet Union. Today, although the Soviet Union no longer exists, most large-scale airborne forces are still based at Leningrad.

The first experiments in the field were made in 1929 under General, later Marshal, Mikhail Tuchachevsky, a leading and farsighted Soviet military theoretician, who commanded the district at that time. His theory was an improved and modernized version of the German assault troop tactics that had been practised at the end of the First World War. But the true originator of the concept was an American, Colonel 'Billy' Mitchell, commanding the US air contingent in France, who had previously suggested dropping soldiers of the 1st Infantry Division behind the German lines, in an attempt to overcome the static trench warfare. However, due mainly to the short-sightedness of the general staff, the idea was shelved.

Proposals for a sample aviation/motorized division were forwarded to the General Staff in Moscow, then known as the Soviet Revolutionary Council and, on 2 August 1930, the first try at using airborne troops to seize an 'enemy' headquarters was made in the course of manoeuvres. A detachment of twelve men was dropped from two Farman-Goliat biplanes near Voronesh, while three R-1 reconnaissance aircraft dropped supplies by parachute. The assault team then went forward and surprised a divisional HQ and its staff officers.

After the First World War Marshal Tuchachevsky was the first man to recognize the importance of the third dimension – airborne troops – on the tactical battlefield. After his concept was accepted, the Red Army went on to address the issues of training and equipment. Their Training Directorate put out a series of directives that outlined training requirements for airborne units, subdivided into parachute, glider, airlanding and combined operations. Special parachute platforms were designed to paradrop heavy equipment from modified TB-1 and TB-3 bombers, which were used as airborne transports.

The four-engined TB-1 Tupolev – the Red Air Force's first heavy bomber – made its maiden flight in December 1930, one of the earliest projects of the fledgling Soviet aircraft industry. The use of corrugated sheet metal for its fuselage and wings made it a design far ahead of its time. As locally made engines were not available, the designers used two Napier 450hp Lion power packs, later replaced by German BMW VI Dietrich engines. However, when it was used to drop paratroops, the technique for the drop was both crude and dangerous: it required the men to climb on to the wings, holding on to handles, and then slide off and free fall!

Once they had the aircraft, the Soviets began to practise this new skill. In September 1933 at Luga in the Leningrad Military District, the 3rd Airborne Brigade, as it was later designated, conducted a tactical exercise under Tuchachevsky's personal supervision. Operating in extremely poor weather conditions, with low clouds and strong winds, a paratroop force dropped from 500 feet into a heavily defended 'enemy' rear zone to block the movement of reserves to the front. The surprise drop which, according to plan, began only when 'friendly' artillery barrages had ceased so as not to endanger the dropping paras, succeeded in driving off the enemy and blocking the passage of reserves.

Following the successful exercises, the 3rd Airborne Brigade was officially formed with one parachute, one motorized and one artillery battalion, supported by an air group which consisted of two squadrons of modified TB-3 bombers. Another squadron of R-5 Poliarkov reconnaissance aircraft was also added. By the end of 1933 the Red Army fielded, apart from the brigade, 29 airborne battalions and four aviation-motorized detachments, totalling some 10,000 trained men.

To bolster recruiting the Soviet government encouraged civilian parachuting facilities near large cities, where jumping towers were constructed. The sport of parachuting became extremely popular throughout the Soviet Union during the thirties, in the same way that gliding for sport ws practised in Germany between the two world wars to encourage flight training while remaining within the limitation of the Treaty of Versailles.

The most extensive airborne manoeuvres to date were held in 1935 in the Kiev Military District, many foreign observers taking part for the first time. The scenario involved the penetration of strong defences by a rifle corps supported by tanks and powerful artillery. Following an initial breakthrough, there was a combined assault by cavalry and mechanized forces. It was at this stage that the airborne troops came into action. Two regiments of paratroops, about 1,188 men in all, were dropped to secure a landing zone near Bovary, north-east of Kiev, after which two rifle regiments were airlanded. The airborne force then rushed the River Dnieper and seized several crossing sites. Holding on against enemy counter-attacks, the airborne force was joined by the cavalry which had crossed the river, and together they continued the drive towards Kiev. The airbridge operation was flown at a distance of more than

280 kilometres from the home base to the drop zones – an unprecedented feat for those times and one which greatly impressed Western military observers.

In 1939 the number of fully trained airborne brigades had risen to six, and one of these participated in the Kalchim Gol campaign shortly before the outbreak of the war, but this was fairly small beer. One year later, however, in June 1940, a full-scale airborne attack was mounted by Soviet paratroops during the occupation of Roumanian Bessarabia. A rapid advance of armoured and cavalry units was needed to guard vital strategic installations, and airborne forces were assigned to seize important objectives in the enemy rear, cut off the withdrawal of Roumanian troops and link up with advancing mobile units. Although it involved little actual fighting, this operation clearly demonstrated the effectiveness of Soviet airborne training and tactics, making the airborne concept one of crucial importance. Compared to the German Wehrmacht, however, which was also fielding airborne troops and using them with great success in the Blitzkrieg on the West, the Soviet Army failed to capitalize on their large number of airborne units to their full value, and mounted very few such operations.

The first of them was in support of a massive action initiated in January 1942, aimed at pushing the German offensive back from the gates of Moscow. While several Soviet armies attacked westward, General Zhukov, commanding the front, called on his parachute forces to strike into the Germans' rear zone, thus blocking their retreat along the strategic Warsaw–Moscow highway near Vyazma. The great airborne strike arm, which had performed with such success in exercises in the thirties, was now to be tested in battle for the first time.

Prior to the major engagement, however, there was a tactical paradrop into the German-held Traeva Sloboda area on 15 December 1941. It passed almost unnoticed, but did succeed in destroying some bridges and harassing German columns retreating from the Klim sector. The next drop, to take place on 3 January 1942, was much more impressive, involving a parachute battalion from 201st Airborne Brigade, a battalion of rifle infantry and an airlanding force from the same regiment. Commanding the operation was a Major Soldatov. The landing zone chosen was near Medyn, an important communications centre in the German Fourth Army Sector.

The first assignment was to capture an airfield near Bolshoy-Fayanovo, and the mission was given to a battalion led by Major Starchak, while Captain Surzhik's contingent from the 201st Airborne was to jump north-west of Medyn to capture a bridge over the River Shanya, thus cutting an important supply route between Yuhnov and Medyn. On the night of 3 January, Starchak's battalion jumped into the airfield perimeter. Because of strong enemy anti-aircraft fire, inaccurate drops scattered his men over a wide area, but the major managed to gather sufficient numbers of his men to attack the German garrison. Several hours later, with sporadic fighting still going on below, the Russian transport aircraft returned, but were unable to land the reinforcements they were carrying. One Russian aircraft which had managed to land took off when Starchak's men ran towards it, as the pilot had mistaken them for Germans! Major Starchak's dwindling force continued to fight throughout the next day and managed to establish a defensive perimeter, but every attempt to disembark the Soldatov's airlanding force was foiled by the determined German defence. The Soviet command therefore cancelled the drop of Soldatov's unit and ordered Starchak and his men to fend for themselves. Many of his men broke through the German lines and reached safely.

Two weeks later another operation was set in motion, this time in the Zhelnaye sector, some 35 kilometres behind the German front. Once again the objective was to cut some important supply routes, those that were still fordable in the prevailing harsh winter conditions. For the airdrop the Red Air Force had assembled 21 PS84 transports – Soviet-built American DC-3 Dakotas – to drop the paratroops, and several converted bombers from the 23rd Bomber Division to drop the heavy equipment.

At 0335 on 18 January the first sixteen planeloads of paratroops took off from Vukovo airfield, and by morning, some 425 men had been dropped between Znamenka and Zhelnaye, where important German logistical installations had been identified by Soviet intelligence. The dropping operation continued the following night, but the weather had deteriorated in the meantime and most of the pilots were forced to abort without dropping their loads. The next day the airhead was dropped and, once in place, guided the transports in, while the heavy bombers had to make do with a snow-covered strip nearby. Several of them bogged down, were unable to take off and were left behind after discharging their cargoes.

Captain Surzhik quickly assembled his battalion and attacked the heavily defended Znamenka airfield. Unable to break through, he disengaged and organized a diversionary landing strip, the location of which he radioed to his HQ. Despite adverse weather the Russian pilots managed to land 1,200 troops in the Zhelnaye area; they began fighting within hours and, as planned, cut the highway, causing great inconvenience to the Germans.

On 27 January the 8th Airborne Brigade mounted its largest airborne operation to date. A forward detachment under Captain Kanaukov was landed near Ozerechnato, west of the Vyazma–Smolensk highway and the railway track parallel to it. These two routes were vital to the Germans for supplying their front line troops, hungry and cold in the freezing Russian winter. As the 1st Battalion, 8th Airborne, assembled, the 2nd jumped near Tabory, with diversionary groups being dropped at various locations.

The German command was almost immediately aware of the extensive Russian operation, but due to the large number and wide dispersion of the drops, the Germans were unable to take prompt action. The Soviet navigation, however, was terribly inaccurate, so that the men were dropped from altitudes which were too high, resulting in their being scattered and difficult to assemble.

By the evening only 476 of the 700 dropped were able to rally with Captain Kanaukov. All their supplies were lost, including the vital radios, so the commander had no option but to move his force to Ozerechnato, linking up with some other men from the battalion, and together they attacked the German garrison. After a vicious fight the Soviet paratroops overwhelmed the defenders and prepared the landing zone for urgently needed supplies.

Meanwhile at Kaluga, previously a German-held airfield, the remainder of 8th Airborne took off as planned, although HQ still had no information as to the whereabouts of its forward detachment on the ground. Once again the drop was inaccurate and scattered. Moreover, the Luftwaffe, familiar with the airport which they had so recently left, launched a massive airstrike just as the heavily loaded Russian transports were taking off. Several aircraft were destroyed and the entire operation was interrupted, adding to the grave situation at the already hard-pressed landing zone. The Soviets switched to an alternative airfield and continued with the operation later, but the number of aircraft available was sharply reduced.

By the end of January the weather had deteriorated drastically, with temperatures dropping to minus 45° C, but the Soviet paratroopers, who were used to wintry conditions, remained in their operational area fighting isolated actions, although no large strategic objectives, such as assisting in the encirclement of the German army, were implemented.

In September 1943 the Soviets carried out their second large-scale operation using airborne troops – which was also their last of the war in Europe. Having repulsed the massive German offensive near Kursk in July of that year, the Soviet forces counter-attacked along the entire front. Heavy fighting was going on in the bend of the River Dnieper south of Kiev. The German command considered the river to be a valuable asset where they could build their defences to stem the Soviets, and were therefore trying hard to reach the southern bank before the Soviets could arrive. In order to secure the bridgehead over the river and prevent the Germans from establishing themselves on the southern bank, the Soviets decided to drop an entire airborne corps into the river bend in the area near Bukrin.

The landing, to be spread over two nights, would require 50 PS-84 transports, 150 Il–4B–25 aircraft and a glider force. The aircraft would airlift the force from Smorodino and Bogodukhov airfields near Lebedin, where the airborne troops assembled and trained – some 200 kilometres from the designated drop zone. The 1st and 5th Guards Airborne Brigades were assigned to jump during the first night, while the 3rd would be landed the next, together with the gliders carrying their heavy equipment, including artillery. Another 35 transports were allocated to ferry supplies into the airhead. The first objective was a bridge near Kanev – the only passage over the Dnieper for many kilometres. Once taken, it would deprive XXIV Panzer Corps of its withdrawal route and close it in a trap east of the river. The Germans knew this, too – and the race was on!

General Nehring, commanding XXIV Panzer Corps, stood near the bridge, watching his armour crossing over. To his amazement there were no Soviet aircraft to be seen. For hours on end, German columns passed across the bridge, absolutely unhampered by the Russians, until at last all units were safely across. The general gave the order to blow the bridge and within minutes it exploded with a thunderous roar and clouds of dust. At that moment – and much too late – the Soviets arrived! While the Soviet vanguard approached the eastern bank – preceded by an artillery barrage – scores of heavily loaded transport aircraft appeared overhead, flying in perfect formation as if on parade at 600 metres' altitude. Just below fighter-bombers attacked German anti-aircraft positions, flying at almost ground level. It was dusk and the Russian pilots switched on their landing lights to comb the ground. Soon they started dropping hapless paratroops by the hundreds, who floated down slowly into the well-aimed German tracer bullets. Several transports were hit by ground fire and exploded in mid-air; others, frantically attempting to evade the deadly fire, dropped their cargo wide of the target area. The chaos became even greater when two Soviet airborne brigades scattered over a wide area, many of the Russians dropping straight into German-held positions.

5th Airborne Brigade was immediately engaged in heavy fighting with the German 19th Recce Battalion commanded by Major Guderian, youngest son of the famous general. The 1st Brigade jumped north of Nehring's HQ over the Rossava river marshes, and soon tangled with mobile forces which routed them before they could rally. One group of Soviet paratroops jumped slap into an advancing panzer formation which was rolling through the village of Balyka. The carnage which followed was terrible, not many Russians surviving the next few minutes.

This was a clasic example of how *not* to conduct an airborne operation. Not only had the lessons of Vyazma not been learned, but the execution of the drop was even worse. Although the planning was basically good, the operation was carried out too late, when the bridgehead over the river was already in German hands, the vital bridge blown and the widely scattered Soviet paratroops too weak to fight a serious battle once on the ground. As soon as the first two of these factors were known, the Soviet command should have cancelled the drop, thus saving the lives of hundreds of men.

Once the scale of the disaster became clear to the Soviet high command, they cancelled the planned second drop which included the heavy equipment. The surviving troops were once again left to fend for themselves, and not many made it across the river back to the Russian lines.

Just like the Germans after their disaster at Crete, the Russians were discouraged from initiating any more massive airlanding operations, but in one final attempt to use their airborne troops they did mount one combined attack against the Japanese to capture the Far Eastern Sakhalin and Kurile Islands in 1945. In a well-coordinated effort, using naval infantry, paratroops and mobile units together, a lightning strike gained all its objectives in record time. A string of seaborne landings captured the heavily defended islands. Launched by the Soviet Pacific Fleet with its two flotillas, and supported by long-range guns from Kamchatka, the Soviets landed two rifle regiments on the islands, forcing the Japanese to surrender.

In another combined assault, Russian armour raced for objectives in Manchuria while paratroops were dropped in a surprise attack on Pyongyang, which was seized by *coup de main*, to link up with the advancing tanks. The Far East campaign, at least – and at last – showed the Soviet airborne concept at its best.

12. SECRET MISSION TO NORTH AFRICA

On Sunday, 17 October 1942, Major General Mark Clark was called urgently to his office in Grosvenor Square, Central London, the HQ of the US Forces in Europe. At 46 years of age, he was one of the youngest generals in the US Army and was deputy to General Eisenhower, i/c American Forces Europe.

On arriving at General Eisenhower's office, Clark saw the reason for all the fuss – a red-hot message straight from Washington, signed by General George Marshall, the American Chief of Staff. It made fascinating reading. The cable was for the most part the text of another cable which Robert Murphy, then in Algiers on a special mission to French North Africa, had sent to Washington. Murphy's plan seemed outlandish, but if it came off it might make all the difference to the success or failure of Operation 'Torch', the planned invasion of North Africa, and save many lives. The two American commanders decided to discuss the idea with Winston Churchill, the British prime minister, whom they knew would be delighted with it. A quick call to Chequers, where the great man spent his weekends, and he agreed to return to London and meet them at Downing Street that very afternoon. In the meantime, the Americans sent for charts of the North African coast and experts on North Africa, and studied the cable in detail.

Murphy had reported that he was in close touch with General Charles Emmanuel Mast, the French commander in Algeria and the Allies' best contact in North Africa. Mast had suggested that an American delegation should come secretly to a pre-arranged rendezvous near Algiers to discuss plans for Allied co-operation in French North Africa. The plan envisaged the possibility of avoiding armed conflict between the former allies. It was implied that General Henri Giraud, the senior French general who had only recently made a dramatic escape from the well-guarded German prison at Königstein castle, and who was highly regarded by Free Frenchman, could become a key figure in the discussion, if he could be brought over from Vichy France.

Specifically, the rendezvous was stated to be a house standing alone on the shore at a definite latitude and longitude, about 120 kilometres west of the city of Algiers, and the Americans were able to pinpoint the house on their charts. The date of the meeting was set for the night of 21 October, only four days away. General Mast had stipulated that the American delegation should travel by submarine and that it must include a senior general, which was how General Clark came into the picture.

The War Department cable suggested that the officer in charge of the mission be accompanied by one man thoroughly familiar with the details of Operation 'Torch', one expert on supplies, one naval officer and a political agent – the latter to be fluent in French. Brigadier General Kyman Lemnitzer, head of the Allied Force Plans Section, Colonel Al Hamblen, the shipping and supply expert, Captain Jeraud Wright, the Navy liaison man on 'Torch', and Colonel Julius C. Holmes, a former State Department officer, fulfilled all these requirements. All were known to General Clark and he relied fully on their expertise.

The Americans sat until late afternoon, working out details of the mission, naturally in conditions of the utmost secrecy. The party would be flown to Gibraltar in two B-17 Flying Fortresses. This part of the plan did not please the Air Force officers, as such large aircraft had never before landed on Gibraltar's short runway, but in the circumstances they agreed. As several aircraft had been lost flying over the Bay of Biscay en route to the Rock, two aircraft would be taken with the party split between them to make sure that at least some of them would get to these important talks. From Gibraltar the Americans would go aboard a British submarine which would take them to the predesignated location on the Algerian coast, about which the cable was very specific: some 15 miles west of the tiny port of Chechel. On the night of 21 October the submarine was to surface off that point; a single white light would be flashed from a seaward window of the house, indicating that the coast was clear for them to land. There was no alternative date given in the message.

With their plans worked out, the two American generals arrived at Number 10 Downing Street, to find about as dazzling an array of British diplomatic and military presence as could be imagined. The Prime Minister was in superb form. As soon as he heard the first details from Eisenhower and Clark, he smiled broadly, puffing on his big cigar as he listened to the final contents of Murphy's cable. The Americans then discussed the fine details of their mission with Admiral Mountbatten,, no novice at this sort of game, and he gave them some expert hints on how to go about their task. Churchill concluded the meeting by emphasizing how much the success of their assignment could contribute towards the Allied cause by saving thousands of Allied lives in the forthcoming invasion of French North Africa. As Churchill escorted them to the door, he offered any help they might need for the job, assuring them how much value he placed on its success.

When they returned to Grosvenor Square they were told that the Air Force had already provided two B-17s which were standing by with specially selected crews. The weather people had advised that takeoff be deferred until the following morning, so that the men could rest for a while and make their final preparations without the pressure of time.

At dawn next day, 18 October, General Clark and his colleagues assembled at the 8th Air Force bomber base at Polebrook, north-west of

London. No one at Clark's headquarters had been notified of his trip, most of his staff thinking that he was going to Scotland on an inspection tour. In addition, to make him less conspicuous on the airfield, Clark had replaced his stars with the insignia of a lieutenant colonel. The weather had deteriorated; several hours were wasted waiting on the cold and windy airfield, while the men tried to keep out of sight of personnel working nearby. Clark was worried about the difficulty of communicating with Robert Murphy and, through him, with the French who by now would already be on their way to the rendezvous. If the American party were to be delayed, the French might take offence and leave, with unknown consequences for 'Torch'. There was also the question of their personal safety: no one could be certain that the meeting was genuine; it could well be a trap to capture some very important personalities whose combined knowledge of Allied military plans would be very useful to the Germans.

At 0630, the takeoff was finally cleared and, after a hasty breakfast, the men climbed into their draughty bombers which immediately took off without an escort to avoid attracting too much attention en route. But the gunners were confident that they could outgun any fighters coming at them, as they had done in several daylight raids over Germany. General Lemnitzer carried all the secret documents for the meeting in a weighted tube. The pilots had received strict orders not to land on Spanish or Portuguese territory under any circumstances, since they had received word that German fighters were patrolling the area along that coast.

General Clark's aircraft, 'Red Gremlin', was piloted by Major Tibbets, who a few years later was to fly 'Enola Gay' to Hiroshima and drop the first atomic bomb there. Breaking above the clouds, Tibbets flew his aircraft perfectly for three hours. Then the clouds broke and below they sighted fishing vessels somewhere off Portugal. Even before they identified the Rock of Gibraltar, RAF Spitfires which were expecting the Forts came along and escorted them in to land. Lemnitzer's plane 'Boomerang' went in first and landed safely on the small strip. One of the pilots was already climbing out of his hatch when a British officer rushed up and motioned everybody to remain inside. He explained that the Gibraltar airfield was under constant German observation from the nearby Spanish village of Linea and all landing aircraft were photographed with special zoom lenses to identify the passengers. The arrival of two B-17s of a type never before seen would certainly arouse suspicion and generate immediate reports to Berlin. The British officer suggested that the Americans leave their overcoats and hats behind and descend one by one, getting into a car which would wait as near to the aircraft as possible. All went well and soon the American officers had met the British Governor and senior British naval officers.

General Clark conferred with the latter who obviously thought that the whole adventure was completely mad. They talked of thick inshore patrols, they talked of spotting planes, but they finally agreed to take Clark and his group in. In contrast to their marked lack of enthusiasm was the alacrity displayed by the submarine commander, Lieutenant Norman Jewell of HMS

Seraph. His boat was small and quite slow, but Jewell was a fine submarine commander with much experience who knew the African coastline well. Clark took a liking to him right away, and the confident young officer recounted a few of his previous exploits. He also informed them that there were several Commandos with their folboats (a kind of collapsible canoe) aboard, just to make sure that everything would go as planned.

There was no time to be lost, so the men went aboard, Clark having sent a last message off to Washington before he left. In it he requested that Colonel Eddy, the US representative in the international zone of Tangier, forward a request to the French reception party to wait for them from 2100 on the 21st until daylight. Should the landing be delayed for technical reasons, another landing would be made the following night.

The submarine was very crowded, and the distinguished passengers were given the officers' quarters for the duration of the trip. A British destroyer led the way for the first part of the trip. Jewell was concerned that he could not make the rendezvous on time if he had to travel submerged most of the way so, studying his charts carefully, he found a route which would enable him to sail on the surface, ready to crash-dive if they were spotted.

General Clark discussed the embarkation with the officers of the Commando force, studying signals and possible actions on shore should the need arise. The submarine would go in as close to the shore as possible after the beach had been scanned by periscope in daylight. The radio operator stayed on the alert for any last messages from Robert Murphy, but no change in the operation was indicated. Late in the afternoon a rehearsal of the embarkation techniques was held. Captain Livingstone of the Commandos and Colonel Holmes launched first. The sea was choppy but they managed to step into the frail and wobbly craft on the dry deck. They paddled noiselessly away and tried out the infra-red signal light from a distance. Then they returned to the submarine and General Lemnitzer and another Commando officer had a go. The general got pretty wet but seemed to enjoy himself and returned in good spirits. Then the rest of the party rehearsed and all went well.

The exercise successfully completed, the submarine got under way again, but when they got closer to the North African coast, the skipper decided to dive and continue submerged. It was not until the early morning of 21 October that they came within sight of the coastline. It was still dark and through the periscope a single light could be seen in the correct position, but it was already too close to dawn to risk a landing. The party was thus forced to spend another boring day pent up in the narrow confines of the submarine. When it was light enough the periscope was run up and the house on the shore observed. Two Algerian fishing boats could be seen on the beach which was to be the designated landing point.

During the day a message came from Murphy which, to Clark's relief, confirmed that the French would await them that night, and arrangements were made with the skipper of the sub that when they had landed successfully they would signal him by turning off the guide light, which would be turned on again when they wanted to re-embark. The submarine would remain in positiion offshore, directly in front of the house, for two nights and wait for the signal.

When darkness fell they surfaced, but there was no light from the house on the shore. For several hours, with tension rising, they waited in vain. At 2230 General Clark decided to retire, but was awakened at midnight by an excited Jewell and told that the guide light was on. Working feverishly, the men got the small boats on deck and into the water and the submarine drifted inshore until it came within four kilometres of the beach.

The embarkation went off well, the officers calmly following the drill they had practised under the supervision of the Commandos. The party approached the beach in vic formation, with Holmes and Livingstone in the lead. As he rode the surf, Clark saw the letter 'K' flashed by a torch – the signal that the first boat had landed and all was well. The others followed and stepped on to dry land in good condition, although they felt rather exposed on the lonely beach, with no one to meet them. There was a steep bluff at the far side of the beach, covered with shrubs and knotty olive trees and they ran there for cover. Then, just as they reached the edge of the cliff, Robert Murphy and his French associates welcomed them to Africa!

They climbed a steep, stony path up the bluff to the house they had been waiting to see for the last three days. It was a typical French colonial villa, built around a stone-walled courtyard. The main highway to Algiers was only ten metres distant. The owner had sent his Arab servants away so that the parties would be undisturbed. General Mast and his staff officers were not in the house when the Americans arrived, but Clark was told that they would arrive early next morning. Clark ordered the British Commandos who had been waiting on the beach to bring their 'folboats' up to the house and hide them in a downstairs room, away from prying eyes. The British themselves were to keep out of sight, as the French were not feeling any too friendly towards the British after the bruising naval encounters at Mers-el-Kebir.

At 0500 General Mast and his entourage arrived, and the discussion started off fairly amicably over a continental breakfast with Murphy, the diplomat, expertly circumventing any difficulties. Some frank conversations followed which covered most aspects of the forthcoming Allied invasion.

As the talks went on, General Clark was thinking that it would be impossible to re-embark that night and, as the afternoon wore on, a strong wind built up, making the sea extremely rough. Suddenly the telephone rang and one of the Frenchman shouted that Vichy police were on their way. Officers began to run in all directions. Some of the Frenchmen changed into civilian clothing; one of General Mast's officers ran to his car, briefcase in hand, and took off in the direction of Algiers; others jumped out of the windows and disappeared into the brush along the beach. Finally only the Americans were left, looking at one another and feeling pretty alone. The French owner of the house, however, kept his head. He motioned the Americans towards a trap door which led to the wine cellar and they got down there. Not a moment too soon – the policemen were already at the main door. As they hid in the cellar, the General and his associates could hear Robert Murphy, who had remained upstairs, identifying himself as the American Consul in Algiers, and telling the suspicious policemen that there was a small party in progress and some women upstairs – something that every good Frenchman could understand. They left without making a search. When all was quiet, the Americans came out, but as the police might return at any moment it was decided to leave at once.

Captain Livingstone made contact with the submarine commander and told him that an urgent pickup was needed. The Commandos got the boats out and took them down to the beach, but the sea was now extremely disturbed and so were the Frenchmen who were still with them and were obviously wishing them gone. So, although the waves were almost unmanageable General Clark decided to try first. Stripping to their shorts, he and Captain Courtney, the most experienced of the Commandos, started paddling one of the small boats towards the submarine through the huge, rolling waves. They soon overturned and this abortive attempt persuaded the general that they would have to find some other means of getting away. Someone proposed driving to Spanish Morocco, but this was thought to be too risky.

There was still contact with the sub, though, which had ventured inshore, dangerously close, almost to the surf's edge and, after midnight, with the help of Murphy and the Frenchmen, who stood in the water and steadied the boats, the group did manage to cross the surf and, rolling over metre-high waves, reached the waiting submarine, soaked and exhausted. The skipper broke out the emergency rations for a celebratory tot of rum. Then, having sent a message to General Eisenhower, the party was taken off by flying-boat and flown home via Gibraltar. Jewell and his crew gave them a cheer as they left. It was well deserved: when the Allies invaded North Africa, on 7 November that same year, there was only token resistance from the French forces there – a clear sign that the secret mission had succeeded.

13. RESCUE FROM THE GRAN SASSO

Benito Mussolino had been supreme ruler – Il Duce – of Italy since his Blackshirts had marched on Rome in November 1922 and seized power from the King, Victor Emmanuel. On 24 July 1943, however, his dominion came to an end when he was deposed by the Fascist Grand Council and succeeded by Marshal Badoglio.

The Italians, who had never shown much efficiency in the past in dealing with such matters, now showed a surprising turn of speed. The Italian police spirited Mussolini out of Rome and sent him off in a corvette to Ventotene, but, when they found a German garrison there, they moved him to Ponza, in the Isole Ponziane, a group of small islands west of Naples in the Tyrrhenian

Sea. There the dictator celebrated his 60th birthday, his first in exile. But on the night of 6 August some mysterious lights were observed out at sea and, as a precaution, the Italians conveyed their prisoner even farther west – to a remote naval base at Fort Maddalena on the northern tip of the island of Sardinia. No army personnel knew his whereabouts, not even the most senior Italian officers, and the new Italian authorities thought their captive was secure.

Hitler was stunned by the overthrow of his closest ally; he felt that if one dictator could be removed so easily, his own hold on wartorn Germany could be in danger too. Furthermore, the prestige of the Third Reich was at stake. Il Duce must be found, and rescued, as soon as possible.

On 25 July Hauptmann Otto Skorzeny was lunching with a university don on holiday from Vienna at the luxurious Hotel Eden in Berlin. Both men were enjoying an afternoon cigar, but Skorzeny had a nagging feeling that something was wrong, and he went to a telephone to call his office, to find that his staff had been frantically looking all over Berlin for him. Skorzeny was urgently required at the Führer's headquarters in East Prussia and a special plane was standing by to fly him there within the hour. Arriving in record time at Tempelhof airfield in the centre of the city, he met his second in command, Lieutenant Radl, who had brought Skorzeny's uniform and gear with him. Changing quickly, he boarded the Ju-52 which immediately took off and flew eastwards. The assignment which he was about to receive would make him a legend in undercover warfare – and one of the most dangerous men in the German armed forces.

The 35-year-old, Austrian-born Skorzeny was an ardent disciple of the Nazi Party and had joined the Waffen SS, fighting in France, Yugoslavia and Russia. In 1943 he had transferred to Hitler's personal security forces and created a special unit for undercover work. So far, however, he had never come close to the Führer himself.

As soon as they landed at Loetzen airfield in East Prussia, Skorzeny was taken by car to Hitler's personal lair, well hidden and carefully guarded in the middle of a wood. The young captain did not have to wait long. Hitler came straight to the point. He told Skorzeny that Benito Mussolini had been arrested and that Skorzeny would be responsible for his early release. He would have full powers to implement the mission although, nominally, he would be under the command of General Kurt Student, the airborne leader, already famous for the raid on Eben Emael, who was waiting for Skorzeny in the next room.

Skorzeny, although impressed by the importance of the mission, was not a man to waste much time in pondering over the grandeur of the moment and, as soon as Hitler dismissed him, he met General Student and discussed with him the details of the mission. Then he went into the office which had been assigned to him and communicated with his own HQ in Berlin, where his staff was waiting for his instructions.

He ordered Radl, his lieutenant, to select 50 of their best men for a special mission. They were to travel light, but with maximum firepower. Each section was to be equipped with two light machine-guns, each man with his own Schmeisser machine-gun, and lots of British-made egg-shaped hand-grenades, not the bulky potato masher type which would take up too much space. Two pioneer corps units would carry the highly efficient plastic explosives of the British type. The officers were to be Italian speakers if possible; in the event, one of them, Lieutenant Warger, was an ideal choice, being both fully proficient in Italian and a skillful mountaineer. The list of requirements was long, sent in several sequences over the hot wire of the teleprinter machine. Radl performed near miracles in getting things organized and by the next morning the combat team was ready to move. They were ordered to fly to the South of France, where they would join Student's airborne division, already getting ready to deploy to Italy, with Rome its final objective.

After a sleepless night, Skorzeny met General Student on the bleak and breezy airfield, where they boarded a waiting twin-engined He-111 bomber. While the general took a nap, Skorzeny, sitting in the co-pilot's seat, enjoyed the scenery en route to the south. On landing at the city airport near Rome, the two officers were taken to Field Marshal Kesselring's headquarters.

Three days later, Skorzeny's 50 men arrived with the paratroopers and reorganized at Practica di Mare airfield, and Lieutenant Radl joined Skorzeny in the Villa Tuscullum at Frascati, overlooking the splendour of the Eternal City. But the two men had no time to enjoy the superlative view. They had to find out where Mussolini had gone. No one at Kesselring's headquarters had any idea as to his whereabouts, although rumour was rife, some of it disinformation spread by the Italian police.

One evening, Skorzeny, feeling restless, decided to make a *tour d'horizon* himself. In a bar he overheard someone telling someone else, as Romans do, that a third someone – a fruit vendor who travelled frequently to Ponza – was sure that Mussolini was being held there. Later he heard some talkative Italian naval officers saying that the Duce had recently been transferred by cruiser to La Spezia. A few days later, he heard that the Italian dictator was actually being held in a villa in Fort Maddalena on the island of Sardinia. Skorzeny thought that this information seemed authentic, and decided to act on it. He flew to the island with Lieutenant Warger and they went on a sortie to see the villa for themselves and perhaps catch a glimpse of the prisoner. Disguised in seamen's clothes, they went to a nearby house from which they could observe the villa and Warger actually saw the Duce sunning himself on the terrace.

Back in Rome, Skorzeny decided to fly a recce mission over the villa to plan his attack. On 18 August he boarded a He-111 at Rome airfield which set course for Maddalena. On the way they were attacked by RAF Spitfires and forced to ditch in the sea, but all the crew managed to escape and sat for some hours in a dinghy until they were picked up by an Italian warship. Skorzeny transferred to a motor boat heading for Corsica, where he discussed his tentative plans with the head of the Waffen SS formation which was to take part in the operation.

The plan was shaping up now. A flotilla of minesweepers and motor boats with the SS formation from Corsica would enter the harbour and anchor at the main mole across the bay from Maddalena. At dawn the ships would leave the harbour as if on manoeuvres, while the troops who had been hidden in the ships, Trojan horse style, would storm ashore and, led by Skorzeny, would march for the villa, freeing the Duce with the aid of surprise and momentum. He would then be spirited away to a fast motor boat which would crash through the harbour defences. It was a bold plan but Skorzeny thought that he might be able to pull it off.

However, just as Skorzeny was shipping out from Anzio and Radl was ready to move off with the SS formation from Corsica, word came that Mussolini had been moved once again and taken to an unknown destination that very morning by seaplane. Skorzeny, of course, called off the operation and signalled Radl to stop everything and meet him in Rome.

Now there started another search and, once again, luck was in Skorzeny's favour when, after a few days of fruitless inquiry, information was received that the Duce might be held in a former ski hotel at the foot of the Gran Sasso plateau. The Gran Sasso d'Italia is a remote and mountainous region, ideal for the hiding of such an important prisoner. In fact, the Albergo Rifugio had been turned into a military installation, its only approach, by cable car, heavily guarded by the Caribiniere, who had sealed off the entire area. Skorzeny sent one of his officers, a doctor in civilian life, to reconnoitre the area on the pretext that he was looking for a convalescent home for wounded soldiers, but as soon as the doctor arrived at the lower cable station, he was turned away by armed guards, who told him curtly that the hotel had been requisitioned for top military commanders.

This was enough for Skorzeny; he was sure that Mussolini was on the Gran Sasso and a rescue operation must be mounted as soon as possible in case the Italians decided to move hin again. Skorzeny commandeered an He-111 and flew a photographic sortie over the mountain resort, taking pictures with a hand-held camera. He could see some very interesting ground features, among them a triangular patch of grass, which he thought would be ideal for a glider landing near the hotel. If the patch were really flat, several gliders could make it down there. He arrived back in Rome, having just missed a massive bombing attack by American heavy bombers which caused heavy damage to the German barracks near Frascati. The Luftwaffe photographic laboratories were among the buildings destroyed, so Skorzeny had to develop his important photographs in a makeshift lab, resulting in some very poor prints. Still, the hotel was clearly visible, together with the small plateau and the top station of the cable car near by, and Skorzeny was able to brief his men with the aid of a diagram which he and Radl prepared.

Twelve DFS 230 gliders came in from Marseilles for the raid, towed by He 126 transports. As soon as they landed at Rome's Pratica di Mare airfield the tow planes were refuelled and made ready for takeoff, which was planned for 1300 on 12 September. Just half an hour before takeoff, as Skorzeny and his men were about to board their gliders, the air raid sirens wailed and bombs came crashing down on the airfield. Only two gliders were slightly damaged, though, and none of the men hit; when the all clear sounded everyone reassembled, ready to move, which they did exactly on time.

Skorzeny had asked to take with him a senior Italian general so that when they landed, one of the first men out would be a figure well-known to the Italian guards. The man chosen was a General Ferdinando Soletti, who had been persuaded to join the venture. Now he shared the flight with Skorzeny, none too happy in his cramped seat in the flimsy glider.

The plan this time was for a surpise landing by Skorzeny's assault force with, on the ground, a *coup de main* by a parachute battalion to capture the lower cable car station and seal off the area. The latter part of the scheme was the responsibility of a Major Mors, already under way with his motor transport.

During the flight the glider pilot, Lieutenant Meyer, called out to Skorzeny that he had lost contact with the gliders ahead of him. They were now flying through thick cloud and he was afraid that he would lose his bearings. Skorzeny pulled out his Commando knife and hacked away at the flimsy canvas that clad the glider until he could see out. The clouds had cleared and he could see below the reassuring sight of the advancing motor column of Major Mors' paratroop battalion.

Soon the hotel came into view and he ordered the glider to break its tow, but as the glider banked to the right, Skorzeny received a severe shock: he could now see clearly the triangular patch which he had selected on his recce flight as a suitable landing field. What he saw from close up was totally unsuitable: not only did the patch slope downwards, but it was rocky and uneven. An on-the-spot decision was called for if disaster were to be averted. Meyer looked at Skorzeny for help, knowing that landing there would be terribly dangerous. General Student, in his final briefing, had given categorical orders that under no circumstances should a crash-landing be undertaken; if no suitable landing place could be found, the gliders were to land in the valley below. Skorzeny, however, for whom the assignment took priority over safety, realized that there was no chance of attacking from the valley and that not landing near the hotel meant aborting the mission completely. He therefore made a snap decision, choosing to disobey Student's order, and shouted to his pilot to dive towards the hotel and crash-land as near to it as possible. The pilot did not hesitate and they hurtled towards the mountain, the parachute brake whipping from their tail. In an instant the glider was pitching over the boulders like a dinghy flung upon a reef. There was a shudder, a jolt, the noise of ripping canvas, and then the glider came to rest less than fifteen metres from the hotel.

Skorzeny and a companion, Sergeant Schwert, broke out of the wrecked glider and raced for the first doorway they could reach in the clifftop hotel. From a window above them, the Italian guard commander, Guiseppe Gueli, watched in amazement, frozen by shock. He did not even draw his revolver from its holster. Near the doorway stood another Italian sentry, also rooted to the spot. No one fired a shot as Skorzeny and his small group entered the hotel. Inside, an Italian radio operator was tapping frantically on his transmitter. Skorzeny booted him from his chair and smashed the transmitter with his rifle butt. Seeing that the room led nowhere, he ran outside again, making for the main entrance.

Just then he saw the familiar head of Mussolini looking out of a second floor window. Skorzeny shouted to him to take cover, and jumped over a low wall to the terrace, followed by some of his men who had now come pounding up to the house. Clubbing their way through a crowd of stupified Italians, Skorzeny and Schwert ran inside and, three steps at a time, flung themselves up the stairs and into room 201, where the Duce stood, flanked by two more astonished Italian officers. Less than four minutes had elapsed since the glider had crash-landed.

Two heads now appeared in the window – Radl and another man who had scaled the wall to make sure that Mussolini was unharmed. Meanwhile, three more gliders had landed, a fourth having crashed into a ravine causing the only casualties so far, and these men now arrived at the hotel and started to disarm the Italian guards, who offered no resistance. Mussolini himself was surprisingly calm and offered his liberators some Italian wine while Radl organized matters outside, and Major Mors arrived from the lower cable car station, reporting the area to be secure.

Skorzeny had successfully executed the first phase of his mission; now he faced the second part, no less dangerous. An evacuation over land was out of the question, as Italian troops still occupied large sectors on the way to Rome; the only way to get the Duce out would be by air. There had been three contingency plans for an aircraft getaway: one was a *coup de main* capture of a nearby Italian airfield, the second a landing by light aircraft in the valley, and the third a landing by Captain Heinrich Gerlach – Student's personal pilot – of his Fieseler Storch on the supposed airstrip near the hotel. Skorzeny realized that the first option would be a waste of valuable time; the second came to nothing when the pilot of the light aircraft made a faulty landing in the valley and smashed the undercarriage disabling the aircraft. The only choice remaining, therefore, was for Gerlach to land on the Gran Sasso plateau.

Gerlach, a superb pilot, flew round once to search for a landing strip and then put his Fieseler Storch down in a perfect landing. Radl immediately organized a party of Italian prisoners and cleared a takeoff strip. Gerlach dissented from Skorzeny's demand that all three of them, including the Duce, should squeeze into the tiny aircraft, but was overruled by Skorzeny, who pulled rank to get his own way. The pilot gave in only reluctantly, thinking about taking off with all that weight, but Mussolini, who was an experienced pilot himself, remained calm as he got into his seat, with Skorzeny squeezing into the luggage space behind him. Radl and his men held on to the wings as the pilot revved his engine for maximum power. There was hardly any space for a run as the small airplane bounced forward over the uneven ground and Skorzeny held his breath, grasping the steel spars until his knuckles were white as the pilot fought the controls. Finally he raised the tail and became airborne, although he smashed a landing wheel on a rock before he pulled the aircraft into the air. As they shot over the edge of the cliff, a thousand-metre cravasse yawned below and the aircraft, hit by a thermal current, was forced downwards. The aircraft disappeared from view, and the men on top gasped, believing that it had crashed in the valley. But Gerlach brought off a miracle of flying skill; he caught the diving aircraft and forced it under control barely thirty metres from the ground! After that, anything else would have been an anticlimax and the rest of the flight seemed positively smooth. Soon the Storch landed intact at Rome airport despite the lack of one landing wheel.

Skorzeny and Mussolini, after receiving a formal greeting from the senior staff, boarded a waiting He-111 which flew them straight to Vienna. On Hitler's personal orders, Otto Skorzeny was decorated on the spot with the Knight's Cross. He had made his mark in a single operation. It was not to be his last.

Mussonlini's end, however, was not so heroic. Captured by Italian partisans at the end of the war, he was shot by a firing squad and hung by his heels in Milan's Piazza Loretto.

14. THE BRIDGE AT BENOUVILLE

J ust before midnight on 5 June 1944, Squadron Leader Merrick took off from Harwell Airfield and set course for France with a distinguished passenger in the co-pilot's seat: Air Vice Marshal L. N. Hollinghurst, commanding the air transport group which was to play a vital role in the forthcoming invasion of Normandy. Merrick's Albemarle was the first of six aircraft carrying the 22nd Independent Parachute Company, the pathfinders of the 6th Airborne Division, whose task was to capture the eastern landing zone of the invasion area.

In this region three important waterways run from the coast southwards, the Caen and Orne Canal, the River Orne and, farther east, the River Dives. The latter had been flooded by the Germans as part of their defence, turning the entire area into impassable marshes. There were four bridges crossing that river, with causeways allowing controlled access. Over the Caen and Orne Canal, however, there was only a single bridge, at Benouville, about halfway between Caen and the coast. This bridge would have strategic importance, as the Germans would meet it for the passage of their armoured reserves, in order to mount a counter-attack against the invasion forces. If the bridge were in British hands, the Germans would have to concentrate on a defensive posture and would not be able to counter-attack during the critical build-up phase.

For this reason, the British planned a daring *coup de main* attack to capture the vital bridge at Benouville well before the main body of the 6th Airborne Division landed, using complete surprise for the action. The taking of the bridge over the Caen and Orne Canal was the first action of the Normandy invasion, and the difficult task was placed on the shoulders of Major John Howard, commanding 'D' Company of the Oxfordshire and Buckinghamshire Light Infantry, which had become an airborne regiment some time before. Howard, a 30-year-old regular officer, had become increasingly bored with his job as a training officer and, as soon as he learned that his hometown regiment was going airborne, he jumped at the chance to join. With him on the mission was a 20-year-old subaltern, Danny Botheridge, who was also looking for more excitement than he could find on the parade ground.

At about 11 p.m. on 5 June, six combinations of Halifax bombers and Horsa gliders took off from Tarrant Rushdon airfield. In each of the gliders were some thirty men, including sappers from the Royal Engineers who were specially trained to identify and neutralize the demolition charges that were believed to be set on all the bridges. Major Howard and his team travelled in a glider piloted by Staff Sergeants Wallwork and Ainsworth.

The Glider Pilot Regiment had been raised in Britain in the early forties, after German success with such craft had been recognized. It had taken the enthusiasm of two officers, Majors Rock and Chatterton, fighting the conservatism of the top brass, to get the affair going, plus the personal intervention of Prime Minister Winston Churchill who had a flair for grasping the importance of new concepts. Chatterton had taken on the training of the volunteers, turning each of them into a first-class pilot and a fighting man, since he realized that once the glider was on the ground, each man had to fight.

The Horsa glider had a cylindrical fuselage, in which up to thirty men could be seated facing one another on wooden benches. In the cockpit two pilots flew the glider, using flaps fitted to the wings to allow a steep descent. First used in 1942 in an abortive raid to Norway, the Horsas were involved successfully in the airborne invasion of Sicily in 1943. Those used by Major Howard's assault team were specially fitted with arrester parachutes, facilitating a short landing near to the bridge.

Flying at some 5,000 feet over the Channel, the first combination reached the French coast soon after midnight. Patchy cloud darkened the sky, but once over the coast visibility was good enough to identify the targets.

Before the raid the pilots had been thoroughly briefed on a specially constructed model prepared by an RAF artist. He had made a film with a movie camera, which gave the pilots an impression of the approach and made them familiar with the scenery – something like the simulator of today. Wallwork, at the controls of his glider, peered through the darkness and was able to identify the distinct features of the river and canal shining in the moonlight, and was determined to bring his glider as close to the canal bridge as possible. At 0016 the tug pilot indicated cast-off and, having done so, banked sharply to starboard.

With Wallwork now in full control, Major Howard ordered his men to prepare for landing and the troops inside the darkened glider fell silent, each man alone with his thoughts. The tow rope was gone and the speed decreased quickly as the drone of the Halifax faded away. Wallwork dropped the nose and the glider swooped down, bumping through the clouds. Lieutenant Botheridge stood up and, with Howard and a sergeant holding him, swung open the exit door. Cold air streamed in. The men could now see the countryside below.

Wallwork had no difficulty in identifying the bridge as he steered for the ground. On his order his co-pilot, Ainsworth, released the arrester parachute, which billowed behind. Then, warning his passengers to hold tight, the pilot slammed the flimsy airplane into the grass, still at terrific speed. The collision was shattering. Howard could see sparks flashing past the open door as the glider skidded along the ground, timber cracking and splitting, smashing itself to pieces. Both the pilots fought the controls, trying to hold the glider in a straight line for the bridge. Suddenly, with a final crash, the cockpit disintegrated, and the glider tore into the outer fence of the German position – right next to the bridge.

As it stopped, Major Howard and his men jumped out. It was strangely still and quiet. None of the Germans seemed to have noticed their arrival. One had, though: Corporal Helmuth Roemer, a young paratrooper on guard, saw the glider crash but he thought it was a bomber, naturally enough because there was an air raid in progress over Caen. But suddenly, out of the darkness, men with blackened faces charged towards him. The German, terror-stricken, dived for the nearest trench, with no time to call an alert.

Botheridge was already leading his men on to the bridge when suddenly there was shooting. A German sentry had seen them and fired a Very light which flashed up into the night sky. Private Wally Parr raced up and lobbed a grenade into the pillbox on the near side, silencing the machine-gun inside. Someone threw in a phosphorous grenade, which exploded in a blast of brilliant green light, the figures of German soldiers silhouetted against it as they fell backwards. One man who was aiming his rifle fell into the canal, hit by one of Botheridge's men.

On the far side German reinforcements were coming in from their billets, aroused by the ear-shattering noise of shooting. Howard assembled his command team near the pillbox. He saw that Botheridge had crossed the bridge and was now fighting on the other side. Also wandering about there was one of the medics, who had got there by mistake. Howard shouted to him to get over, which he did – fast. All seemed well, so Howard called for the demolition squad leader to get to the girders of the bridge and neutralize the charges before the Germans could blow them. Soon the demolition men were checking the base of the bridge, disconnecting the detonators, and making the charges safe.

Suddenly a German machine-gun started firing from the far side and Lieutenant Botheridge fell, fatally wounded, but his men charged on and silenced the machine-gun with grenades and automatic fire. The two glider pilots had now managed to extricate themselves from the ruins of the cockpit. Wallwork, his face covered with blood from splinters, disregarded his pain and, in the traditions of a soldier trained by Colonel Chatterton, set about offloading the stores still inside the glider.

The attack was only three minutes old when word came from the far side of the bridge that the objective was secure. In one of the paradoxes of war, the runner who brought Howard this news also had to tell him of Botheridge's death. Howard told his radio operator to signal the success message to brigade, and then set about organizing his all-round defensive perimeter.

His initial orders had been to capture the bridge and hold it until relieved, a task that would be far from easy in face of the determined counter-attacks which would surely ensue as soon as the Germans realized that their only access route to the coast had been blocked.

Surprisingly, however, Howard's small force managed to hold on to the bridge perimeter despite several German counter-attacks which, perhaps because of all that was happening that night, were rather tentative and did not break through the vital bridges. At noon the next day, Howard was finally relieved by Lord Lovat's Commandos, who came marching behind their piper up the canal road towards the hard-won Benouville bridge.

15. THE MERVILLE BATTERY

T he most dangerous part of the seaborne assault on Normandy fell to the 9th Battalion of the Parachute Regiment: the destruction of a battery of 150mm guns emplaced in concrete fortifications at Merville, thought to be impregnable to any attack. The capture of this battery was of major importance because the guns commanded the beaches earmarked for the assault of the British 3rd Division; these were on the left flank of the invasion zone. If the German guns were still in action on the landing day the entire seaborne assault could be jeopardized.

Lieutenant-Colonel Terence Otway, who commanded the 9th, was only 29 years old – extremely young for a battalion commander even in the paratroops. A non-conformist, he had an acute military sense which had served him well during his army service in India before the war, and was to serve him equally well in the difficult mission ahead. He had been told of the task allotted to his battalion in April 1944 and had searched for, and found, a suitable place in England to train his men. This was Newbury, Berkshire, whose countryside was similar to that of Merville in France. Within days he had managed to requisition the place, have it fenced off and bulldozed into shape. In it he built an almost exact replica of the gun battery and its defences, with tubular scaffolding taking the place of the guns. With his men largely innocent of the nature of their target, rehearsals were started, first by day and later by night, according to a precise timetable carefully worked out by his staff. After final exercises with live ammunition, every man knew his job.

The Merville battery would be a tough nut to crack. Air reconnaissance had indicated that it was placed in bomb-proof fortifications, surrounded by dense minefields, barbed wire entanglements and machine-gun positions guarding every access route. Repeated bombing attacks had failed to cause any serious damage, although the surrounding countryside was now pocked with bomb craters. The 150mm coastal guns were emplaced in thick concrete bunkers, designed to withstand the heaviest bombs and shells. Earth four metres thick surrounded the casemates. Access was solely by steel doors. Two hundred men defended the compound, its gun positions and wire guarded by minefields.

Colonel Otway's plan called for his battalion to be divided into eleven separate parties, each assigned a special task. One party would jump well ahead; then, at a rendezvous following the main drop, they would collect and organize the assault teams and distribute the weapons, which would arrive by glider. A recce party would move out, reconnoitre the route leading to the defence perimeter, and set up a base where the assault teams would start fanning out. A breaching company, preceded by a party of sappers, would clear the minefields, tape a breached path and lead three assault platoons into the battery compound, followed by a reserve company. Just before the breaches were blown by Bangalore torpedoes, three gliders would come in and crash on top of the battery, adding to the effect of surprise. This last part was a repetition of the German assault on Eben Emael which had been so successful, and Otway believed that their timely arrival would tip the balance.

The glider force carrying the heavy equipment plus the rendezvous and recce groups took off from RAF Brize Norton in Albemarles and Halifax tugs just before midnight on 5 June 1944, while the rest of the battalion set off somewhat later from Harwell airfield. All went well until four minutes before the drop, when anti-aircraft fire caused the pilots to take sharp evasive action, throwing the aircraft violently around in the sky just as the heavily loaded paratroopers were forming up for the jump. The effect was chaotic: Some of the men were thrown to the floor of the aircraft and could rise only with the help of their comrades. Otway, himself thrown down, tried to persuade the pilot to fly a straight course at least for a few moments, only to be informed that the tail section had been hit by flak. Just then the signal turned green and the colonel jumped. As he came down he recognized some of the features which he knew almost by heart from photographs, but with considerable alarm he saw that he was being carried by the wind towards the German battalion headquarters, not exactly the most suitable place to land!

By now tracers were whistling past him, some tearing through his parachute, but there was little time to worry for soon he hit the ground, on top of a wall. As he jumped down into a garden, he was greeted by two of his men. A German upstairs opened a window and looked out, but failed to see Otway and his men in the darkness. Someone picked up a brick and threw it, apparently with good aim: there was the sound of breaking glass and the head of the German disappeared abruptly. Otway and his men raced to the back of the house and out of the garden, while some Germans rushed out at the front.

Otway's small group now made for the rendezvous arranged in a small wood nearby, where he was greeted by his second in command. The major informed him that the drop had been chaotic. It was nearly 0200 and only a small fraction of the battalion had assembled. As time went on more men straggled in, but the final tally was only about 150. The rest were missing. Moreover, all the heavy equipment, apart from a single machine-gun and some Bangalore tubes, was also gone. There were no engineers, no medical supplies, and no radios.

Although Colonel Otway's meticulous plan had allowed for many contingencies, he had hardly envisaged a situation as bad as this. He faced a terrible dilemma: to attack under such circumstances would be suicidal; but not to attack might have serious implications for the entire invasion. He had little choice but to mount the attack with the resources he had.

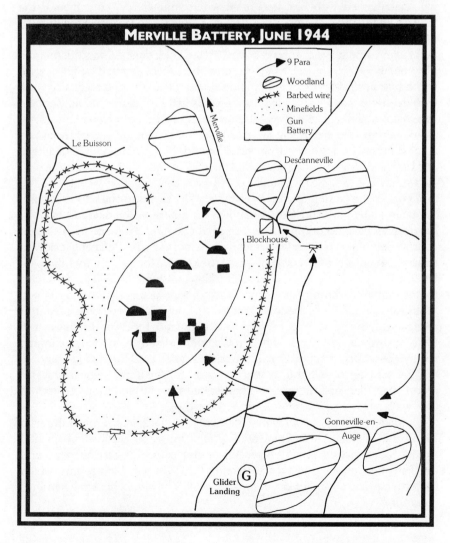

MERVILLE BATTERY, JUNE 1944

9 Para
Woodland
Barbed wire
Minefields
Gun Battery

Le Buisson

Merville

Descanneville

Blockhouse

Gonneville-en-Auge

Glider G Landing

At 0250 the men moved out, skirting a German flak battery which was firing on gliders coming in to the east. Some of the men wanted to fire on the battery, but were stopped by their officers, who literally grabbed at the guns as they were being aimed and shoved the men back into line. Just afterwards Otway encountered Major Smith, the leader of the recce party, who brought him up to date. Smith's men had undergone a really harrowing experience when they dropped. Some Lancasters on a bombing raid were overhead at the same time and the Lancaster pathfinder, mistaking the location of the battery, had dropped his markers right on to the dropping zone of Smith and his men. As a result, bombs whistled past them as they dropped, exploding beneath their feet. Not a single bomb hit the battery compound. However, he and his recce group had already cut the outer fence, crossed the large minefield and pinpointed the German machine-gun positions. The engineers who had landed with him had breached the minefield, searching for the mines with their bare hands as the mine detectors had been lost in the drop.

Heartened by this news, Colonel Otway and his 150 men reached the outer wire without incident, undetected by the defenders. All was quiet, apart from one panicky moment when some terrified cows, aroused by the bombs which had fallen, stampeded right through their line, causing more than one man to jump back very swiftly indeed. Now the colonel could see the casemates outlined distinctly against the dawn sky, but, glancing at his watch, he was alarmed to see that it was 0430, the time when the gliders should be coming in. He had no mortar flares with which he could signal the gliders in and, precisely on time, he saw two of the gliders with their tugs approaching above.

One of the combinations, flown by Staff Sergeants Bone and Kerr, with the team leader Captain Gordon-Brown on board, was already in trouble. Tracer was pouring into it as the tug pilot struggled to keep the glider on course. Suddenly the arrester parachute opened in mid-air, making it slow to control. As no starshells could be seen, the glider pilot thought that the plan had gone wrong. Seeing the ground fire, Bone mistook the village of Merville for the battery and turned too soon, landing eight kilometres from his target. Staff Sergeant Kerr did better, managing to put his glider down only 100 metres from the outer fence. As he came in to land, however, he saw out of the corner of his eye a sign written in German: 'Minen'. Shouting a warning, the two pilots just managed to lift the glider and cleared the danger, landing just behind the minefield in a sunken road, nor far from Colonel Otway's group. The men quickly emerged and joined up with the paratroopers – a very welcome sight.

Immediately the colonel gave the signal to attack. The gaps in the wire round the perimeter were blown by Bangalore torpedo tubes which had already been placed, and the assault parties crawled over the gaps and stormed the battery – just the beginning of a savage, bloody fray which started with fierce gunfire on both sides and went on to become hand-to-hand combat.

Three German machine-guns were destroyed by accurate bursts from the Vickers. As soon as they were cleared, the men went for the big guns. As Otway led the reserves into the compound, it looked like a scene from Dante's *Inferno*: German soldiers were running wildly over the compound, and black-faced paratroopers seemed to be everywhere, firing their weapons through the apertures of the casemates, throwing grenades. The whole scene was blacklit by flashes from the mortar, and accompanied by all the noise of war. Three of the 150mm monsters were destroyed by Gammon bombs, while others were neutralized with German bombs stuffed into the breeches. Paratroopers battled their way through the trenches and gun positions and, after twenty minutes, it was all over.

Colonel Otway fired his Very pistol to signal their success; an aircraft circling overhead conveyed the news to HMS *Arethusa* – just in time; she was about to open fire. Lieutenant Loring, the signals officer, pulled a carrier pigeon from his jacket and sent it off in the air. Only 80 men were still on their feet but the mission had been a success.

16. RANGERS AT POINTE DU HOC

One of the many noteworthy feats performed early on D-Day, 6 June 1944, was the scaling of the heights at Pointe du Hoc, a few kilometres west of what came to be known as Omaha Beach. The 40-metre-high mass looks forbidding today, almost fifty years later, as it juts out into the sea, its steep walls of solid rock falling straight down to a narrow strip of beach. The cliff walls face in three directions, seaward, east and west – a perfect site for a coastal gun emplacement.

In fact, that was exactly what the Germans had in mind when they built the massive fortifications on that great pile of rock. It was part of the Atlantic Wall defence conceived by Field Marshal Erwin Rommel, who had overall command. Allied intelligence had estimated that a fixed gun position with 150mm guns was housed within a reinforced concrete bunker, its field of fire covering up to 23 kilometres; this range would include the beaches of the projected American assault as well as assault ships which would be offshore, making them a perfect target for such artillery. Some intelligence researchers surmised that the Germans might have placed even bigger guns, like the giant 240mm coastal guns, which would considerably increase the danger. The planners of Operation 'Overlord' had enough to worry about without giant guns on the flank of their assault, and decided to get rid of them first, if at all possible.

Chosen for the task of silencing the guns on Pointe du Hoc was the 2nd US Ranger Battalion under the command of Lieutenant Colonel James R. Rudder. A 34-year-old Texan, he was just the man for such a tough job. His men, all volunteers and eager for action, had been trained to the peak of perfection at Bude in Cornwall, where they had practised by scrambling up cliffs of a similar height. Colonel Rudder had planned his assaults in great detail and had also acquired technical equipment which would enable his men to scale the cliff in minimum time from the moment they landed on the beach.

Just before midnight on 5 June, Rudder's 2nd Rangers, part of the great armada which sailed for the shores of Normandy, were fighting seasickness in the swell which battered their ships and bounced them around the sea like balloons. Most of the men were thoroughly miserable and eager to land, although they knew what was awaiting them at the other end.

The three leading assault companies were due to land at H Hour, set at 0630, on the narrow, gravel-covered strip of beach below the chalk promontory which loomed high above. The offshore naval vessels had already opened up a deafening bombardment, with the battleship USS *Texas* sending 355mm shells into the clifftop and medium bombers dropping their bombs for good measure. Under this impressive cover the Rangers, having boarded their landing craft in extremely difficult conditions, started for the beach. Some of the boats pitched so badly in the swell that they filled with water; for the men, who had already endured hours of stormy seas, that last stretch was probably the worst they had encountered.

The three companies assigned to the assault numbered some 230 men. The rest of the battalion, along with Lieutenant Colonel Max Schneider's 5th Rangers, were scheduled to land with the 29th Infantry Division on Omaha Beach, farther east, waiting offshore for a signal from Rudder that he had the point secure. Failing that signal, Schneider was to land some eight kilometres east, fight his way inland and go for the guns from their rear – a strategy that was almost hopeless from the start, in view of the German defences there.

Rudder placed himself in the leading assault craft which headed for the beach. The Channel ran high and the flimsy craft pitched sickeningly over each huge swell, a dreadful ordeal. Added to that was the earsplitting din as heavy shells pumped into the cliffs, and fighter-bombers roared low overhead strafing the gun positions.

The men, however, fine tuned for the fight, ignored all that; as soon as the landing craft touched the beach, they scrambled out of the boats and raced forward. No enemy fire was evident at first, but suddenly the Germans opened up from the clifftop; bursts of machine-gun fire hit the landing craft and the first casualties fell into the water. More boats were coming in all the time over the heavy surf, their skippers attempting to avoid the obstacles strewn in the water offshore and, as soon as the Rangers had reached the beach, leaping for cover towards the cliff wall, the colonel, right up there with his men, urged them to begin the climb.

The Rangers had been well prepared for their mission. Eight of the landing craft had been specially fitted with three pairs of rockets that could lift heavy ropes attached to grapnels up the cliff. Others carried tubular ladders in sections which could be placed on the cliff wall. Two DUKWs even came in with 30m turntable ladders lent by the London Fire Brigade for the job, but with a pair of Lewis guns mounted in place of the fire hoses. The Rangers themselves were sent in lightly burdened, with only personal weapons and ammunition, to allow them a fast climb. However, in the heavy seas some of the landing craft foundered, among them one which carried vital supplies.

As the Rangers assembled for the ascent, gunners in the landing craft directed fire at German troops on the clifftop to chase them away. Then the first pair of rockets went off, sending the lines upward to where the grapnels should hold, but the ropes, heavy with seawater, failed to lift and did not pull enough line to hoist the rope ladders. The men became more determined with every setback and fired their hand rocket lines, which finally caught hold. Soon the men were climbing like goats up the sheer rock face, which was filled with lines as more and more Rangers poured up.

Behind them in the water another drama was being enacted as three amphibious tanks which were supposed to give fire support became targets of anti-tank guns whose shells ripped their amphibious skirts to shreds. Within minutes the huge war machines had become no more than steel coffins, their crews frantically scrambling up the hatches trying to escape. Not all of them made it; most were trapped inside and drowned. At the same time great spouts of water were to be seen as the landing craft became the targets of German artillery. Although Allied destroyers skimmed back and forth to fire support for the hapless landing craft, pounding the German guns, the Germans still kept firing.

By now the ascent of the cliff wall was in full cry. Men were scrambling up the cliff wall in scores while again and again the rockets soared, shooting up more and more climbing ropes and ladders. Shells and machine-gun fire from the offshore boats raked the cliff top, shaking down great chunks of earth and stone on to the men as they climbed. Here and there at the top, Germans were throwing down hand-grenades and cutting the climbers' ropes from their grapnels, and automatic Schmeisser fire could be heard as German gunners shot down some of the climbers who had nearly made it to the top.

Some of the Rangers did not even wait for the ropes to catch the grapnels. Weapons slung over their shoulders, they cut handholds with their Commando knives and climbed up the nine-storey-high cliff like flies, while Germans kept cutting the ropes and Rangers went tumbling down to the bottom, only to start right up again. Some tried it two, three or even more times until they finally made it to the top.

One example was Private Harry Roberts: his rope was cut twice, but on his third try he finally got to a cratered niche just under the edge of the cliff. From there, hidden from the Germans, he could even hear their breathing as they leaned over and fired their Schmeissers.

Another tale was that of Sergeant Bill Petty, who scaled the wall by climbing hand-over-hand on an ordinary rope. Although an expert free climber, he could not grip the rope because of the wet mud covering it, and slid downwards. He tried scaling a ladder, got about halfway up, was hit in the shoulder by a rock and fell down again. Despite the intense pain, he tried once more, only to have his ladder cut by a German soldier. The determined

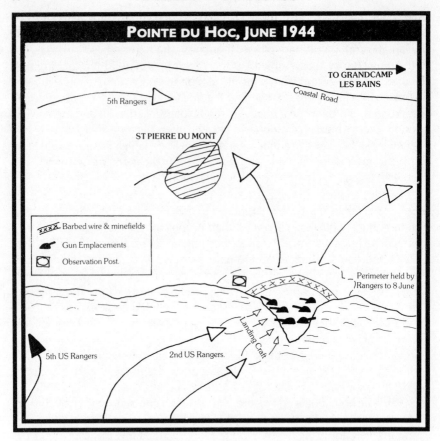

POINTE DU HOC, JUNE 1944

TO GRANDCAMP
LES BAINS

Coastal Road

5th Rangers

ST PIERRE DU MONT

Barbed wire & minefields

Gun Emplacements

Observation Post

Perimeter held by
Rangers to 8 June

5th US Rangers

2nd US Rangers.

Landing Craft

sergeant now started upwards one more time and, by dint of cutting holes in the cliff with his knife, he finally made it to the top, almost exhausted.

Now men were scrambling in scores up the wall, throwing themselves over the edge and into shell craters. Private Martin Corrado, perched on a saddle just below the summit, picked off two German gunners who were busily trying to dislodge grappling hooks. Other Rangers who reached the top came face to face with a German machine-gun dug into the cliff only a few inches away from them. Two of them lobbed grenades into the weapons pit and silenced the gun, but one grenade fell short, rolled down the cliff face, and exploded at the bottom. Luckily no one was hurt.

Another cliff edge position was even harder to take. Here two Germans lunged forward to push one of the Rangers off the cliff, but both were gunned down by another man who was on a ladder nearby. One of the Germans lost his grip and plunged headlong down the rock, but he took with him another Ranger who was on his way up.

The naval gunfire, which had been pounding the cliff top incessantly throughout the climbing phase, now stopped, signalling the start of the next phase. With loud battle cries, the Rangers threw themselves over the top and raced forward to the first German trenches. Sergeant Fred Morton led the first section. A German rose from his trench and lunged at him with a submachine-gun but, before he could fire it, Morton threw his knife at him and the German pitched over the cliff. A Ranger coming over the top saw Germans running inland. Unslinging his assault rifle, he fired a long burst and dropped them. It was not all one-way, however. From the aperture of a bunker, a machine-gun blazed away with deadly accuracy, covering all approaches, only a few centimetres above the ground. Two Rangers raced forward, but dropped dead within a few steps. Another tried his luck and fell, wounded crawling behind a rock and into one of the hundreds of shell craters which pitted the ground, making the landscape look eerily like the surface of the moon. Many Rangers had reason to be grateful to those craters, to which they owe their lives.

Colonel Rudder, who had established his command post in a niche at the edge of the cliff, decided that the machine-gun bunker had to be taken as a priority. A sergeant and two men crawled forward, inching their way from crater to crater, until they got within throwing distance of the bunker. All three lobbed bombs into the aperture, killing all the Germans inside, and the gun never fired again.

Now the Germans were running for their lives inland, some even throwing away their weapons. The Rangers followed, cautiously approaching the concrete bunkers which, according to their intelligence, held the big guns. None of them had fired so far, which Colonel Rudder found strange. Just before the men entered the first gun emplacement, a grenade was thrown in. It exploded, but the interior sounded hollow. The first man ventured in, his rifle pointed, but, as the dust settled, he called out that the bunker was empty; no guns were mounted, nor were there any signs that they ever had been! The next bunker was also empty. The guns simply were not there! For the last two hours men had been dying on the beach and the cliff for nothing, to silence guns which did not exist, at least in that place.

Of more than 200 Rangers who had scrambled off the landing ships that morning, fewer than 90 were left, lying exhausted in shell craters on Pointe du Hoc. In the haze that covered the hilltop, tired men walked about, the smell of cordite still stinging their nostrils. Some who sat near the cliff top could watch the astounding sight as hundreds of assault craft neared the beaches of Omaha.

Some hours later, when Colonel Rudder ordered an advance inland to take up a defensive perimeter against enemy counter-attacks, a recce patrol found a five-gun battery in a camouflaged position, with shells stacked round the guns. Surprisingly, they were unguarded, nor was there any evidence that the guns had been manned at any time.

The enigma of the Pointe du Hoc guns has never been solved. It is assumed that the guns were intended for the point emplacements but that the order for their mounting had not arrived and with the German love of order and discipline, they had just left them there.

As the day wore on, Rudder's Rangers had to fight off several counter-attacks; all were beaten off with no further casualties, but the 2nd Rangers were now totally exhausted and reinforcements were urgently needed if the point was to be held. Finally, Colonel Max Schneider's 5th Rangers came in from the east with the rest of Rudder's men. It was high time. Joining up with the 116 US Infantry Regiment of the 29th Division, the Rangers pushed on inland, fighting in the 'battle of the hedgerows' until they broke out into central France several months later.

17. THE BRIDGE AT ARNHEM

B y the middle of September 1944, the German armies, which four years before had overrun Belgium and France so swiftly, were now retreating even more swiftly towards their own borders. More than a million British and American soldiers with many hundreds of tanks were bursting out of the congested bridgeheads of Normandy and pushing the Germans before them.

While these battles were being fought, three Allied airborne divisions were kicking their heels in Great Britain, waiting for their chance to fight. Among them was the 1st British Airborne Division which, now at full strength, had missed the great paradrop of Operation 'Overlord' and had not seen action since the Sicilian Campaign of 1943. Sixteen times had General Frederick Browning, commander of the 1st Airborne, proposed airborne operations of some magnitude, and sixteen times had the ground troops overrun the objective before the paratroops could be inserted.

The British Second Army had now crossed the River Seine, advanced to Brussels and started penetrating into Holland, and here the airborne troops were to get their chance at last. After much argument, General Eisenhower, commander-in-chief of all Allied troops in north-west Europe, finally agreed, with the help of a little persuasion from Field Marshal Montgomery, to let the 1st Airborne Division loose. A bold and imaginative battle plan was worked out by which a combined armoured and airborne thrust across Holland would bring the Allied armour to the threshold of Germany itself.

Operation 'Market Garden', as it was code-named, was to be the largest airborne operation of the war, and would clearly demonstrate the over-whelming Allied supremacy in both the technical and the operational fields. For the invasion of Normandy some 17,000 airborne troops had been used; 'Market Garden' was to involve more than twice that number. More than 2,000 transport aircraft and gliders were to be used to fly in the 35,000 men in a massive airlift of unprecedented scale.

The main task of the airborne assault would be to capture three major bridges, a mission which fitted the capabilities of the highly trained troops like a glove. The US 101st Airborne Division commanded by Major General Maxwell Taylor would drop near the two southern bridges along the main advance route from Eindhoven and Veghel; the 82nd Airborne Division, commanded by the young Major General James Gavin, would parachute at

Grave and Nijmegen, capture the high ground to the east and secure the bridges between the Maas and Waal, the most important task being the high girder bridge over the River Wall at Nijmegen, which would be a vital factor in the result of the operation.

The most difficult objective, however, would fall to the British 1st Airborne Division, led by Major-General Roy Urquhart, a 42-year-old Scot, whose men would have to capture and hold the vital bridge over the lower stretches of the River Rhine at Arnhem – the last bridge in Holland before the German border. First Airborne had under its command the 1st and 4th Parachute Brigades, an airlanding brigade and the 1st Polish Parachute Brigade, commanded by the indomitable Major-General Stanislav Sosabowski.

During the planning stages, one important factor was determining the site of the landing zones in the Arnhem area. The German fighter airfield at Deelen, just north of the city, was believed to be heavily protected by anti-aircraft guns. Slow transport aircraft flying over that area in daylight would stand little chance, so the airmen in the planning group were quite determined that the landing zone must be well clear of that danger. This meant a forced march of up to ten kilometres before the first troops could reach the bridge itself, fighting all the way even if only modest opposition were encountered, as indicated by Allied intelligence reports that only second-class troops were to be found in the Arnhem region.

This was encouraging, but at the last moment agents near the town noticed two extremely disturbing changes: first, Field Marshal Model had established his headquarters at Oosterbeek, a few kilometres to the west of Arnhem; secondly, German armoured units were now thought to be in the vicinity, potentially lethal to airborne troops without anti-tank weapons and armoured protection.

General Browning and his staff, however, really wanted to go ahead with what they considered their last chance to get into battle, as did the airborne divisional commanders, so the danger of a strong German presence was played down. Only two men, a young British intelligence major, Brian Urquhart (no relation to the General) and a Polish general, realized the acute danger of German armour situated so close to the 1st Airborne landing zone, leading to a possible slaughter of the unprotected paratroops, but their anxiety and reservations were ignored during the last briefing, as all the other officers wanted to proceed.

As the airborne troops went on with their briefing and preparations back in England, the Germans in Arnhem, unaware of what was about to befall, were busy with other problems. Field Marshal Walter Model, commander of Army Group 'B', had recently sent Lieutenant-General Wilhelm Bittrich's SS Panzer Corps to the Arnhem area in order to rest and reorganize for the last defence of the borders of the Reich. Bittrich's forces had been badly mauled during the fierce Normandy battles. Tank losses had been appalling; his men, whose ranks were sorely depleted, were short of ammunition and other supplies were exhausted. He had two SS panzer divisions under his command, but these were combat forces only on paper. A rest might work wonders, as would the arrival of reinforcements but, so far, he had received only promises, most of which were never kept.

At his headquarters east of Oosterbeek, Bittrich held a conference with his two division commanders, Brigadier General Heinz Harmel commanding 10th Frundsberg and Lieutenant-Colonel Walter Harzer, in temporary command of 9th Hohenstaufen Panzer Division. Both men were in their mid-thirties, tough armour leaders who had fought in Russia and France against great odds, but now they were nearly at the end of their tether. Harmel's division had no tanks left at all, but Harzel's could still boast a few runners and, with 9,000 men in its ranks, was also much stronger in manpower. Now GHQ in Berlin had sent orders that Harzer's division should hand over their equipment in order to equip Harmel's. He and his men were then to entrain for Siegen in Germany for reorganization. The date for this move was 18 September 1944. It was to be a day of destiny for both men.

They were both furious as they faced their commander. Bittrich himself was far from happy with the orders from Berlin but he had no choice. Harzer, however, was a resolute man, familiar with the ins and outs of the German military bureaucracy, and he had no intention of handing over his last tanks without a fight. Moreover, he had a little secret stock of them which he had not entered on any lists. Back at his own HQ he ordered his technical adjutant to remove the tracks from most of the self-propelled guns and tanks so that he could report them as unserviceable.

Meanwhile, Bittrich decided to send Harmel to Berlin to report the situation and use his status as a frontline officer to demand reinforcements. Harmel left immediately. Bittrich in the interim organized his remaining forces into small alarm units of company size, which would be as mobile as possible, armed with the best equipment available. By 17 September, as the great Allied air armada was taking off from 25 airfields in southern England, the SS Panzer corps could field ten such company formations on immediate standby in the Arnhem area.

Sunday 17 September 1944 was a bright autumn day and thousands of people came out of their houses when they heard the thunder of the endless aircraft formations passing over, craning their necks to watch the transports and gliders gleaming in the sun. Horses and cattle stampeded in the fields near the glider bases in Oxfordshire and Gloucestershire. From 25 airbases American C-47 Dakotas, British Halifaxes, Stirlings and Albemarles pulled almost 500 gliders on their 300-feet ropes. Swaying behind were the smaller Wacos and Horsas as well as the massive Hamilcar gliders, each packed to maximum capacity with the thousands of airborne forces who would have good cause to remember this day. Above and below, scores of fighters patrolled the sky, watching out for any German fighters which might have ventured over, but none came.

First to drop was the 101st Airborne Division, which came in low over the Eindhoven corridor, as the tanks and halftracks of XXX Corps were assembling in battle order along the highway ready to link up, as planned, with the paratroops. In the lead were the Sherman tanks of Liutenant-Colonel Joe Vandaleur's Irish Guards, who was ordered to go flat out for the first bridge and link up with Taylor's paratroops.

The 101st dropped and landed almost without opposition, the few Germans in the area being utterly surprised as thousands of paratroops jumped on them. Although some flak was encountered over Eindhoven, little damage was done and as soon as the men assembled they raced for the bridges across the Vaart Canal at Veghel and captured them. Only a single bridge, that over the Wilhelmina Canal at Son, was blown up in the faces of the paratroops.

General Gavin's 82nd also had a relatively easy drop around Grave and Nijmegen; one of his battalions dropped right over the bridge at Grave and took it within the hour. Enemy opposition was quickly overcome as the troops advanced towards the high ground in the east, but as he pushed his men towards the great Nijmegen bridge enemy forces began to show considerably stiffer resistance, defending the area from well-placed and fortified positions.

1st Airborne Division, tasked with the bridge at Arnhem, included some 9,000 troops and 1,100 glider pilots. Unable to fly in the entire division in one haul, Urquhart decided to put down 1st Parachute Brigade and 1st Airlanding Brigade on the first day and follow up with the 4th on the second.

Since the area around Arnhem is covered by woods, unsuitable for parachute or glider landings, one parachute and two glider drop zones were located north of the Arnhem-Utrecht railway line while a third – a mixed one – was placed south of Wolfhezen with a supply drop zone to the north-east, near the village of Warnsborn. The seizure of the Arnhem bridge was to be carried out by 1st Para Brigade with Lieutenant-Colonel Frost's 2nd Para Battalion leading the attack, going in along the northern bank of the River Rhine. Preceding the battalion would be Major Freddie Gough's reconnaissance squadron with twin Vickers machine-gun jeeps which would come in by glider and, once ready, go flat out for the bridge and take it in a *coup de main*.

At the outset all went well. The weather was near perfect as Major 'Boy' Wilson's pathfinder force dropped from twelve converted Stirling bombers and marked the dropping zones west of Arnhem. Only a few Germans were encountered, who scattered when they saw the paratroops descending on them. Soon after, the drone of hundreds of aircraft engines could be heard as the formations of Dakotas and glider tugs came into view. The sky filled with billowing parachutes as 1st Para Brigade dropped. The gliders landed on schedule, although many crashed, among them several carrying Major Gough's precious jeeps. General Urquhart's divisional headquarters, though, came in safely. Throughout all this, not a shot was fired; all around him, the general could see his troops in orderly assembly. It appeared that the plan was working well – even better than during exercises – and he was pleased. But not for long.

Field Marshal Model was having dinner with some of his officers at the Tafelberg Hotel in Oosterbeek when the sound of aircraft engines was heard.

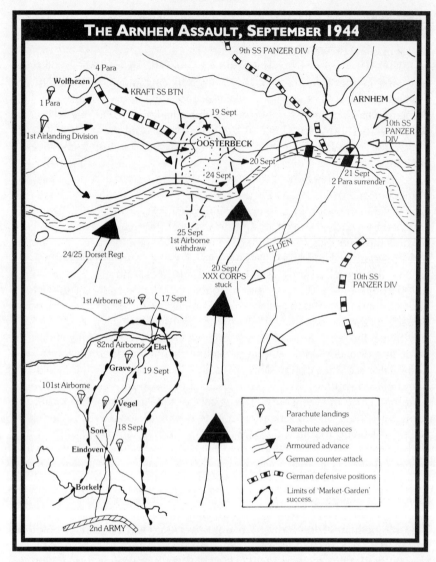

THE ARNHEM ASSAULT, SEPTEMBER 1944

They ran out to the terrace of the hotel and were amazed by the large number of aircraft overhead. Suddenly the sky filled with parachutes, and gliders could be seen landing only a few hundred metres from where they stood. Model called for his orderly, raced for his car and sped away to the north while his staff quickly collected some of the more important documents and followed him. The Field Marshal – potentially a big prize for the Allies – had slipped through their fingers with only minutes to spare.

Thirty minutes later he stormed into Bittrich's headquarters, only to hear reports coming in of numerous parachute descents all over the countryside. The Allies seemed to be everywhere at once, from Eindhoven to Arnhem. When the Marshal departed, Bittrich made urgent phone calls to his divisional commanders. Estimating that the two major targets would be Nijmegen and Arnhem bridges, he ordered his alarm units to set off. Harmel's deputy, standing in for his commander who was still in Berlin, was ordered to send a strong mobile force towards Nijmegen and hold the bridge there at all costs, while Harzer was told to move immediately to the Arnhem road bridge and defend it.

The alarm companies started almost immediately and soon there was confusion in the narrow streets of Arnhem as troops struggled through them to the bridge. Harzer, who had previously ordered the tracks to be removed from his armoured vehicles, now urged his men to put them on again quickly. Meanwhile, at Oosterbeek, Major Sepp Krafft, commander of a panzer-grenadier training regiment, pulled his raw recruits into a defensive position between the railroad and the Utrecht-Arnhem highway. None too soon; British paratroops could already be descried advancing along that road. As the panzergrenadiers took up positions and began firing, troops from an alarm unit led by Corporal Helmut Buttlar came up. Storming along the railway siding, he led nine of his men into the fray, meeting a British team from 1st Air Landing Brigade head on. As they came up, Buttlar opened fire at point-blank range and felled two paratroopers with the first burst of his Schmeisser. A British machine-gun fired low, raking the street where they stood, and Buttlar, first lobbing two hand-grenades, jumped up and went for it, firing his submachine-gun as he went. Two of his men followed, but fell dead. Two more came, but as he closed in on the machine-gun, Buttlar fell wounded.

Meanwhile, 2nd Para, led by Colonel Frost, raced forward along the river bank. Freddie Gough's recce squadron had already gone forward, fighting off men of the SS anti-aircraft alarm company which was also racing for the bridge. Back at Division HQ, no communications were working, and General Urquhart was completely out of touch with his brigades. He had received the bad news that Gough had lost his jeeps, but had no word from him as to where he was or whether he could reach the bridge. It was now up to John Frost and his seasoned 2nd Para to capture the bridge before the Germans got there. At the same time General Bittrich was urging Harzer to speed up his troops to go for the bridge before the British could reach it.

Frost, leading in the race, approached the railway bridge, which was about two kilometres west of his goal, but just as he was ordering one of his lieutenants to lead a team across, German sappers blew the bridge in their faces. Second Para continued along the river road, but were hampered by a joyful crowd of Dutch citizens, who greeted the paratroopers with fruit and cake. Suddenly a German armoured car appeared around the corner and began to fire, scattering the crowd. The paras took aim with a PIAT, but the armoured car managed to escape. Colonel Frost then ordered more speed and, pressing forward, soon reached their destination, the Arnhem bridge, still intact. The bridge looked strangely empty. Taking up position on a roof overlooking it, Colonel Frost sent an officer and a platoon towards the far, southern side. As the men moved cautiously across, the Germans who had been hidden there came to life and, raking the troopers with deadly automatic fire from a pillbox, they soon stopped the advance.

Now it was the turn of Captain Mackay and his sappers; they went into action with a flamethrower which they aimed from the top floor of a house overlooking the pillbox. The flames blew up a nearby ammunition dump and screams of agony came from the German position as men were roasted alive. The whole bridge seemed to be ablaze. Then two troopers with a PIAT advanced and fired straight into the pillbox. The firing stopped and only the crackling of flames could be heard.

Still, Frost and his battalion held only the northern end of the bridge, a fact which would prove crucial. At 1800 an SS alarm unit commanded by Captain Brinkman advanced from Elden in the south towards the bridge with 30 halftracks. He had not been told that 2nd Para was already holding the northern end. Coming within the range of Frost's anti-tank weapons, the German column was destroyed in minutes, their burning vehicles blocking the way. However, Frost and his men themselves were now coming under heavy fire from all sides as more and more German troops entered the area held by his battalion, and more British troops also arrived, among them Gough and some of his recce squadron, who had finally fought through the German cordon. The situation was confusing and, to make matters worse, Colonel Frost could not get through to brigade or any other headquarters, as none of his radios were functioning.

During the night he organized his defence around the houses over-looking the bridge, hoping to hold on until the rest of the brigade could link up with them, and awaiting XXX Corps' armour coming up from the south along the Nijmegen high road. But he was not left alone for long.

Another German armoured attack took place during the following morning. Halftracks and armoured cars came into view, racing over the bridge straight for Frost and his men. A savage fight ensued, several German vehicles being destroyed. Then came two Tiger tanks, however, which fired pointblank into the houses where Frost's men were positioned. The heavy 88mm guns were devastating; losses mounted quickly. Some British gunners edged forward and fired their anti-tank rifles, but failed to penetrate the heavy armour plates of the steel monsters. At last a lucky shot managed to set one Tiger on fire but the other crashed through the rubble and disappeared into the streets of Arnhem.

In the town, the rest of the brigade was fighting fiercely against German resistance. Brigadier Gerald Lathbury, the commander, was wounded and the battalions were unable to break through to join Frost's men at the bridge. More and more German troops were coming into the area, thanks to Field Marshal Model, who grabbed every man and every tank he could lay hands on, both in Holland and in Germany, and sent them into the battle.

For several hours 1st Airborne Division was leaderless, when General Urquhart was trapped in a Dutch house, surrounded by Germans. He managed to escape, however, and join his HQ, only to be told that there were no communications with his troops, with XXX Corps, or with the RAF.

Above: German Stormtrooper Infantry make their way along a ditch during an attack. The penultimate man is carrying a Wex Flammenwerfer as part of the unit's special assault equipment. Note the British tank which appears to be a knocked out Mk V. (PJH)

Below: German assault troops seen in the standard rubber dinghy used frequently in river crossings during the early years of the Second World War. Carrying an average of ten equipped troops, they were used at Eben Emael to form the secondary assault, together with the airborne troops. (Lucas)

Above: A British Commando looks down from Maaloy Island on the burning buildings in Vaagso. The Germans, although initially taken by surprise, quickly reorganized to put up a spirited defence.

Top right: Aftermath at Crete: a solitary German airman surveys the wreckage of many Ju-52 transports, shot down during the fiercely contested invasion of the island. The Luftwaffe could scarcely afford such losses: neither could the Paratroop units who were never used on the same scale of operation again. (Lucas)

Right: An SAS troop pictured before a long-range patrol. Note how the jeep is loaded with supplies – notably petrol jerry cans – and the extra radiator cooling unit on the front grille which was vital for desert conditions.

Above: The target: low-flying photographic reconnaissance aircraft took this pre-raid picture of Dieppe centre, 36 hours before the assault. Note the German sentry at the bridgehead.

Below: Destruction at Arnhem: the key bridge held by 2 Para over the Neder Rijn in Arnhem centre which was vital to the success of the operation, aiming to seize and secure a corridor to the industrial heart of Germany, the Ruhr.

Above: A typical view of the Burmese terrain: long winding roads snake their way through the hills, which are otherwise virtually impassable due to the thick jungle. It was here that the Chindits operated.

Right: The Israeli 202nd Parachute Brigade leaves the DZ and begins the march to the assembly point, prior to seizing Mitla Pass.

Above: The terrain in which battle took place in Aden, as seen from a commanding GPMG position.

Right: Radio men in the Golani Infantry Brigade pause to establish positions behind a good covering wall.

Right: The attack on the main terminal building at Entebbe. As support Hercules transports fly in, the leading assault teams disembark from the lead aircraft and make for the vital control facilities at the airport.

Below: The assault team seen just before attacking the radar target at Ras Gharib.

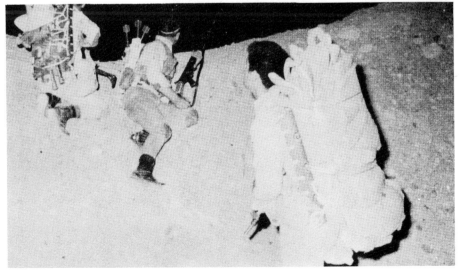

Left: Royal Marine Commandos pass Two Sisters on their way to Port Stanley. The inhospitable terrain seen here well illustrates the difficulty of conflict in the Falklands.

Left: US Marines from the 2nd Light Armored Infantry Battalion and 1st Fleet Anti-Terrorist Security Team conduct operations from armoured personnel carriers in Arrijan, Panama.

Above: US Marines from the 2nd Light Armored Infantry Battalion and 1st Fleet Anti-Terrorist Security Team conduct operations in Arrijan, Panama.

Right: A special Forces FAV (Fast Assault Vehicle) is down-loaded from a CH-47 Chinook Helicopter in the Gulf. Ideally suited to desert conditions, these vehicles roamed deep inside Iraq during the covert war against the enemy.

Top right: The type of target Bomber Command targeted for low-level daylight attacks. This is the Knapsack Power Station at Cologne, being bombed by RAF Blenheims in August 1941.

Bronze
Workshops

Main Diesel
Engine Factory

Top left: Lancaster bombers were only just entering RAF service when the Augsburg raid took place. Squadron Leader Sherwood's Lancaster is here seen crashing during the raid.

Below left: The target for the remarkable daylight raid was the MAN works in central Augsburg. The main workshops and production sheds were all clearly identifiable, but the failure of many bombs to explode meant that many men died in vain.

Right: The results of the unique attack by 617 Squadron's Lancasters on the Mohne Dam, one of the most important in Germany. Repair work to the breach took many months.

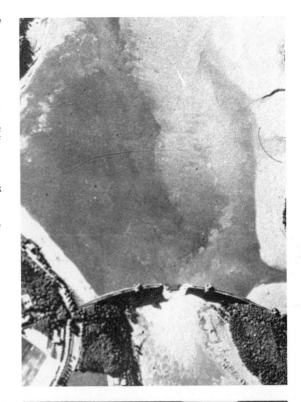

Right: A remarkable photograph taken during the raid by US Air Force B-24 Liberator bombers on the Ploesti oil refineries in Roumania. Despite the extremely low level at which the raid took place, flak and static defences combined with Luftwaffe fighters to shoot down almost one-third of the bombing force.

Above: Israeli Air Force F-16 fighter-bomber, seen here with full reheat on take-off and armed with a pair of air-to-air missiles on the wingtips. Aircraft of this type successfully destroyed the nuclear facility at Baghdad.

Below: X-Craft seen running trials in home waters before the attack on the German battleship *Tirpitz*. After an eventful voyage to the target, the explosive charges of two X-Craft caused serious damage to the warship, but failed to sink her.

Above: Modified by the removal of armour plating, mid-upper gun turret and bomb-bay doors, the Lancaster heavy bomber eventually sank Tirpitz with the 10,000lb Tallboy bomb, seen here moments after release. Two direct hits and several near-misses sealed the fate of Hitler's last battleship.

Below: Italian frogmen successfully penetrated the defences at Alexandria harbour using these Maiale, or 'Human torpedoes'. Small, silent and difficult to see when running almost awash, their removable explosive charges caused extensive damage to Royal Navy battleships *Valiant* and *Queen Elizabeth*.

Above: Israeli naval Commandos seen disembarking from their parent craft, in this case a guided missile frigate. Note DP gun turret and quadruple Harpoon missile-launcher to the port of the boat.

Partially as a result of this, hundreds of transport planes came over and dropped their precious supplies into the German held zone.

This was bad, but worse was to come. Frost and his depleted battalion, running short of ammunition and supplies, were trapped on the northern side of the bridge, under heavy fire from the south and from inside the town, and were soon surrounded. More and more German troops were thrown into the battle by Harzer, whose SS troops were fanatical in their efforts to dislodge Frost from his hold on the bridge. But Frost doggedly held on to the position for six terrible days until, overcome by superior firepower and sheer exhaustion, his – mostly wounded – paratroopers finally gave up and went into captivity.

At that time XXX Corps was only 20 kilometres from the bridge at Arnhem, having taken Nijmegen bridge with a *coup de main* attack by Major Julian Cook and his brave men, who crossed the River Waal under withering fire in flimsy boats and reached the bridge just before it was to be blown.

All this courage was already lost. General Urquhart's dwindling division withdrew into a defensive perimeter to the east, near the line of the river, where an attempt was made to drop General Sosabowski's Polish unit and link up with them, but their drop was a complete failure and the hapless Poles were slaughtered before they even reached the ground. During the night, the Polish general made another effort to cross the river, but this was beaten off by heavy German fire, causing yet more casualties.

With Colonel Frost and his surviving men in captivity, General Urquhart had little choice but to try and save the remainder of his division and, under cover of darkness and in pouring rain, he led his men over the Rhine to reach the British lines. General Urquhart had taken more than 10,000 men into Arnhem on 17 September and came out, less than a week later, with just over 2,000. More than 1,000 were dead, the rest captured, mostly wounded. The Germans had lost close to 4,000 men, some of their best troops.

John Frost's gallant stand became a legend in the annals of the British Parachute Regiment. Although he spent the remainder of the war in a German prison, Frost, who had already won a DSO and MC for his exploits in Bruneval and Sicily, was to become a major-general of great distinction and one of the finest soldiers Britain ever produced.

18. WINGATE'S CHINDIT RAIDERS

I n the spring of 1942 the situation of the British Forces in the Far East was deplorable: the Japanese had ejected them from Burma, and India itself was in danger, with disastrous consequences if the Japanese did succeed in invading its territory. The British were eager to recapture Burma but it seemed an almost impossible dream with the Eastern Army in such a bad state. They needed unconventional men, and unconventional methods, to break the seemingly invincible Japanese. One such man was already there, waiting for his chance.

Colonel Orde Wingate was only thirty-eight years old but he had already become known in military circles as one of the most extraordinary officers in the British Army. Full of physical and mental energy, Wingate was an unorthodox soldier and an outstanding exponent of unconventional warfare. He was born into a military family in 1903. He studied Arabic, which he spoke fluently, a fact which helped him during his service in the Sudan. In 1936 he was sent to Palestine, where he gained his first experience in unconventional methods of war while fighting bands of Arab marauders and rebels. For this purpose he raised the Special Night Squads in which selected Jewish fighters and British soldiers waged a tough campaign against the Arab bands. It was during this tour of duty that he gained a reputation as a nonconformist because, in contrast to the majority of the British Mandate forces, he had very close relations with the Palestinian Jews, who adored him (and, in fact, still do).

General Sir Archibald Wavell, commander-in-chief India in 1942, had been Wingate's commander in Palestine, and had been rather concerned about that unorthodox relationship. Right now, though, he was looking for exactly the sort of man who could think for himself and such potentially brilliant commanders were hard to come by in India at that time.

Quickly promoted to colonel, Wingate was given command of all guerrilla operations behind the Japanese lines of Burma. He established his headquarters at Maymyo, where the Jungle Warfare School was located. Its commandant, Major Michael Calvert, also a superb soldier, was a man after Wingate's own heart and was to become one of his most successful commanders. The two men put their heads together and began to work out battle plans. Their basic theory was that in a jungle covered terrain formations could remain in enemy territory for indefinite periods provided that they were continually supplied from the air – a concept which was completely new at that time. Wingate considered that covert operations by small groups in the enemy rear zone would pay enormous dividends. He thought that the troops should operate in columns, each large enough to inflict severe damage on the enemy but small enough to escape when outnumbered.

General Wavell liked Wingate's ideas, and authorized the creation of a brigade-sized force to include a British infantry regiment, a Gurkha battalion and 142 Commando, as well as an RAF liaison party with high-powered radios, which would accompany each column and keep in touch with the RAF for air support and supply drops. Wingate named his force the Chindits after a mythical creature which guards Burmese temples. They would operate in strong company columns, each commanded by a major, self-contained to survive deep in enemy territory, and including a mule train to carry the heavy loads, weapons and signal equipment. Each man would carry his own individual gear plus a jungle carbine – a lightweight version of the service rifle.

The Chindits' first mission was to infiltrate into Burma, which was defended by more than five Japanese infantry divisions, commanded by

General Renya Mutaguchi. In mid-February 1943, the Chindits moved out in two groups of several columns each, Wingate, now a brigadier, leading the larger. The two groups were to cross the wide River Chindwin at two points, Tonhe in the north and Auktaung in the south, some 70 kilometres apart. They were to cross the hills to the Pinbon-Naungkan area, where the strategic north-south railway line ran, and blow it up, with a number of important viaducts as special targets.

So the great adventure began. Both groups crossed the Chindwin without enemy interference and the first air drops were received on time. The first brush with a Japanese patrol occurred on 18 February, when the southern group hit an enemy outpost near Mainyaung, but they managed to disengage, avoiding combat by making a wide detour. Wingate, with the northern group, pushed on until they reached Pinbon on 1 March, and established his forward base there. He sent off two of his columns, one commanded by Major Calvert and the other by Major Bernard Fergusson, a New Zealander and son of the High Commissioner, both of them outstanding officers.

On 5 March Major Fergusson's column reached the railway line and, after a short, bloody action with a Japanese force, dynamited the railway bridge near Bongyaung. The muleteers held tight to the animals to prevent them from bolting when the explosions came; the other men were under

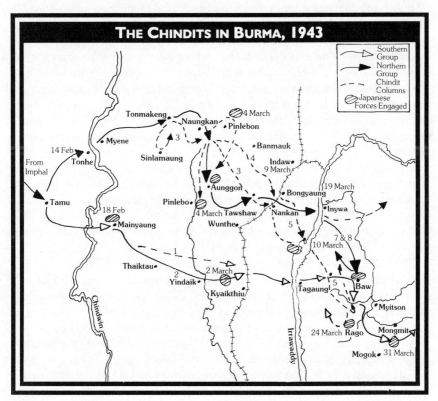

cover, watching. Suddenly there was a flash iluminating the entire hillside, then a thunderous bang as the bridge exploded. The mules plunged and kicked, while their muleteers struggled to hold them fast. The column then went on to dynamite a nearby gorge, blocking the railway line with tons of rock and earth. That same day, Major Calvert blew two bridges near Nankan to the south.

At General Mutaguchi's headquarters the news of the railway's demolition caused grave concern, especially as no indication of the British infiltration had reached the frontline commanders along the River Chindwin line. Patrols sent out to investigate repeatedly reported that there were no signs of British lines of communications to support guerrilla movements. Puzzled, the Japanese high command decided to seal off the river crossings and to increase their own forces in these locations in order to cut off any possibility of retreat. Only one officer, General Tazoe, an airman with more imagination than most military men, guessed that the British forces might be supplied from the air, but the high command ignored this suggestion.

On 6 March Wingate reached Aunggon, halfway to the second river for which he was heading, the two-kilometre wide Irrawaddi, which presented a tremendous obstacle. He knew that if they crossed this one the Chindits would find it very difficult to get back again, with two wide waterways to cross, if they decided to withdraw and return to India.

Wingate had made his decision, however, and he pushed on until, on 19 March, he crossed the great river with the main body of the northern group. Fergusson met with no resistance. Major Calvert, after a battle in which he lost nearly all his mule train, got over with most of his men, and linked up with the second column south of Hmaindaing. There they received orders to destroy the Gokteik viaduct, an important target because it linked up with the strategic main jungle road to the south.

By now, however, the Japanese had discovered that the Chindit columns were being supplied by air, and had switched their tactics accordingly. The Chindits were being hunted relentlessly. Moreover, Wingate was in for a shock when he crossed the Irrawaddi. Instead of finding the humid jungle which he had expected and for which he had trained his men, he found to his horror that the area was a hot, arid triangle where armoured vehicles could operate and harass them considerably.

A trying period now ensued. The troops had to fight their worst enemy yet – the dry, strength-sapping heat, which taxed their already exhausted bodies. The need for water became their most urgent problem, dominating their tactics. Air support became difficult, too, as the long distances made it more and more tricky to fly in supplies. After consulting his superiors, therefore, Wingate was convinced that their only chance of surviving was to withdraw quickly and leave the waterless triangle before it was too late.

First, however he wanted Calvert and Fergusson to blow up the Gokteik gorge bridge. Their two columns set out, but found the entire area infested with Japanese patrols. Wingate sent in bombers for air support, but this move did not achieve much; Fergusson was forced to make a wide detour in order to obtain some urgent supplies, and thus was unable to make his rendezvous with Calvert's column. Calvert was then ordered to demolish the viaduct himself, but before he could start both columns received urgent messages from Wingate, recalling them and ordering a withdrawal.

Calvert and Ferguson acted as rearguard for the entire group and, to make the withdrawal more viable, they decided to split up their columns and operate in smaller teams, each led by an officer. The journey back was a nightmare. Most of the men were already ill with malaria and other tropical diseases, some too weak to march. The jungle was infested with insects, and food was scarce, as most of the mules had been lost. The worst disaster hit Major Fergusson's column while crossing the River Schweli. Tricked by a Burmese boatman, the men found themselves marooned on a sandbank in the middle of the wide, fast-moving river. Some men drowned when they attempted to swim the rapid stream; others sank into quicksand and disappeared. The shrieks of those unfortunate men rang in the ears long after they had gone. With no boats to ferry the men, Fergusson led the way himself, swimming to the far river bank, but was forced to leave some forty men behind. Most of those remaining eventually reached Imphal safely – but totally exhausted.

Wingate himself with his men made an unopposed crossing over the Irrawaddi and then swam over the River Chindwin, having discarded most of their equipment. Only four of his 43 men were lost, but other groups were less fortunate: of the 3,000 men that Wingate had led into Burma only 2,200 returned, many too ill for duty. Although there had not been many tangible gains, the Chindits, nevertheless, had achieved something much more significant by operating behind Japanese lines, raising the morale of the dispirited British forces, and showing the way to the victory which was to follow.

PART TWO
Postwar Elite Actions

19. ACTION AT THE MITLA PASS

The date was 29 October 1956, the time 1659 hours. Major Rafael Eitan stood at the open door of his DC-3 Dakota, which hovered at 1,500 feet over Parker's Memorial at the eastern end of the Mitla Pass. The green lights flickered on and he jumped out into the Sinai Desert, followed by 395 of his paratroopers. The Sinai Campaign, also known variously as Operation 'Kadesh' and the Suez Adventure, had begun. Its aim, according to Israeli government sources, was to stop the continuous terrorist incursions over the Egyptian border into Israel, and to prevent Egyptian attacks on Israel's lines of communication.

Rafael Eitan, known to every Israeli as Raful, an infantryman to the core, was totally fearless and very popular. He had already fought as a platoon commander in the tough battles for Jerusalem in the War of Independence of 1948 and was seriously wounded there. A born leader of men in battle, the stocky farmer did not speak much, but when he did it was usually to the point. He was now commanding the parachute battalion of the 202nd Airborne Brigade but his courage and motivation would take him right to the top. After helping to stem the Syrian onslaught during the opening days of the Yom Kippur War in 1973, he later served as Israel's Chief of Staff during the 1982 Lebanon War where, as usual, he fought alongside his troops.

But now he was jumping out of an aircraft, 300 kilometres from the Israeli border, not far from the entire Egyptian Army at the Suez Canal, right into the Mitla Pass, a crack in the great black hills that loom over this part of the Sinai. As they drifted downwards in the evening sky, Eitan and his men were surprised to see a party of Egyptian road workers who, on their descent, welcomed them: they had mistaken the Israelis for Egyptians on manoeuvres. Not bothering to disabuse them, Eitan set about organizing his men into a defensive perimeter where they would stay until relieved by Colonel Arik Sharon and his brigade.

Sharon himself, in the southern Negev on the long trek over the barren Sinai desert, was concerned about Raful's battalion, completely isolated in the middle of enemy territory. Until the link up could be made the paratroopers were dependent on their own weapons, and had no heavy anti-tank equipment. Even the air support on which they were optimistically counting was not very likely at this stage, in view of the fact that the Egyptian Air Force had its main bases nearby in the Canal Zone. Moreover, a strategic route stretched from the Canal to the Sinai Peninsula, so that strong mechanized forces of the Egyptian Army could reach the Israeli paratroops within a very few hours. For the time being, however, all was quiet; the men dug in without hindrance and went about their chores.

While Raful's men were preparing their defences, the rest of the brigade was already on its way; long columns of halftracks and trucks were churning the dry desert and sand into great clouds of dust, visible kilometres away. The vanguard took the first Egyptian outpost, at Kuntilla, in a surprise attack; the garrison there fled in panic when the Israeli soldiers came upon them, but the next post, at Temed, was not so easy. Surrounded by a strong minefield and defended by well-concealed gun emplacements, it needed a stronger assault. A battalion commanded by Aron Davidi was given this job and, attacking from the east with the sun behind him, Davidi drove his halftracks straight into the Egyptian compound. After a sharp battle which lasted for forty minutes, it was all over. The Egyptians suffered fifty dead, the Israelis four. The next Egyptian position, at Nakhel, fell that same afternoon. The road was now clear for the link up with the paratroops.

That evening, exactly twenty-four hours after his jump, Eitan welcomed Sharon and his forces. To their surprise the Egyptians had so far made no move. Later that evening, however, some inaccurate mortar fire and isolated strafings from MiGs indicated that the Egyptians were aware that they were there – and were concerned. During that night two infantry battalions from the Egyptian 2nd Brigade were sent from their base at Shaloufa in the Canal Zone. Crossing the pontoon bridges there, they advanced along the track to the Mitla Pass to establish a defence perimeter at its western exit. However, the Israel Air Force had observed the move, and jets strafed their vehicles, most of which were left burning fiercely while the Egyptian troops escaped, mainly unhurt, and scrambled into the hills, setting up their defences in the caves on both sides of the mountain pass, unnoticed by the elated Israeli pilots watching the blaze down below. When Sharon's headquarters learned of the successful air attack, they had no reason to doubt that the pass would be undefended. Eitan, however, a cautious man, sent a reconnaissance patrol into the pass, which returned having found no evidence of enemy forces near the eastern entrance.

As evening fell reports began coming in from Southern Command, although they were sporadic due to static, indicating that an Egyptian force at least the size of an armoured brigade was advancing eastwards along a central road from Ismailiya, some seventy kilometres to the north. Sharon realized that their position near Parker Memorial was extremely vulnerable, and would become untenable if the Egyptian armour turned south. He preferred to move his brigade into the pass itself and establish a stronger defence inside. His request was denied, but a senior officer, sent by Piper Cub to land near Sharon's HQ, saw the situation for himself and was convinced that something should be done. He finally authorized a limited reconnaissance in force into the pass, but made it clear that under no circumstances should the patrol get involved in any serious fighting.

Major Motta Gur's 88 Airborne Battalion was given this assignment. Gur chose his men carefully and organized a motorized patrol of halftracks, weapons carriers and three AMX-13 light tanks. A battery of 120mm mortars went too, as did the brigade reconnaissance squadron, led by Captain Micha Kapousta. As the patrol set off at midday, Major Davidi and Lieutenant-Colonel Hofi, the deputy brigade commander, decided to go along as well and jumped into one of the halftracks.

The lead carriers entered the pass warily, the long column winding behind them along the narrow track. Radio contact soon became fitful, since the hills screened the FM radios. Men could be seen outlined against the sky on the hill tops but they were thought to be Israeli paratroopers. The hills now became steeper and the track even narrower; it wound its way into a defile, the mountains closing in on both sides, the slopes very steep, the scene very reminiscent of a John Wayne western.

As the head of the column reached a wadi which intersected the track, they came under fire, not very accurate – at least at the beginning. At this point, where the cliff overhangs almost to the surface of the road, some Egyptian vehicles which had been destroyed in the air attack littered the road and had to be moved and, while the men were doing this, the Egyptian fire became heavy and accurate. The driver leading the column lost his nerve and tried to move around a wrecked car, skidding into the wadi. Heavy machine-gun fire caused several casualties as the men emerged from their halftracks and ran for cover behind rocks.

At this moment of panic, one man, still inside his vehicle, risked his life by radioing Major Gur to stop all movement of the patrol, so as to evade the ambush. Another man tried to return fire with his machine-gun but could not angle it high enough and, shot from above, fell dead at his gun. An officer got some of the men together and tried to rush the Egyptians on the lower slopes with a grenade attack, but they were forced back.

Then Major Gur came forward on foot, accompanied by his radio operator. Ducking the enemy fire, Gur set up his command post behind a rock, in an empty foxhole. Some of the vehicles farther back in the column were coming into the turn, not having received news of the Egyptian attack. Gur sent an officer to signal the drivers to stop, but as he dashed out into the open he fell.

Meanwhile the radio operator tried to establish contact with brigade but could not get through. The signals officer, Danny Shalit, took the radio set and set off uphill, defying the heavy fire, and managed to raise Major Davidi, still in his halftrack. Gur sent a message to Davidi, asking him to send the reconnaissance squadron over the hills, outflanking the enemy position on the hilltop.

The commander of the company of light AMX-13 tanks, Captain Zvika Dahab, now forced his way through with one of them and reached the wadi.

MITLA PASS, OCTOBER 1956

Directing his guns on the Egyptian positions he began firing, but once again they were too high up the hill for effective results.

Gur and his men were pinned down, unable to move. As he watched, some halftracks and tanks crashed through the pass, moving so fast that none of the men noticed Gur trying to signal to them. In one of the vehicles was Colonel Hofi, the deputy commander. The small group got as far as the western exit without stopping and only then did they realize that something was wrong at Gur's end. Hofi immediately turned round with the purpose of helping Gur, only to be stopped by heavy fire. Unable to raise Sharon on his radio, Hofi decided to place his force into a defensive position, stay where he was and wait for the situation to clear.

Major Gur was still unable to identify the source of the fire which was coming from above, as most of the Egyptians were hidden from sight in their caves. At last, however, Sharon had managed to contact them by radio and been informed of what was going on in the pass, although he did not realize that Hofi and Gur were in two different places. He discussed the options with Raful Eitan, who suggested that they attack through the defile itself, but this was overruled, as Sharon preferred an attack over the northern hills, where the terrain might be better.

Meanwhile Major Davidi, who had heard Motta Gur's urgent calls over the radio, sent Captain Kapousta and his men towards the northern hills. Kapousta, a veteran soldier, formerly of the élite 101 unit, immediately collected his men and, leaving their cramped positions in their vehicles, they set off uphill, guided by the sound of the exploding mortar shells. As he reached the northern ridge he saw in front of him some stone emplacements facing south and he and Lieutenant Dov Tamari raced for them, firing their submachine-guns and lobbing grenades into the weapon pits. Some of the Egyptians who had been hidden there bolted, terrified by this sudden assault from the rear. Kapousta and his men stormed over the northern ridge and down the slope on the other side, where they came under heavy fire from the southern ridge facing them. Some of the men fell, but others found cover among the boulders and began to return fire.

From their present position Gur's men could not be seen, so Davidi urged Kapousta to continue his advance, only to be told that he and his men were pinned down too. But Major Gur's situation was now getting really serious, and Davidi did not mince his words in explaining this fact to Kapousta, who immediately leapt to his feet and, followed by some of his men, ran down the slope through heavy fire. Some of his men had disappeared and, while trying to round them up, Kapousta saw the caves in the hillside for the first time, and now realized where all the fire was coming from. Casualties were mounting every minute, as the Egyptians were sitting in their caves, actually firing into the backs of the Israelis as they ran.

By this time, 1500 hours, the recce squadron had already suffered nine dead and fifteen wounded, terrible losses for such a small force, but still none of the senior officers was aware of their plight. As the recce team fought its way along the cliff, another combat forces was advancing along the upper ridge in the opposite direction and there was imminent danger that they would run into each other. Davidi, who could see both groups from his position, tried in vain to raise Kapousta on the radio and, when this failed, unable to contain his impatience he called for a volunteer to drive a jeep into the defile. Racing through the curtain of fire, he was wounded, and his jeep careened into a ditch and overturned.

Micha Kapousta and his men now attempted to evacuate their wounded, but at exactly that moment four Egyptian Meteors appeared overhead, zooming low, and began to strafe the defile. Then, in a second pass, the jets blasted the only mortar battery still functioning. Its ammunition was hit, causing a huge explosion. Kapousta's men, still pinned down, looked at their leader and, seeing no way out, he opted to carry on downhill and try to reach the track. Shouting to his section leaders to stay with him, Micha rose and ran – but was immediately hit. Tamari took over – and was also hit. A sergeant took command. Urging the men on, he scrambled down the steep cliff, followed by those who could move. One of the men stumbled, fell, and rolled all the way down the rocky hill, but there was nothing anyone could do to help.

Davidi, from his position at the end of the patrol column, sent in a force which managed to evacuate some of the wounded men, including Kapousta and Tamari, and it was only when Davidi met Kapousta at the dressing-station that he realized for the first time that the enemy were entrenched in caves on the southern slopes. Darkness was falling, enabling the Israelis to mount a night attack to rout out the Egyptians from their caves. A two-pronged strike was ordered, to drive in from east and west simultaneously.

Just before dark, the lone tank held by Motta Gur was sent by him to the western exit, as it was his only way of making contact with Hofi, who was still there. Hofi was asked to turn around and attack the Egyptians in an eastward direction.

Thus, as night fell, the Egyptians, who had been reinforced and now numbered almost two infantry battalions, were completely surrounded in their caves. The night battle which ensued was a vicious one, as the Egyptians defended with determination. In one of the actions Captain Oved Lidjinsky, commanding a paratroop company, selected a team of 25 men and led it along the southern ridge, beginning to clean out the caves one by one. When they reached the top of the cliff they shouted to Major Gur below to let him know they were there.

In another sector Lieutenant Eli, a platoon commander, was suddenly confronted by a dark figure. He aimed his gun, but luckily, saw in time that it was Captain Nadel, the brigade operational officer, who had come to warn them that there was a machine-gun position inside the cliff wall. Yigal Graber, a section leader, edged forward carefully, locating the position by the flashes from the guns. The position was almost completely covered by sandbags and stones, but, wriggling uphill on his belly, he got close enough to the opening to throw a grenade. Unfortunately he missed and it exploded harmlessly against the sandbags. Another man came up and clinging on to the rock face with one hand, threw in a grenade. The waiting men heard a tremendous explosion.

As Captain Oved Lidjinsky and his men advanced along the edge of the cliff, they saw the flashes of another machine-gun emplacement firing from above them. The captain warned the men that he was throwing a grenade, but it fell short, rolled back – and exploded on the narrow path where they were. Seeing what was about the happen, Lidjinsky threw himself on the grenade, taking the full blast. The men, mad with grief for their fallen leader, just stood up and raced for the machine-gun cave, disregarding the deadly fire from above. Forcing their way inside, they sprayed the cave with their Uzis, killing eight Egyptian soldiers who had been firing Spanish Alpha machine-guns from their elevation.

With the machine-guns silenced, the way was clear for the assault and it was all over in an hour. The Egyptians died to a man, with no quarter being asked or given. The paratroops lost 38 dead and 120 wounded.

The rest of the night was spent in extricating the wounded, who were evacuated the following morning, when several Dakotas landed on a makeshift airstrip near the Parker Memorial. The survivors of this terrible ordeal, although exhausted and shaken, went on fighting. The battle for the Mitla Pass was the airborne brigade's first major combat action. A lesser force would have crumbled in face of such an ambush, but training and individual acts of extreme courage decided the battle – the first of many.

20. THE BRITISH IN ADEN

Aden's only natural asset is the wide, deep harbour lying at the southern entrance to the Red Sea. An important maritime crossroads, it is one of the most unpleasant places on earth, with a temperature reaching 50 degrees Centigrade at noon in hot weather, dropping to a mere 15 degrees at night, coupled with high humidity.

Behind the waterfront of Ma'ala stands the extinct volcano Shamsan, in whose airless crater the Adenis chose to build their city. For centuries its proximity enabled it to live and prosper on the slave trade – a small key in the harbour is still called 'Slave Island'; the slave route from Aden led through Yemen into Arabia.

In 1513 the Portuguese besieged the town, unsuccessfully, but in 1839 the Royal Navy bombarded it into surrender, thus acquiring a strategic base whose importance increased with the opening of the Suez Canal. For many years it was a busy coaling station, and today is still one of the most important strategic locations in the region, although its status decreased with the ending of the cold war between the Superpowers at the end of the 1980s.

The British Crown Colony of Aden extended only a few miles from the harbour, but beyond that boundary lay a largely desert hinterland which stretched away to the Rhadfan massif. The only good communication with the interior was a single surfaced road built on the tracks of a long abandoned railway extending as far as Lahedj; beyond this point the road degenerated into a rough trail which followed the old slave route as it wound through the mountains to the border with Yemen. The track might have been all right for camels, but it could batter the life out of a normal cross-country lorry within six months.

In 1941 the British Army used Aden as a base for the reconquest of Somaliland, and after the Second World War, with Arab nationalism on the increase, the British were forced to mount periodic expeditions into the Rhadfan area to restore order among the unruly inhabitants; by far the most important of these actions was caused by the civil war in Yemen. Because of their links with Saudi Arabia, the West supported the royalist side, which controlled the country; their opponents in the East began arming and training Rhadfan dissidents.

In August 1963 the 4th Royal Tank Regiment, commanded by Lieutenant-Colonel Bryan Watkins, arrived in Aden. This armoured regiment, especially converted to armoured cars for the mission, deployed two mixed Saladin and Ferret squadrons in Aden, while a third was dispatched to the Persian Gulf.

By this time Aden had become the major strategic British base east of Suez, but the main combat force was still the Federal Republican Army, formerly the Aden Levies, now commanded by an ex-officer of the 16/5th Lancers, Brigadier Lunt. It consisted of three infantry battalions supported by an armoured car squadron. At the end of that year fighting escalated when Egyptian troops based in North Yemen joined the dissidents, frequently helped by Egyptian jets which flew overhead, strafing villages and republican outposts.

The RAF had a complete three-squadron wing deployed at Khormaksar airfield, but in order to get at the hit-and-run Egyptian jets operating out of Tajiz, the RAF Hunters needed more than quarter of an hour to reach the area. This gave the Egyptians ample time to escape back to their base. The sole means of retaliation was to fly sporadic raids on the Egyptians' border forts at Harib, but results were fairly equivocal.

For this reason, and to clear the Aden-Dhala road, blocked for months by the local tribesmen, the 22nd SAS were moved into the area. Heavy fighting went on in the hills and the British soldiers, who were greatly outnumbered, received air support from the Hunters at Khormaksar which would swoop in almost at ground level, raking the Arab positions with rockets and cannon fire. This type of anti-terrorist operation went on for several weeks.

Early in 1964 the major rebel force, armed with mortars and light machine-guns, overran a small British post, beheading the two survivors. They went on to occupy several commanding heights, from which they retired each night to their villages, according to their normal method of tribal warfare. These heights were recaptured in a brilliant night operation carried out by the British Commandos and parachute troops, and a sharp punishment was administered to the village where the perpetrators of the atrocity lived.

The level of hostile activities remained high, but a British brigade group stationed at Thumeir, in the central Rhadfan, managed to contain them. For a while the rebel tribesmen came every night to the base, infiltrating between the outlying pickets and the main camp in an attempt to start a fire fight, and occasionally the fighting became quite serious. However, the surrounding villages were evacuated by the British authorities, thus depriving the dissidents of local support, and daily actions in the surrounding wadis, with artillery and air support, gradually eroded their will to continue the fight. By autumn of that year the back of the revolt had been broken.

A major factor in the fighting was the six-wheeled Saladin armoured car, the 75mm gun of which had a long reach and packed a punch hard enough to dismantle the most stoutly constructed sangar. Rebel attempts to obstruct the use of these vehicles by mining tracks and wadis failed, as the Saladin was able to lose two complete wheel assemblies and still drive on.

Also in 1964, the Federal troops mounted a well-planned operation, code-named 'Nutcracker', which involved four infantry battalions, backed by a troop of Centurion tanks from 16/5th Lancers and armoured cars from 4 RTR. The aim of this operation was to establish control over wide areas of the hinterland where guerrilla forces, supported by North Yemen and Egyptian forces, had been operating almost uninterrupted. A base camp was established at Thumeir, close to the North Yemen border, to the west of the Barri ridge on the road from Aden to Dhala. From this location British forces operated in the hills and wadis – ambushing and routing guerrillas who were attempting to infiltrate across the border. Although the FRA achieved some initial success, however, the well-armed dissidents – who considerably outnumbered the thin ranks of the FRA – gained the upper hand after several weeks of fighting and forced the British to withdraw from the area.

The British Army now came under pressure from the local government to reinforce their troop level in Aden, but their forces in the region were sparse, mostly concentrated in Cyprus and the Far East, where they were badly needed. However, the crack 45 Commando Battalion did come from East Africa and 3 Parachute Battalion from Bahrein, bolstering the two infantry battalions in place. After their arrival a brigade headquarters was established, under Brigadier Blacker, the Thumeir base was reorganized, and combat patrols supported by Saladin armoured cars – now rearmed with a more powerful 76mm gun – began penetrating into the mountain fastnesses of the rebels. Working under extremely difficult conditions, they succeeded in knocking out several enemy outposts with the aid of RAF Hunters when necessary.

Heartened by these successes, the British next planned a larger attack, on Wadi Misrah, to destroy guerrilla forces in that area. A mixed armoured car and Centurion tank task force, supported by artillery, moved out. Things went badly at the beginning: some of the tanks lost their tracks on the rocky ground, while the armoured cars' tyres were ripped to shreds. However, when they did get to the rebel strongholds, the Centurions' 105mm guns blew them to pieces, fire being directed at long range by Auster observation aircraft which flew overhead. Finally, the paratroops moved in to mop up. This operation, and others which followed, managed to restore some order to the wild outback, and the infiltration was stopped, for the time being.

The years that followed, however, were marked by growing civil unrest in Aden itself and naturally the morale of the local police and the FRA, both of which were inflitrated by rebels, suffered heavily, leading to mutinies and the loss of many British lives. The low point of the entire Aden story was reached when the authorities decided, against their better judgement, to abandon the Crater sector to the terrorists. The reason given was the desire to prevent a blood-bath, but the terrorists immediately took over the entire sector, and marched in a victory parade, sporting sticks and weapons in defiance of the local police.

Encouraged by their gains, the guerrillas now began to attack British troops in the open. In one ambush near an army camp, several soldiers were killed and wounded when their convoy was fired upon by automatic weapons and grenades. The lack of British response to this made it clear to all that the British would soon be leaving, a situation which only increased the venom of the National Liberation Front (NLF) and other dissident factions.

In June 1967, following the dramatic events of the Six Day War, Arab nationalism heightened, which meant automatic hostility to all Western forces, not only Israel, and increased their demands for freedom from colonialism. Thus even a small incident, of which there were several almost daily in Aden, could set off a chain reaction ending in further violence. There were several mutinies in the ranks of the FRA and the local police and, although they were quickly suppressed, the firing which was heard led to wild rumours that the British forces were slaughtering their former comrades in arms.

On 20 June a company of the Royal Northumberland Fusiliers, which controlled the sector, was in position just outside Marine Drive, one of the exits from the Crater, with armoured cars from the Queen's Dragoon Guards in support. Lieutenant John Davis was making routine rounds when he noticed suspicious activity inside the police barracks. He heard shots being fired and, after reporting the matter to his superiors, decided to take a longer route, avoiding the police barracks. At this stage contact was lost and the company commander, Major David Malcolm, concerned about the safety of his patrol, went to look for them with a mobile force travelling in two Land Rovers. As they arrived near the police barracks the small force was riddled with bullets, the vehicles set alight and most of the soldiers killed outright, including Major Malcolm. Only one man survived. Lieutenant Davis, hearing that Malcolm and his men were out looking for him, dismounted with three of his men and, in turn, went in search of Malcolm. All four of them disappeared and, in spite of continuous attempts to find them by their comrades, they were never seen again.

A number of Saladin armoured cars entered the Crater but were forbidden by the authorities to use their main armament. All-round small arms fire was directed at them and soon their optical vision blocks were smashed, making it impossible to fire accurately. A Sioux helicopter which had been hovering overhead was shot down, and the situation deteriorated rapidly. As darkness fell on what had been the bloodiest day the British had ever seen in Aden, all troops were withdrawn from the Crater. The mutinous local police, fearful of retaliation, opened the prison, and issued arms to all and sundry. That night the hysterically rejoicing mob began to fight among themselves, turning the party into a bloody riot. All control seemed to have been lost, and the army did the only thing possible: it sealed off the Marine Drive exit from the Crater to prevent the riots from spreading outside and endangering even the nearby airport and brigade HQ.

In order to ameliorate the situation and restore some respect for the British Army, a counter-attack was mounted on a junction just inside the peninsula, but the troops, without fire support from artillery and armoured car cannon, were pinned down by heavy fire from an old Turkish fort in the Crater, and they had to fend for themselves.

The authorities turned down various proposals to retake the Crater since they wished to maintain a low-key policy to prevent further escalation. Only sniper fire was allowed so, during the next few days, several terrorists were picked off by sharpshooters firing from rooftops just outside the Crater. At night patrols penetrated the enemy positions and managed to bring out the British dead for a decent military funeral.

On 21 June the Argyll and Sutherland Highlanders took over control of the sector. Their commander, Lieutenant-Colonel Colin Mitchell, was a born soldier, who had joined the Home Guard at the age of fourteen, but joined his regiment, in 1945 right at the end of the war, just in time to see action in Italy. Wounded in Palestine after the war, he had also fought in Korea, Kenya and Borneo, soon becoming known for his bravery and fierceness in battle. His devotion to his regiment and to his men were qualities which earned him their unstinting loyalty.

Here in Aden, Mitchell would not accept a situation in which his men would be mauled by the Arabs without retaliation. Sizing up the situation, he came up with his own plan to retake the Crater. The authorities hesitated at first but Mitchell persisted and gradually won them over. On the afternoon of 3 July 1967, one of his companies was heliported on to Ras Marshag peninsula, which was still in British hands. From there the men advanced to link up with troops coming from the direction of Marine Drive. To the terrorists the move seemed nothing out of the ordinary. With the Argyll pipers skirling in the background, Colonel Mitchell's companies moved off into the darkness, supported by a squadron of the Queen's Dragoon armoured cars and, in the darkness, they entered the Crater. Near a place called the Sultan's Waterfront, the first exchange of fire occurred, two Arabs being killed and, suddenly all the terrorists melted away, surprised by the determination of the attack, which had been unknown in earlier skirmishes.

His first mission a success, Mitchell requested permission to widen his hold and by 0300 the battalion was in charge of all objectives. The Argylls had restored British authority over the problematic Crater without losing a single man. The Scottish pipers brought the surprised Adenis out of their beds with the Long Reveille, which echoed around the ancient volcanic cliffs in the morning air.

21. THE GOLANIS STORM TEL FAHAR

On 5 June 1967, after months of rising tension between Israel and the surrounding Arab states, Israel found herself at war again, fighting concurrently on three fronts: Egypt, Jordan and Syria.

One of the Israel's main objectives was to stop the ceaseless bombardment of Israel's northern settlements from the Syrian Golan Heights. These bluffs, ascending steeply above Israel's Hula Valley, were packed with strongly fortified strongholds armed with heavy artillery, from which shells and mortars rained down almost daily on the civilian population of northern Israel.

On the afternoon of 9 June 1967, the Barak (Lightning) Battalion of the crack Golani infantry set out to capture one of these strongholds – Tel Fahar.

Blocking access to the northern slopes of the Golan, it was one of the key points of the Syrian defence system, containing several 57mm anti-tank guns, recoilless guns, three Guryonov heavy machine-guns and a battery of medium mortars. All these were well dug-in to the hillside and almost invisible from below – or, indeed, from above. At that time it was guarded by a company of the Syrian 187th Infantry Battalion. Some 1,500 metres to the north-west and below Tel Fahar was Tel Azaziat, also hewn into the rocks, and a smaller defence post, Burg-Bavill, guarded a minefield to the south. Most of the Syrian 11th Infantry Brigade was located higher up the mountain slopes, in the fortified villages of Ein Fitt and Zaoura.

Quite apart from the advantages of its geographical position, Tel Fahar had been extensively constructed to present an awesome challenge for any would-be attackers. Situated on two opposing hillocks, it had fortified trenchworks criss-crossing between them, each surrounded by wire and mine obstacles; bunkers, covered from the top, overlooked access routes, all of which were blocked from below by dense minefields. This was the mission of the Golanis.

Their orders were to follow tanks of the 8th Armoured Brigade up the slopes along a prepared track. At a certain point, the turn-off north of a village named Na'amush, the armour would turn south-east while the Golani halftracks and Sherman tanks would continue north and north-east, eventually to storm the Syrian 11th Brigade high up in their villages of Ein Fitt and Zaoura, thus opening the northern route to Mount Hermon, the peak of the Golan Heights.

The Israel Air Force had absolute control of the skies by this stage in the war, and now began strafing the Syrian positions. But the Syrian emplacements had been well designed; only their openings were visible above the ground, even those being camouflaged, and the Air Force bombs were not seen to inflict much damage.

The Golanis now began their climb and soon reached the Na'amush turn-off, from where they arrived at Tel Azaziat from the rear; after a short but difficult fight they captured it. The Barak Battalion was briefed to carry on, and assault Tel Fahar from the east, using a road, now disused, which once had conveyed oil from the Trans-Arabian pipeline, to approach the fortification. But the word 'road' was only approximate; it was now nothing but a dirt track, very difficult to see. The connecting track, which had looked so good on the map, was completely invisible, and the unit commander who was in the lead missed the turn-off and went on to the wrong dirt-road, immediately coming under heavy fire from Syrian positions above it.

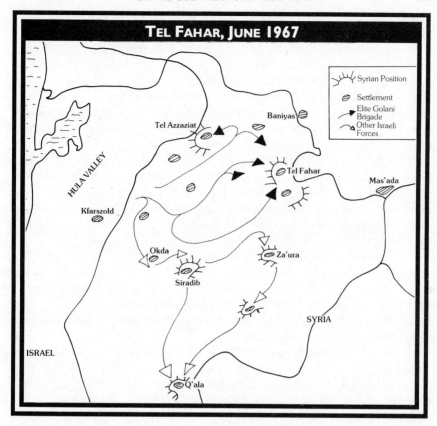

TEL FAHAR, JUNE 1967

Syrian Position
Settlement
Elite Golani Brigade
Other Israeli Forces

Baniyas
Tel Azzaziat
Tel Fahar
Mas'ada
HULA VALLEY
Kfarszold
Okda
Za'ura
Siradib
SYRIA
ISRAEL
Q'ala

They were in serious trouble, and it would last. Three of their Sherman tanks broke down, blocking the track for those following, and the Syrian fire increased, wounding many of the men in their halftracks. Eventually Lieutenant-Colonel Moshe Klein, the battalion commander, crashed right up the hill, circled the Syrian gun positions from the rear, ran down again, and regained the road. Many, but not all, of the other halftracks followed; some of the drivers were simply not experienced enough to negotiate those rocky hills.

Moshe Klein, known as Moussa, was a veteran infantry commander, adored by his men who would have gone through fire and water as long as he was leading them. A simple man, thickset, with a bashful smile which hid the ruthless determination of a fighter, he would share everything with his men, and took a deep interest in their wellbeing. Now he was leading them into battle and, finally, to his own death.

The Syrians began to bring artillery to bear on them. Splintered rocks caused by their shelling was falling in all directions, and casualties mounted. The men, packed close together in the halftracks, were sitting ducks as one after another the carriers were hit. It seemed for a while as if the entire battalion would be killed there.

Some of the men managed to jump out of their halftracks, and raced for cover among the rocks, but Colonel Klein rallied his men and urged them on, standing erect in his carrier as an example, a true example of the Israeli officer's motto: 'Follow me!' As the front of the column neared Tel Fahar, however, it became apparent that – because they had been on the wrong dirt-track – they had approached from the wrong angle and the assault would have to go in against the strongest position of Tel Fahar instead of the weakest as originally planned. Klein, however, realized that there was no option but to continue with the mission, since not to do so would endanger the success of the entire operation. Calling to his men to attack, he raced forward, losing contact in the process with most of his men.

The battle for Tel Fahar was like nothing one could read about in the text books. The junior officers, realizing that they would have no contact with their commander, showed the courage and initiative for which the Golani troops were famous. Assembling the survivors from the burning halftracks, they sent medics to attend to the wounded, and formed the rest of the men into small units. 'A' Company, under its deputy commander Lieutenant Schmiel, reached the outer defences and split into two sections. The men panted uphill carrying their heavy combat loads, dodging fire from the bunkers above them. Since much of the fire was coming from a Guryonov machine-gun emplacement, one man crawled up until he was just below the slit of its opening – then threw a grenade inside. There was an explosion followed by silence. Those guns did not fire again.

Soon the Golani men were inside the trenches. The Syrians were determined defenders, though, and it seemed as if every inch of ground had to be disputed. All over the trenches and bunkers groups of two, three of four men could be seen fighting in hand-to-hand combat while losses mounted on both sides.

The main bunker was a source of agony to the Israeli soldiers, spitting lethal fire on every side. Finally, they were near enough to assault it and four men, led by a young corporal, stormed up, reached the apertures and hurled in two grenades. When the dust settled after the explosion, they entered to make sure that all the Syrians had been killed. Emerging and running along a trench parallel with the main bunker, they suddenly met their battalion commander, quite alone. Calling them to follow him, he ran forward, ducking bullets, and shooting a Syrian soldier who abruptly appeared in front of him. Followed by the men, he reached the northern part of the position but there, hit by a sniper's bullet, he fell, dead.

For a moment the men were stunned by the loss of their much-loved commander, but an artillery captain came forward and rallied them once again. Encouraged by seeing more Golani fighters coming up the hill to join the battle, they began to mop up the Syrian positions. The Syrians were beginning to feel threatened and withdrew to the southern section to muster their men and establish a defence, but, at this point, with the Golanis running out of ammunition and the small groups unable to contact one another, they also felt the urgent need for assistance. One officer managed to reach one of the halftracks which had been abandoned on the way to Tel Fahar. Finding that its radio was still working, he established contact with his brigade HQ and soon the brigade's Recce Squadron appeared from the south-east and was guided into the northern section of the tel.

Seeing that the battle was at a crucial stage, Captain Ruvke, the Squadron commander, lost no time. He and his men stormed over to the southern compound and the last bout of savage fighting took place. The final mopping-up took some time, but to all extents and purposes the battle was over.

The victorious – but exhausted – men of the Barak Battalion proudly raised their flag on the branches of a tree pockmarked by bullets. Twenty-two men, including the colonel, had been killed in the battle, but the road to the Hermon was open.

22. A HIT TEAM TO BEIRUT

On 10 April 1973 at 2130 a flotilla of Israeli Navy missile boats floated silently over the horizon and entered the coastal waters of Lebanon. Close to midnight black dinghies launched from two of the vessels, *Cherev* and *Eilat*, glided noiselessly to the beach of the Beirut suburb of El Uzai, a luxurious and beautiful holiday resort in better times, known as the Lebanese Riviera. The occupants leapt to the shore. They were members of an élite Israeli Commando unit led by Lieutenant-Colonel Ehud Barak (now IDF Chief of Staff), and their mission – probably the most daring in Israel's history – was to kill highly placed members of the PLO's military wing who had been responsible for many terrorist acts inside and outside Israel, and to destroy as many of the PLO's huge arms caches as possible.

Waiting by the roadside were several cars whose drivers, dressed like European tourists, nevertheless greeted the night raiders warmly – in Hebrew. Once the Commandos were in the cars, they were given a guided tour of the busy night traffic of Beirut, which the drivers obviously knew well. They headed for the exclusive district of Ramalat el Baida.

Minutes later, another pair of ships, *Misgav* and *Sufa*, landed more dinghies on the same beach. They brought more troops – a landing party commanded by Lieutenant-Colonel Amnon Shachak (now a major-general and deputy Chief of Staff to Barak). More limousines took this party, too, to Beirut, but they headed for the Beirut neighbourhood of Sabra in the heart of the city, occupied largely by Palestinians.

At 0129 six black sedans then entered the prosperous neighbourhood of El Biada. Barak, who had (and has) a misleadingly baby face, and one other team member were dressed as women, complete with blonde wings. Others wore expensive suits bought the day before in an exclusive Tel Aviv mall. Though well made, the suits seemed rather too big for their wearers – with reason, since beneath them were pistols, Mini-Uzis and lots of ammunition. They raised no suspicion, though, looking just like any other group of happy couples returning from a night on the town after visiting some of the many night clubs still flourishing in downtown Beirut.

Three cars continued to Ibn-El Walid Boulevard and stopped at a nearby parking lot; eight people left the cars, while two remained behind to watch their backs. Barak's deputy, Muki Betzer, took his assault team to a tall condominium, seeking out the apartment of a high-ranking officer of the terrorist group Black September, Muhamad Najar. Surprisingly, the door to the lobby was wide open, the doorman sound asleep and snoring, and Betzer had no trouble locating Najar's apartment. While he was preparing the explosives to break down the door, shots were heard from the street below. Barak and a member of his team had seen a suspicious movement in a parked car. They shot instantly, killing one guard sitting in the driver's seat, but the other managed to bolt, disappearing into the dark street.

On hearing the shooting, Betzer lost no time in setting off the charge. The door fell open inwards and the team poured into the apartment. As they entered the bedroom, they saw the terrorist reaching for his gun, but managed to shoot him before he could grasp it.

At a nearby apartment house, a second assault team went up to the second floor, the dwelling of Kamal A'Duan, another PLO military leader, while a third team went up another floor to the residence of Kamal Nasser, the PLO spokesman. One of the team members, Malek, placed explosives on A'Duan's apartment door, but once again shots were heard from the street. Instinctively Malek backed off and with one kick opened the door. As it swung open he saw a big Arab pointing a Kalashnikov rifle straight at him. But the Arab hesitated, and it cost him his life, as several Uzis fired simultaneously by the Commandos riddled his body.

As they entered and began to search the apartment, they could hear the explosion of the third team breaking into Nasser's flat. The smoke cleared; the room seemed empty. The team searched everywhere, finding only two terrified women hiding under blankets, who were spared. The team leader was sure that Nasser was in the apartment, but he could not find him – could he have slipped away at the last minute? Then, in the kitchen, one of the Commandos spotted a movement behind the refrigerator, but Nasser managed to get off a burst from his Kalashnikov, wounding the Israeli who, before he fell, got Nasser with an accurate round of automatic fire. Nasser fell dead and the team regrouped downstairs, entering their waiting cars, whose engines were already warm and running smoothly. Just as they were moving off, a Lebanese police jeep arrived. Well–aimed automatic fire killed one of the policemen, but their jeep continued to advance; then another bullet hit the driver, who lost control of the vehicle, and it crunched into a doorway.

Now the first team led by Betzer came down into the street, to be met by fire from another police car. They tried Mini-Uzi rounds, but missed, as this weapon is not effective at long range. The Lebanese, however, cautiously kept their distance.

The group in the other three sedans, with Shachak in command, went to the Sabra sector, to hit the headquarters of the Popular Front, another terrorist organization, located in a large apartment building. They reached their target slightly ahead of time and waited until H–Hour. Shachak gave the order and the lead section – Avida Shur and Hagai Mayan – cautiously approached the building. Twenty metres behind were Shachak himself, his command team and the demolition section – a car loaded with 120 kilograms of explosives. Shur and Mayan were detailed to make the first contact and neutralize the Arab guards.

Four guards were on duty east and west of the building, covered by a Russian-made heavy machine-gun mounted on a pick-up truck. The Israelis approached the guards, asking for a light for their cigarettes. As one of the guards searched his pockets for matches, Mayan closed in and killed him with his silenced pistol. Shur took the other guard, but was not so lucky. The second Palestinian was fatally wounded, but released an ear-splitting scream before he died, raising the alarm all over the neighbourhood. The machine-gun crew opened fire, and two Arabs dismounted from their truck and took up positions at the side of the road, firing assault rifles. The Israelis were immediately hit, and contact between them and Shachak's command team behind was lost. Shur was dead and Mayan fatally wounded, but yet another victim of the shooting was Yigal Presler, a member of the main command team. The second man in his team immediately responded by pulling out his Uzi and eliminating the guard with a long, well-placed burst.

Obviously the element of surprise had now been lost, but Shachak decided to continue with the mission and they moved in, while the terrorists threw grenades from the upper windows. Evaluating the situation quickly, Shachak decided to close in from the west and sent a group of men to check the situation on the far side of the building, which still seemed quiet. They were also told to secure the main staircase, holding the entrance open for the assault of the main party.

The Commandos charged forward, under cover of fire from a rifle grenade-launcher which blazed across the street at the upper floors and, simultaneously, the car packed with explosives was called into service, driven into the parking lot right under the building. Just then, the Israelis guarding the front entrance to the building saw that the lift was coming down; racing forward, some sprayed the cabin with gunshot, while others tossed grenades and tear-gas bombs into the staircase. When the lift doors opened at the ground floor, it was filled with the bodies of Arabs, their Kalashnikovs littering the floor.

Now working against time, the sappers placed their demolition charges, guarded by the security team. As they completed their task, shots were heard all round them, bullets pinging only inches away. More of the PLO were trying to get down the staircase, firing their weapons at the same time, but held back by the Israelis who were firing from below.

The moment the demolition chief activated the fuzes – at a delay time of three minutes – he shouted a warning to clear the area, and all the Commandos raced for their cars, keeping the Arabs at bay as best they could. Casualties were loaded, and the limousines left the scene, the Commandos lobbing smoke bombs behind them as they rounded the corner of the street and, mingling with the rest of the traffic, disappeared into the crowded downtown area.

Meanwhile, a team of frogmen dressed in black diving suits, members of a crack naval Commando unit led by Lieutenant-Colonel Shaul Ziv, had come in across the dark sea. Hitting the beach south of the designated point, there were no cars waiting, and they had to rush to their meeting-place on foot. Since they were loaded with weapons and explosives, they arrived, panting, forty-five minutes late.

The target seemed deserted; all was quiet. Ziv placed his command team – himself, a radio operator and a doctor – close to the shore, facing the target: the PLO command facility and a nearby shack holding leech mines, which was found abandoned. Civilians found on the first and second floors of the building were quickly evacuated, the charges set and activated, and the naval Commandos left the area. Ony five minutes had elapsed.

There were still two more assignments that night: a warehouse holding arms in the port area was destroyed, and ambushes were placed on the main road to Beirut, north of Sidon.

By 0200 the operation was over; the Commandos returned to their collecting points and were taken aboard their vessels. They had suffered four casualties: two men killed and two wounded. It was a complex, well-planned raid and meticulously carried out, probably one of the most ambitious ever executed.

23. THE ENTEBBE RESCUE

M any of the Israeli special forces' bravest deeds have never been told – even to their own people. One of their finest operations, however, did receive worldwide coverage – the amazing rescue operation from Entebbe airport in Uganda.

The Entebbe story began on 29 June 1976, when Air France Flight 139, en route from Tel Aviv to Paris via Athens, was hijacked by Palestinian terrorists and others working under their aegis. They forced the captain to fly to Benghazi airport in Libya and, after refuelling, to take off again, heading for Uganda in the heart of Black Africa. Landing later that evening at Uganda's national airport at Entebbe, the passengers were taken to an old terminal building under heavy guard, where they remained.

During the seemingly endless week that followed, they were visited frequently by the Ugandan dictator Idi Amin, a man who could rightly be called 'the smiler with the knife'; the non-Jewish hostages were released and flown to safety but the Jews – together with the courageous French crew, who chose to stay with them – were told that they would not be freed unless the Government of Israel acceded to the terrorists' conditions. These – the liberation of 54 convicted terrorists – were unthinkable; the Israeli authorities knew that if they gave in on this, the terrorists' demands would never end. It seemed at first as if the hostages might all be killed, as threatened by the terrorists: their deadline – midnight, 4 July.

To this seemingly insoluble dilemma, however, a military option was moted: to free the hostages by *coup de main*. To any other government, the suggestion would have been almost ludicrous, if the circumstances were not so serious. Entebbe, almost 5,000 kilometres from Israel, was guarded by the Ugandan Army, as well as the terrorists themselves, who were heavily armed with automatic weapons and explosives – sufficient to kill the entire hundred and more hostages who were crowded into the terminal. Nevertheless, Chief of Staff Motta Gur, himself a veteran paratroop commander, with many missions to his credit, had confidence in his men although at first he regarded the various proposals with some misgivings. Having been won round to the idea, though, Gur delegated the planning stage to a group of experienced officers: the ground role was placed in the hands of Brigadier-General Dan Shomron, the 36-year-old commander of paratroops and infantry, assisted by Israel Air Force chief General Benjamin Peled, who had led the IAF during the Yom Kippur War's air battles three years before. Peled, himself a seasoned fighter pilot, was the very man to plan such a difficult mission. At once thorough and daring, he began to search for unconventional approaches to the problem, knowing that whatever they decided would tax his transport aircraft to the utmost.

The final plan, which was approved by Israel's cabinet at the very last moment, involved a hand-picked team of paratroops and Commandos to be flown out to Entebbe in four C-130 Hercules transport aircraft. Once the aircraft had landed on the old runway, nearest to the terminal where the hostages were kept, the troops would rush out, storm the terminal, disposing of both guards and terrorists, and then escort the hostages to the Hercules waiting to fly them home.

The leader of the assault team, Lieutenant-Colonel Jonathan Netan-yahu, known as 'Yonni', was a unique mixture of intellect and guts. Brought up in New York by Zionist parents, he returned to Israel on reaching the age of 18, to join one of the élite units of the IDF. He rose quickly through the ranks, distinguishing himself in the Six Day War of 1967 and in the Yom Kippur War of 1973, when he fought on the Golan Heights during the crucial early days. On one of those days, Yonni rescued his best friend, the commander of an armoured battalion, who had been wounded and lay on the battlefield at the mercy of the advancing Syrians. Yonni made it back, but was badly wounded by enemy fire. In spite of being discharged from active service with a high disability rating, he returned to serve, convincing the Chief of Staff to let him command his old unit, a crack Commando force. Now, having brought his highly trained unit to perfect pitch, he was to set off on his most famous operation.

The first C-130 Hercules, piloted by the squadron leader, Lieutenant Colonel Shani, rumbled down the runway and took off at 11 p.m. on 3 July 1976, setting course southward. Inside the cargo compartment, a black

Mercedes was lashed down, and sitting in the Merc were Yonni and some of his officers, putting the final touches to the plan. The Mercedes had been the bright idea of one of Yonni's officers who had served as an instructor with Idi Amin's forces and knew them very well. He thought that if the attackers were to use a black Mercedes and Land Rovers in Ugandan colours, wearing camouflage uniforms similar to those worn by the Ugandan soldiers, they might pass for Amin himself or at least one of his senior officers, on a routine visit to the airfield, thus achieving complete surprise during the first moments of their arrival, always provided, of course, that the aircraft could land in the dark unobserved by the control tower. During rehearsals some senior Israeli commanders had watched the Hercules land and, although they knew they were coming, could not hear them approach at all, which gave the mission commanders confidence. Also travelling in Shani's aircraft were the commander of the ground operation, Dan Shomron, and a senior officer, Colonel Matan Vilnai, another top paratroop commander, who was acting as his deputy. Four aircraft were off to Africa: Shani's led, then the Hercules flown by Natti, transporting two armoured personnel carriers and some of the paratroops; the third aircraft carried two more APCs and a contingent of Golani fighters, while the last one hauled fuel and bowsers with a ground crew to service the aircraft at Entebbe. It was planned to leave the material there and use the empty transport to load the hostages on their way home.

The first leg of the flight was to Sharm el Sheikh in southern Sinai, where the IAF had established a forward airfield. There the Hercules were to refuel and await last-minute clearance by prime minister Yitzhak Rabin who was in constant session with his senior ministers. The flight to Sharm was a bad one. The aircraft flew at near zero altitude to evade the Jordanian radar and strict radio silence was observed to avoid their flight being spotted by the Soviet intelligence ships present in the Red Sea. But flying so low over the desert caused severe turbulence, the aircraft rocking violently, and many of the passengers were airsick.

Once on the ground, however, the Commandos were able to rest while they waited for Rabin's 'yes'. It finally came, and the four tranports took off, setting course for the African coast, flying over the international airways route into Ethiopia. Take-off temperature was high at 40 degrees Centigrade but, as they climbed over the African highlands, it dropped very low, taxing the pressurized cargo interior to the maximum. The men settled down to a long flight in their cramped bucket seats; many of them, exhausted, slept throughout the entire journey in spite of a heavy African thunderstorm which hit them en route. They flew on – up to the border of Kenya and Uganda, where the pilots began to look for a final navigation point. This was a significant feature, a bay near the town of Kisumo in Kenya. Over this bay blew the very heart of the thunderstorm, with rain up to 50,000 feet. The pilots had no alternative but to go on. They penetrated the thick clouds, and found hail, lightning and thunder, as well as strong winds, which made several course corrections necessary. It was far from pleasant. But eventually they were through, and on their last leg: over Lake Victoria, heading straight for Entebbe airport!

Over the radio a conversation between a British Airways jet and the control tower could be heard distinctly. All seemed well; there was no hint that their presence had been detected; the voices were calm and professional. Colonel Shani turned into his final approach and lined up on the fully lit runway. Visibility was near perfect with only light rain as he settled down for the landing. The pilots virtually stood on their brakes, fighting to stop the heavy aircraft quickly in the middle of the runway. The rear loading ramp was already lowered, and Yonni ordered the engines started before the aircraft even came to a stop.

The second they had landed, the black Mercedes with Yonni and his group drove off, followed closely by the two Land Rovers and the rest of the assault party. As the motorized party drove off in the direction of the terminal, Colonel Shani directed a special team to race up the runway and place torches near the flarepath. None too soon, for another Herc was already landing as the runway lights went out, but all three aircraft managed to land safely.

Yonni's group drove steadily along the runway and the Mercedes purred past two astonished Ugandan sentries who challenged them. One of them, mistaking them for VIPs, saluted and stepped back; the other, more suspicious, brandished his rifle. Yonni and one of his men shot him with a silenced gun, but the other sentry, now fully alerted, began to run towards them firing his own rifle. Alarmed by the noise, Ugandan troops began to fire from near the control tower and from one of the Land Rovers a paratrooper, aiming carefully at the muzzle flashes in the darkness, shot the source.

The motor column, all headlights now blazing, continued towards the terminal, only 150 metres away. The shooting had stopped, and all was quiet again. The three cars stopped near the terminal and the men stormed out, forming into a triangle as they, with Yonni and his deputy, Captain Muki Zur, in the lead. So far not a shot had been fired from the terminal but suddenly one of the terrorists came out of the building. It was the blond German who, upon seeing them, shouted loudly to the Ugandan soldiers. Muki shot the German with a quick and accurate burst of automatic fire, and the Commandos killed two Ugandan guards who were guarding the door. Only four minutes had passed since the cars had rolled down the ramps of the aircraft.

Now, for a second, and only a second, Yonni's men hesitated. Yonni had already anticipated this – it was normal in such operations. Shouting to Muki to follow him, he ran towards the terminal. The men immediately rallied and stormed after him. From the right came a Ugandan soldier, firing as he ran; he was killed by concentrated fire from one of Yonni's men. Then came the sound of crashing glass, as a terrorist broke a window and started firing through it. A single bullet from his gun hit Yonni, who fell, fatally wounded, near the doorway.

He had given strict instructions that under no circumstances was the operation to halt, even to tend the wounded, until the hostages were freed. Thus no one stopped, and the assault party continued on in to the building. As the leader kicked down the door, he came face to face with a terrorist who was lying on the floor firing his Kalashnikov, but the Arab was surprised and his shots went astray. Sergeant Amir, who was just behind his leader, fired a short burst, killing the man from close range. According to the agreed procedure, Amir then turned right as he passed through the doorway. Avner, who followed him, turned left. Out of the corner of his eye, he could see a terrorist rise from the back of the hall and aim his rifle, but he was shot before he could fire. Two more terrorists, one a woman, were crawling towards them on the floor, aiming their guns, but Avener spotted them and killed them both in a split second. Rushing forward, he kicked their rifles away in case they were still alive. Another Israeli soldier, Amos, spotted a terrorist hiding behind a pillar, gun in hand. Amos fired, but probably missed, and Captain Muki Zur, coming up behind, finished him off. All four of the terrorists who had been guarding the hostages were now eliminated, and with them the danger for the hostages, who had been lying on the floor, trying to shelter from the crossfire. Amir took his loudspeaker and, speaking first in Hebrew and then in English, told them that they were Israelis. The joy and relief were great, but sadly a headcount established that three of the hostages had been killed during the shooting. The assault forces had paid a heavy price, too, with their leader dead and one of their comrades badly wounded. That man, a private named Sourin, would remain paralysed for life from a bullet that hit his spine.

From the far side of the airfield, the area was suddenly lit up by a spectacular firework display as the Golani troops demolished the line of MiG-21 fighters of the Ugandan Air Force standing on the runway. Getting the signal, the Commandos hurried the hostages into their waiting Hercules, which took off immediately, and set course for Nairobi in Kenya for refuelling. The others took off, too, and they all reached Israel without further incident.

On the morning of 4 July 1976 the four Hercules transports flew over southern Israel to land at Ben Gurion airport, to a scene of wild rejoicing rarely seen before. While everyone else celebrated, a band of sad soldiers filed inconspicuously from their aircraft. As some of the Commandos were carried shoulder high by the jubliant crowd, others carried the lifeless body of their commander, Lieutenant-Colonel Yonni Netanyahu – a man who had now passed into history.

One year later another rescue operation took place, this time involving the German GSG 9, the anti-terrorist unit of the Federal Republic of Germany, set up after the 1972 massacre of eleven Israeli athletes at the Munich Olympics by Palestinian terrorists of the Black September organization.

At noon on 13 October 1977 Lufthansa Flight 181, Boeing 737 Charlie Echo, took off from Palma di Majorca and set course for southern France. One hour later while in flight, captain Juergen Schumann reported that his aircraft had been hijacked and ordered to fly to Rome. A near hysterical voice broke in; he called himself Mahmoud, said he was the terrorist leader, and, in broken English, announced his demands, among which were the release of the Bader Meinhof Gang and several million dollars in ransom.

While the aircraft was being refuelled in Rome, the captain managed to signal the authorities that there were four terrorists aboard, but before any use could be made of the information, the jetliner took off and headed for Cyprus, on the first stage of a journey that would take it all over the Middle East until it made its final stop at Mogadishu airport in Somalia; Mahmoud had killed Captain Schumann on the way for allegedly communicating with the authorities during a stop in Yemen, and co-pilot Juergen Vietor was forced to fly the aircraft on to Mogadishu with his dead colleague on the flight deck.

In Germany the authorities were determined not to let the terrorists get away with it and Colonel Ulrich Wegener, in charge of the GSG 9 Commando group, was ordered to prepare his men for a rescue operation. Wegener was a very competent officer who had trained with the Israeli secret service and studied the Entebbe raid thoroughly. Considered an expert in anti-terrorist operations, he was eager to demonstrate the capabilities of his small but well-trained force. Wegner had been following events from Cyprus to Dubai, but had been unable to do anything. Now he and a selected assault team flew to Mogadishu and by 17 October had established a forward tactical command post there.

Mahmoud now threatened to blow up the aircraft if his demands were not met forthwith and, to prove that he meant it, he dumped Schumann's body on to the tarmac, in full view of the on-the-spot camera teams. In order to gain time, the German authorities offered to release some of the Bader Meinhof Gang, while two SAS men, Major Alistair Morrison and Sergeant Barry Davies, were flown to the scene to help. Then, towards midnight a small group of German Commandos crawled out into the desert and from behind a sand dune, some thirty metres from the jetliner, studied the scene through their infra-red binoculars. This observation confirmed that two of the four terrorists were in the flight cabin, but the location of the others was not clear.

After midnight on 18 October specialists armed with grenade-launchers moved out to the desert while the two SAS men prepared some 'fireworks'. The operation began at 0150. While two of the terrorists were kept busy on the radio discussing terms for the release of the hostages, Wegener's men rolled a flaming oil drum on to the runway in front of the airliner, which attracted the terrorists' attention. Meanwhile other Commandos reached the aircraft and placed ladders against the emergency doors, setting magnetic charges. The charges were blown simultaneously and, while the SAS men threw stun grenades which detonated deafeningly with blinding flashes, the German Commandos charged into the aircraft. Colonel Wegener was first inside, quickly followed by his men, some of whom clambered over the wings. Shots rang out, and two of the terrorists were killed, the passengers hitting the floor to avoid the bullets. Mahmoud, appearing from the flight deck, was totally surprised; he was shot by several Commandos, but before he fell he dropped two grenades, which fortunately did not cause any casualties. As soon as the terrorists were neutralized the passengers were evacuated by emergency procedure in case of an explosion. The whole operation had taken five minutes, and GSG 9 had earned its spurs.

24. HELL AT A SHAU, VIETNAM

After the embarrassing defeat of the French at the Battle of Dien Bien Phu in March 1954, and their subsequent withdrawal from Indo-china, the United States began to maintain a small group of military advisers in South-east Asia. In 1957 a special group of the US Green Berets was sent from its base in Okinawa to Vietnam, as it was now known, to assist the republican forces trying to control communist infiltrations from north to south. These groups, known as A Teams, normally consisted of a captain in command, a lieutenant and ten other ranks, including a medic or two, radio experts, demolition operators and skilled weapons men, trained in handling a large variety of arms of both western and eastern manufacture.

An A Team would enter its assigned region and establish a fortified camp which included bunkers and trenchworks for all-round defence. For their various duties in the country, the Green Berets were trained in the rudiments of the indigenous customs and were fluent in the language, even down to the local dialect, so that they could more easily blend into the terrain and begin organizing the local population to defend itself from communist infiltrators from North Vietnam – the Vietcong.

One thing which soon made the Americans popular was the excellent medical care they provided in regions where none had hitherto existed. The introduction of new medications and health care soon became known throughout the malaria-infested jungle. After a single year operating in the Vietnamese highlands under extremely difficult conditions, enduring the blazing sun by day and the freezing cold by night, suffering frequent spells of malaria and other tropical illnesses, the Green Berets had set up 26 fortified camps and trained some 30,000 locals in the techniques of weapons handling and undercover operations. This was a tremendous achievement and one which never received any media attention while stories of American brutality were capturing front page headlines all over the world. They received, moreover, almost no help from the government in Saigon, who had been reluctant to arm the South Vietnamese Montagnards, fearing that they might become a threat later on.

In March 1963 Captain Rod Paschall, a Green Beret and commander of the A Team assigned to Darlac province, took some selected members of his team to lay an ambush against a Vietcong infiltration route near the Cambodian border. Paschall's raiding party left the camp before dawn and set up their ambush near a number of bamboo huts which, to his experienced eye, looked suspicious. Before dusk the following day, some ten Vietcong soldiers cautiously approached the huts. The Americans were well hidden, so the Vietcong entered the huts quite unsuspectingly and sat down for their evening meal. No guards were about and the A Team crawled towards the huts, unseen. Suddenly one of the Vietcong heard the sound of a rifle bolt and, grabbing his assault rifle, ran out, only to be killed at the door. The other Vietcong had no chance and fell in seconds as the Green Berets stormed in. Nine VC were dead and one was captured, who gave valuable information. As the firefight had been very short and had taken place in a remote area, Captain Paschall decided to eliminate all traces of the action and remain in ambush for further infiltrators who might come to use the hideout. His hunch proved correct – more came, not much later, and met a similar fate.

A much more serious incident took place at A Shau; it was later to become famous as the setting of a film entitled 'The Green Berets', starring John Wayne as the commander of an A Team. Set in a misty jungle-filled valley surrounded by mountains, some of which were 3,000 metres high, A Shau served an important location for observing the enemy's supply route into North Vietnam and Laos. The camp was defended by seventeen Green Berets, led by Captain John Blair, plus some 210 other men including three companies of Vietnamese special forces and a motley gang of others – a mixture which did not inspire too much confidence. Captain Blair requested, and received, reinforcements in the shape of a 'Mike Force' – a force made up of 'Nungs', mercenaries of Chinese descent who had two plusses in American eyes: not only were they better fighters than the locals, but they also hated the communists. They could thus be counted on in critical situations, working as rapid reaction teams.

A Shau was defended all round its perimeter – in theory; trenches had been dug, but many of them needed repair, as they had filled with mud after the last monsoon rains. The barbed wire fences were becoming rusty, and the elephant grass had grown out of control, impeding a clear field of fire. A rampart, made of earth from the excavated trenches, presented some cover from incoming small arms fire, and an area had been bulldozed clear between the outer fence, its adjacent minefield and the jungle, so that any approach could be seen in time. Captain Blair, however, was worried about the state of his fortification and, as was to become apparent, with reason.

On the evening of 8 March 1966 Blair received reports by radio of a possible Vietcong attack and placed the camp on high alert status. At dusk noises were heard near the outer fence, and Blair ordered illumination flares to be set off, following them up with automatic and mortar fire in the general direction of the sounds. The VC scouts melted into the darkness, as usual, but after midnight mortar shells started falling inside the camp perimeter, the onslaught becoming heavier as the aim improved. Some buildings were hit and started to burn, lighting up the entire camp. In the barrage, one American soldier was killed on the spot and a medic badly wounded, but he continued to attend to the wounded until he died shortly afterwards.

The mortar barrage lasted for forty minutes without a pause, then the Vietcong attacked the camp on its southern side, which was the side guarded by the South Vietnamese soldiers – the least trained of the lot. Blair rushed some reinforcements with automatic weapons to the endangered sector, and soon the VC were being hit by withering fire, just as they had begun to cut their way through the wire fences. The Vietcong were repulsed – but not for long. Soon they rallied their men and could be heard shouting to them to search for a weak spot in the camp's defences.

Captain Blair did not lose his nerve, shifting his best men from place to place wherever and whenever an attack came, until he managed to break the assault just as dawn was approaching. The VCs disappeared into the jungle, pursued by mortar fire.

As Blair did not have enough men to launch a ground pursuit, he was on the radio at first light, requesting an air strike to come in and do the job. Weather conditions in the valley were extremely bad, with low cloud making an air attack very dangerous, but mortar attacks on the camp continued, so a USAF AC-47 gunship was sent in to find and attack the mortar position and knock it out with the rapid firing machine-guns they had aboard. As the slow aircraft entered the valley, however, and came in to low level, it was hit by massive automatic ground fire, and the pilot made an emergency crash-landing in the valley. Three of its crew members managed to crawl out of the blazing wreck and were rescued under fire by a daring helicopter pilot who risked his own life to land nearby and get them out.

During the morning, in answer to Blair's ever more urgent calls, some WW2 vintage A-1E Skyraiders, flown by air Commando pilots from the airbase at Pleiku, flew in under the clouds and strafed the Vietcong positions with 20mm cannon, but a 37mm anti-aircraft gun placed on a hillside put up devastating fire as the old piston-engined fighters lumbered along.

The situation inside the camp was now becoming extremely dangerous, as ammunition and medical supplies were running low, and two cargo aircraft were therefore rushed in to paradrop supplies inside the camp perimeter – but lost their way in the clouds, and could not locate the camp. One of the Skyraider pilots, Major Bernard Fisher, was still cruising in the area and guided the C-123s right to the camp, disregarding enemy fire from the ground. The paradrop went in, but some of the containers dropped far outside the fences; some of the men volunteered to crawl out and retrieve them, as every item was badly needed.

More support was now arriving overhead. Major Fisher, still coasting, directed an attack by twin-engined Canberra bombers which dropped cluster bombs on the VC positions. He was now short of fuel, but just before leaving the area, coolly escorted a Medevac helicopter into the camp itself to pick up some of the badly wounded and fly them out.

Suddenly another mortar barrage started falling on the camp, destroying more buildings and causing an ammunition dump to explode. Then the North Vietnamese came in again in a human wave, and the South Vietnamese defending the southern sector lost their nerve and ran. Blair rushed into the gap but was overwhelmed by the sheer numbers of NVA who, having cut through the outer fence, were now storming into the camp. He organized a defence near the command post bunker where he had decided to make his stand, and ordered his best men to join him. As the Vietcong got through, face-to-face fighting began, but the VC with their superior numbers started to get the upper hand. One Green Beret, a sergeant, managed to rally some of the Mike Force in a counter-attack, hitting the NVA just as they started to push Blair's small force inside the communications bunker. Scores of NVA soldiers fell in a crossfire of automatics and grenades, giving Blair just enough time to make a frantic call to his HQ for an immediate air strike on the camp perimeter, and telling his commander that time was rapidly running out for him and his men and that the survivors would have to be evacuated shortly — if at all.

Meanwhile Major Fisher had collected some more A-1Es and they immediately attacked. Two of his pilots were shot down during the first pass, but one managed to crash-land his aircraft in the valley and stepped out of thee burning wreckage. Fisher unhesitatingly decided to pick his man up, and came in to land on the bullet-pocked runway. Major Stafford Myers, the pilot, sprinted to the aircraft, climbed into the cockpit, and Fisher took off, to receive a well earned Medal of Honor.

Shortly afterwards the helicopters came in to pick up the camp's survivors. Escorted by UH-1 Huey gunships which fired their weapons to subdue the NVA, sixteen transport helicopters flew in to land. Just as they came in, however, the South Vietnamese broke. Throwing away their weapons and equipment, they stampeded over wounded and dead bodies towards the waiting choppers, leaving only a handful of men, led by Captain Blair and his Green Berets, to fight off the NVA, who were firing directly on to the landing zone. In the end Blair and the helicopter crewmen had no choice but to fire into the frenzied crowd which was rushing the choppers and threatening to overturn them. They finally managed to get some order into the evacuation and piled into the choppers, which immediately took off. One man who hadn't got to the choppers in time was rescued by a gunship which picked him up, badly wounded, under the noses of the advancing NVA.

Apart from that wild stampede, the South Vietnamese had fought rather well, indeed better than expected. At a body count, some 200 dead were found in the perimeter, some of them still clutching their weapons. But the battle for A Shau was over.

25. MISSION TO RAS GHARIB

A t the end of the Six Day War of 1967, some Israeli soldiers driving euphorically through the Sinai desert had found a radar station just standing there, and had thought it would be a good idea if someone had a look at it. The IAF experts who examined it identified it as a Russian P-10 Kniferest, and were very interested. In September 1969, an Israeli armoured force landed on the Egyptian side of the Gulf of Suez at Ras Zaafrana; they found there a Soviet-made Barlock GCI radar station. Some IAF boffins examined this equipment, too, and were even more impressed. However, in December 1969, the IAF, attacking Egyptian targets along the Suez Canal during the War of Attrition there, took recce photos of a radar site at Ras Gharib. It turned out to be a Russian-made P-12 Spoonrest, believed to be the most advanced Soviet radar in the Middle East, details of which were completely unknown to the West. It was thought to be an extensively modified version of the P-10, designed especially to detect low-flying aircraft – which happened to be the IAF's speciality.

If this were the case, the IAF's offensive momentum against Egypt would be lost and, at first, the planning chiefs decided to lay on a large-scale raid to knock out the radar station. But that all changed when Danny Shalev, a young corporal in IAF intelligence, was interpreting one of the recce photos. He asked his boss why the site had to be destroyed. 'Why not', he asked, 'just bring it back intact?' His commander, Lieutenant Yechiel Halor, thought it over. True, Israeli territory was only a short distance away, on the eastern side of the Gulf of Suez; and it would mean that the Israeli experts, who had been longing to get their hands on it, would get their wish. The officer had a word with his boss, the Chief of Operations, who liked the idea, and the air strike was cancelled for the time being.

A meeting took place between air force and paratroop officers to discuss the technical and tactical aspects of such a raid, which resulted in a detailed plan, submitted to Chief of Staff Haim Bar-Lev at a general staff meeting at Tel Aviv, and the man assigned to command the airborne part of the operation, Colonel Rafael Eitan (later Chief of Staff) was put in charge of the planning group.

It was decided to use a combined force made up of a *Nahal* paratroop battalion plus a special Chief of Staff's assault team. The paratroopers at once started training on a site similar to what they would face in Suez, while the IAF team went into the problems of how to carry such heavy equipment by helicopter. The P-12 Spoonrest was known to consist of two shelters mounted on Soviet Zil-15 trucks; one shelter, the main one, housing the radar set, control and display consoles, was said to weigh about 3.5 tons; the second, with the antennae assembly and the electrical motor unit, about 2 tons. Hundreds of the Zil-15 trucks had been captured by the IDF in 1967 and were now stored in various salvage depots all over the country. Two of them were brought to an IAF base in an attempt to solve the problem of how to lift off the shelters from the trucks without harming them. A field trial to estimate the weight-lifting capabilities of various helicopters, showed that the Sikorsky CH-53D, quite new in Israel, was ideal for the task. Its maximum carrying weight was 19 tons, far more than would be needed, but additional allowances had to be made for extra fuel, in light of the great distance they would be flying and the very approximate nature of their knowledge of the radar's weight.

Preliminary trials carried out by the paratroopers and the helicopter teams worked very well: the chopper pilots were able to lift the shelter and carry it around the base for some distance. The trials were repeated several times, successfully, to everyone's relief, and the paratroops started practising the dismantling procedure and to make it as fast as possible. After several hours, they had brought the time down to half an hour. They also had an extra man doing some trials – a radar expert who was familiar with the Soviet equipment. He was very good at the technical stuff, but had no combat experience at all, so he joined the paratroops for a rehearsal. The poor man panted and sweated along, with a heavy pack of special equipment on his back, together with the rest of the troops as they force-marched over hills and desert at night. But he got through, and earned a word of praise from the sympathetic commander of the paras, Lieutenant-Colonel Aryeh Zimmel.

The Ras Gharib radar site was sited just opposite the oilfields of Abu Rodeis, held by the Israelis since the 1967 Six Day War; the entire perimeter consisted of protective trenches and earthworks, inside which the radar equipment was located, placed in dug-outs for further protection. There were also some infantrymen protecting the site and the Egyptians had grouped significant forces just a few kilometres away down the road. To make matters even more difficult for the Israelis, the Egyptians had an idea something was going on, and had put all their forces on full alert.

On 26 December 1969 the *Nahal* paratroop battalion, commanded by Zimmel, flew in three Super Frelon helicopters to Ras Sudar on the Gulf coast. There Colonel Haim Nadel, commander of the airborne brigade, gave a final briefing, immediately setting out for Abu Rodeis, where the Chief of Staff's party awaited. At nightfall, Zimmel and his men flew out in their Super Frelons, heading for the Egyptian coast with control and panel lights dimmed in order to avoid detection. As they crossed the coastline, IAF fighter-bombers carried out a diversionary raid on Egyptian military camps to the south and north, to keep the Egyptians busy.

The helicopters arrived over their designated landing zone and, as they hovered, the pilots could see the dimly lit radar site about seven kilometres to the north. The first helicopter pilot had to look hard in the darkness for a landing site but eventually, using the antennae of the Egyptian radar as a reference point, managed to come down fairly easily. However, he saw that the other two were having trouble finding a suitable spot, so he sent a para officer to signal them in and finally got them both down. All the men disembarked and set off rapidly, arriving just after midnight at a hill overlooking the radar site, where they hid behind sand dunes. They were so close that they could hear the humming of the generator, so close that when two cars came into view on the road, their headlights blazing, the soldiers thought they were coming for them. The Egyptian cars, however, stopped short of the roadblock that the paras had laid and the lights went out. Perhaps they'd just come out for a quiet smoke!

On a signal from Lieutenant-Colonel Zimmel, the paratroopers crawled forward towards the unsuspecting Egyptian guards and attacked the perimeter, automatic rifles blazing. One guard managed to give the alarm, but even so it was all over in three minutes. One section went to the bunkers, slamming hand-grenades into the ventilation slits. Several Egyptian guards were killed in that phase of the fighting, while others, including the site commander, escaped into the darkness. Another team went to the dugouts and began to dismantle the radar shelters from their trucks. The battle was over, and the whining noises heard were no longer bullets, but the acetylene burners being used on the rigging. The working team had the shelters freed from the trucks in under an hour, with no interruptions from the Egyptian forces.

Once they were clear, all the men helped to make them ready for lifting-off, and at 0243 on 18 December Colonel Zimmel radioed forward HQ at Abu Rodeis that the heavy choppers could come in to take them away.

The first CH-53, flown by Major Nehemia Dagan, arrived overhead soon after and one soldier placed himself on top of the radar shelter, holding on to the rigging. Perfect contact was made between the chopper's electric hook and the rigging, the loader jumped clear, the helicopter lifted the radar off with only the slightest of jerks, and flew eastwards, the coveted radar swaying beneath. The men below, who felt as if they had been holding their breath for hours, let out a relieved sigh.

The second lift-off was almost an anti-climax: as the antennae section of the radar was one ton lighter, it was much easier to lift and was soon away. The pilot, Captain Zeev Mates, however, had quite a harrowing time when, over the Gulf near Abu Rodeis, his radar shelter began to swing, putting the chopper in some danger of crashing. It turned out that one of the paratroopers had opened the door of the shelter, causing a wind tunnel, which in turn caused the swing. However, this was corrected and he – and it – landed safely.

As soon as the helicopters had left, the paras demolished the remaining radar equipment on the site, and withdrew to make their rendezvous with the Super Frelons. They lifted off without mishap and flew home, taking with them four Egyptian prisoners. To their surprise, there had been no Egyptian counter-attack during the entire period of their occupation of the site. Even those two cars were still there on the road.

Major Dagan, piloting the first helicopter, had some uneasy moments while flying home. The weight gauge pointed to 4,300 kilograms, well over the 3,500 kg they had expected. He had lifted off all right, but as soon as he gained flying altitude a red warning light went on in the control console, while the chopper shuddered. Another warning light went on showing a drop in hydraulic pressure. But the pilot decided to try for the far shore anyway, realizing that he did not have much to lose. His gamble paid off. At 0435 both shelters were put down on the beach at Abu Rodeis.

The fruits of this intelligence triumph were later shared with US Intelligence, to the great annoyance of the Soviets, who henceforth were extremely chary of trusting modern and sensitive equipment to the hands of the Egyptians.

26. DELTA FORCE

F ollowing the departure of the Shah of Persia in January 1979 and the rise to power of the Ayatollah Khomeini and his militant Islam, anti-US feeling had been fermented by the restless and volatile mobs who daily roamed the streets of Teheran. On a rainy Sunday, 4 November 1979, this came to a head: a mob of frenzied young Iranians climbed the gate of the US Embassy compound, overwhelmed the astonished Marine guards and, at the point of pistols and Kalashnikov assault rifles, took the entire staff hostage. Seeing the compound filled with rampaging Iranians, some staff members had just had time to send an urgent teletype message to the Pentagon in Washington. The Pentagon passed it on to Delta Force.

When the message came in to the Delta Force duty officer at Fort Bragg, North Carolina, his commander, Colonel Charlie A. Beckwith, was discussing an exercise with his officers at an all-night restaurant; it was thus almost dawn the next day when he received the news that the American Embassy staff was being held hostage in Teheran. Beckwith was an aggressive veteran. As a young captain, he had served with the British SAS going on to become a member of a Special Forces Team in Vietnam. These were groups which were proficient in long-range reconnaissance missions into zones in the rear of the Vietcong. Although he was badly wounded in combat, he volunteered to serve another tour of duty in the Far East.

His real dream, however, was to create in the US Army a special assault team similar to the SAS and GSG-9, both of which had impressed him considerably. The efficiency of the Israelis' rescue operation at Entebbe in 1976 had added fuel to the fire of his determination and he had been advocating the establishment of such a force, to the deaf ears of the Joint Chiefs of Staff, for years.

The German rescue operation in Mogadishu finally gave Beckwith his chance. Jimmy Carter, then President of the United States, asked his military staff to look into the matter and raise a unit for counter-terrorist activities; Beckwith was put in charge with a period of eighteen months to get the unit operational. It was decided to include 250 men, all volunteers, in this élite force but Beckwith wanted only the best and, of the first 185 men who asked to join, only 53 finished the gruelling course, including free-fall parachuting and field training. Himself in perfect physical condition, he led his men through long-distance forced marches and obstacle courses until they could do everything a Commando could do by way of stealth, speed, accurate shooting and rapid reaction. Beckwith wanted his men to be completely expert in every military field, so weapons training on every conceivable rifle, machine-gun and mortar was undertaken until the men could dismantle, fire and repair even the most exotic weapon both day and night with their eyes closed. They also became proficient in working portable radio sets under any conditions, with laser gunsights and night vision goggles. One thing was clear: with training like this, if Delta did go into action, it would be able to perform – and survive.

As soon as Colonel Beckwith had his first team ready he demonstrated its capabilities before a crowd of distinguished onlookers who assembled at Fort Stewart, Georgia. A scenario was invented as follows: a group of terrorists had seized hostages at a friendly airport, some being held in a jetliner while others were in two airport buildings, making a simultaneous assault necessary. After some mock negotiations to gain time, as is usual under such circumstances, Delta Force worked round the clock to hammer out their attack plan. Then Beckwith and his Delta operators struck. using techniques first used by the Israelis and GSG-9, the troops breached all the airliner's doors at once and swarmed inside within seconds, overpowering the terrorists, and rescuing the hostages. At the same time the terminal buildings were assaulted by a second task force which stormed in under cover of some impressive fireworks. It was all a brilliant success, and Beckwith's force was adjudged combat ready.

At dawn the very next day, 5 November 1979, the Colonel was ordered to present himself for his first assignment: the rescue of the American hostages in Teheran. Major General James Vought, the 53-year-old former Ranger commander who was put in overall charge of the operation, knew that he was facing a formidable challenge. The hostages were held in a place halfway round the world, with only limited information available as to the situation in the compound. Failure of the operation would be a terrible blow to US prestige and might mean death for some, or all, of the hostages. Any attempt, therefore, had to be a complete success; nothing less would do. True, the Israeli government and general staff had faced similar problems when considering the Entebbe rescue, but the Israeli troops were much more experienced in that kind of mission, while Beckwith's men had only just finished their training.

Delta Force's mission looked simple enough on paper: to assault the American Embassy in Teheran, take out the Iranian guards, free the hostages, and get everyone safely out of Iran! Really well-trained men could carry out such a mission, but it would depend to a great extent on their real-time intelligence. Beckwith realized that the Israelis at Entebbe had been thoroughly briefed before takeoff and knew exactly where the hostages and their captors were located, whereas he and his force had no such information.

There was no hard information coming out of Teheran about the situation in the compound. The hostages were frequently moved, making it difficult to pinpoint their location at any one time. The same went for the guards, only more so, as these were undisciplined fanatics, impossible to assess by any known military criteria. In the meantime, Beckwith was kept quite busy enough just planning how to insert his force into the area. At first coming in by parachute seemed the most promising method, but lessons learned from major airborne operations since the Second World War showed that a high percentage of the paras would be out of action after the drop and, in such a specialized mission, this would be a loss they could ill afford, since each men would have his own special task to perform.

Other proposals came in thick and fast, among them one to land a task force right in the Embassy grounds but this was soon ruled out as impracticable. Another proposal which at first sight appeared more promising was to truck in by land across the Turkish border; this idea, however, was discarded on political grounds, as the USA did not wish to involve the Turks, and in any case, the roads in that area were few and rough.

In the end, it was clear that helicopters provided the best way to get Delta Force into the country; it was investigated as the optimum solution by General Vought and presented for consideration to Joint Chief of Staff General Davis Jones. Several problems, however, immediately emerged: for example, the type of helicopters, and the best way to use them. Having considered all possible options, the Sea Stallion, a heavy Navy RH-53D chopper, was rated best. This helicopter could take off from a carrier, having foldable tail booms and rotor blades. Although designed for minesweeping, it could carry up to fifty men, depending on the fuel payload and the flight range.

Another issue that immediately ensued, however, was that the Sea Stallion would not be able to fly the entire distance to Teheran without refuelling en route. This, in turn, presented a security problem. Another hurdle was the transportation of the fuel itself to the planned desert rendezvous. At this point an extremely experienced air force officer was introduced into the planning team.

Major General Philip C. Gast knew Iran intimately, having been there shortly before as a military adviser. Himself a veteran fighter pilot, Gast brought with him another officer who was to take part in the mission, Colonel James Kyle, who would be responsible for getting Delta in and everyone out. Kyle was a former air Commando who knew everything there was to know about such operations, having handled the most difficult jobs in Vietnam. Kyle's businesslike approach to the most seemingly insoluble problems impressed Beckwith, who gave him his complete confidence.

Slowly, as for each problem which was raised some kind of solution began to be dimly seen, a tentative plan took shape: on the first night, Delta would be moved into Iran and located somewhere near Teheran; on the second night the assault would take place and Delta and the freed hostages would be flown out. This left one whole day during which the team would have to hide somewhere without being spotted. The journey to the compound from the hideout would have to be by road, as a heliborne operation would be too risky.

Meanwhile more information was dribbling in. The compound was very large; there were fourteen buildings inside which would have to be cleared and made secure. There were known to be fifty-three hostages, but it was still not known if they were all in one place. It was thought that six helicopters would be necessary to fly the mission, so two more would have to be on standby if the operation was to succeed.

One question which was highly problematic was that of the helicopter pilots who were to fly the assignment. The Navy pilots belonged to a mine countermeasure squadron and had absolutely no combat experience. To fly such a mission would tax even the best crews: most of the flight was over uncharted desert where even the best navigators might go off course. To find the desert rendezvous would need precision flying by first-class crews; no navigational aids would be available and the assigned landing point would have to be flown in at first approach with no errors. Even the slightest deviation from the timetable could jeopardize the entire action. A fine-tooth comb search for suitable pilots was therefore carried out and when they were found a thorough training programme was initiated to bring them and their crews up to the highest standards in night flying and navigation.

The next problem to be tackled was refuelling. After experimenting with rubber containers dropped by C-130s, someone came up with the idea that the refuelling tanker aircraft should be flown into the rendezvous itself. To test that idea a STOL aircraft flown by experienced pilots landed at Desert One, the rendezvous which the US intelligence analysts had selected in a remote area of the Dasht-e-Kavir salt desert, some five hundred kilometres south-east of Teheran. A dirt road bisected the site but traffic was estimated as light. The STOL pilots and an Air Force expert checked the ground for eventual C-130 landings and found it suitable. For good measure they implanted beacons into the ground. These were special devices which could be activated by remote control as the transports approached.

For the site where the group would have to hide out the day before the mission, special agents had located a place near Garmsar in the southern foothills of the Elburz mountains, south-east of Teheran, from where a nearby paved road would lead Delta Force to the capital. The plan was for the helicopters to drop their passengers there, then fly on to their own hiding-place, some thirty kilometres north-east, and wait under camouflage nets until they were called by radio. Finally, Manzariye, a disused airfield south-west of Teheran, was picked as the spot where a Ranger force would land and secure the area prior to the raid, preparing on it a pick-up strip on which heavier transport aircraft would land and lift off Delta Force and the freed hostages.

By the end of March, Delta Force had rehearsed the exercise several times and every man knew his exact position at any given time. Beckwith and Kyle agreed that the latter would be in charge of operations at Desert One. Beckwith was still concerned with possible problems in Teheran itself, since it was known that an armoured unit was stationed in an army ordnance depot just a few blocks from the compound, but he was reassured that, with the Iranian Army in its present condition, they would not be able to intervene for several hours after receiving an alert. He was more worried about the ZSU-23-4s, formidable Russian-made anti-aircraft guns, which might cause trouble for the helicopter as they came in to pick up the hostages. To neutralize any armoured or air-defence intervention, two AC-130E gunships were given the task of cruising over the city, taking out the F-4 Phantoms on standby at Mehrabad airport and preventing any troop movement along Roosevelt Avenue, which led up to the compound.

The final plan, code-named 'Eagle Claw', was as follows: Three troop-carrying MC-130 transports would take off from the former RAF airfield at Masirah off the coast of Oman in the Persian Gulf, and head for Desert One, together with three EC-130 fuel tankers. At the same time, eight RH-53D Sea Stallions would be launched from the carrier USS *Nimitz* and head for Desert One to join up with Delta Force as soon as they had landed and refuelled. The assault force would number 118 men, led by Colonel Beckwith; they would head for the hideout near Garmsar, there to meet two special agents who would take Beckwith for a recce tour near the compound. The following day six covered Mercedes trucks would take Delta Force to Teheran. Between 2300 hours and midnight a selected group of operators would take out the guards with silenced guns, and immediately after the trucks with the entire Delta Force would arrive.

There would be three task forces: TK Red, commanded by Major Coyote, with forty men, would be responsible for the western sector of the compound, neutralizing the guards in the motor pool and power plant, and then freeing the hostages held nearby. Blue Element, commanded by Major Logan Fitch, would go for the eastern part to free the hostages confined in the Ambassador's residence, while a small force – White – would secure the main road outside, sweeping any approaching enemy forces with a machine-gun enfilade. Air cover was to be provided by two gunships cruising overhead waiting for a call. Once all the hostages had been mustered TK Red had the task of blowing a gap in the outer wall of the compound. The helicopters would have been alerted by radio and flown from their hideout, flying directly into the compound to lift out the hostages, while the task forces would withdraw to the stadium next door through the gap in the wall. Estimated duration of the attack: forty-five minutes. By this time the Rangers would have secured Manzariye airport, where the helicopters would bring the hostages, thence to be flown out by Starlifters.

The rescue mission was planned to start on Monday 21 April 1980, when Delta Force landed at Wadi Kena airfield in southern Egypt to await transfer to Masireh. At the very last moment before take-off, Beckwith received some valuable information from Washington, where a CIA agent had managed to talk to a recently released hostage. This man knew exactly how many guards there were in the compound and where the hostages were to be found.

On 24 April, Delta was flown by C-141 to Masireh where General Gast was already waiting; four hours later the first MC-130 carrying Beckwith and his command group, Kyle's group and Fitch with his Blue Element took off for Desert One.

They crossed the Iranian coastline at 400 feet to escape radar detection, and set course inland. The low-altitude flight caused stomachs to lurch and the air was suffocating. As they neared the desert strip, the pilot activated the beacons which lit up in the dark, dimly, but just enough for a perfect landing. The minute they touched the ground Kyle contacted Masireh and Wadi Kena via satellite, and heard from General Gast that all eight choppers had taken off from *Nimitz* just as planned.

So far so good. But suddenly a big Mercedes bus, headlights blazing, appeared as if from nowhere out of the clear desert air and drove right on to the site. One of the Rangers fired, and the bus stopped. Major Fitch and his men, who had just landed, surrounded the bus and forced its passengers, approximately forty-five in number, to get down. Then, while they were sorting out these good people, a gasoline truck came into view! Obviously this place was not as remote as they had thought! A Ranger fired a LAW anti-tank missile right into the truck, and it started to burn furiously, while the driver managed to scramble out, also furiously, just before it blew up.

The C-130s stood on the strip, engines idling, while they awaited the helicopters. They were already late, and it was another ninety minutes before the first came in; others arrived one at a time, each from a different direction. This delay upset the schedule completely and Beckwith was furious; his carefully worked-out plan had gone haywire, meaning that his team would not get to the hideout until after dawn.

Worse was to come, however. Only six helicopters of the eight landed; he was told that two had aborted en route, and one of the remaining six was in bad shape, its pilot explaining that he could not fly the mission for technical reasons. Beckwith knew that he had no chance of pulling off the operation with only five helicopters. He discussed the matter with Kyle and General Vought over the radio and, with their concurrence, decided to abort the mission. Beckwith was close to tears with frustration and anger, but his choice was a wise and a courageous one; insufficient transport on a mission like this could have meant disaster.

As Colonel Kyle organized the lift-off, Beckwith explained the changed situation to his officers. All of them were very upset, but Beckwith was adamant. At 0240 some of the C-130 pilots started gunning their engines, as dust swirled around in the wind. Between the gusts, one of the helicopters lifted off and banked to the left, only to slide backwards. There was a terrific explosion and a blue fireball ballooned into the night. The chopper had struck a C-130 tanker aircraft, within seconds, both burst into flames. The helicopter nearest to the inferno would explode, too, if the flames reached it and its ammunition.

Miraculously, all the Delta troops escaped the conflagration and Major Fitch ran to Beckwith to report that his men were OK although one of his operators had been badly burned when he went into the burning aircraft to try and rescue one of the crew. Beckwith now ordered an immediate take-off, telling the Marine pilots to abandon their helicopters and join him in the Hercules. With all accounted for, except the trapped aircrews in their blazing aircraft, and after only fifty-six minutes on the ground at Desert One, Delta was leaving. The big C-130 began to gather speed; hitting an embankment which lifted it into the air with a lurch, it bounced and then flew, as the pilot gunned his engine for maximum power.

Operation 'Eagle Crew' was over before it had really started. Five airmen and three marine aircrew were dead, six Sea Stallions left behind and the commander, Colonel Charles A. Beckwith, was a very sad man as he set off for home.

27. THE ATTACK ON GOOSE GREEN

There are some two hundred islands in the Falklands, covering about 12,000 kilometres of territory. The two largest islands are West and East Falklands, divided by the Falkland Sound, a major waterway, and one which was to acquire both strategic and logistic importance during the campaign to recapture the Falkland Islands, invaded and captured by Argentinian forces in April 1982.

Running across the island from top to bottom is a chain of mountains of medium height which not only afforded excellent topographical defensive features but also controlled approaches to the main British objectives. The southern chain, with Mount Usborene, 705 metres high, overlooking Falkland Sound and San Carlos, as well as Goose Green, provided excellent observation posts. Farther east, the 458-metre-high Mount Kent with its range of smaller hills dominates the Port Stanley area, while Mount Challenger controls the approaches from Bluff Cove to the south. Connecting Goose Green with Darwin and the Port Carlos area to the north there is an eight-by-two-kilometre land bridge – the only land connecting the main island with Lafonia to the south, providing superb defence facilities – high ground for observation and long-range field of fire on advancing attackers.

Sparsely vegetated and inhabited mainly by isolated sheep farmers, the Falklands have little to offer in modern-day military terms. Arctic weather conditions, low ground fog and ice make military operations difficult and demanding, in particular hampering rotor aircraft, which in turn limits support missions for ground forces. The lack of paved roads, vegetation and inhabited settlements demands total self-reliance for food, shelter and *matériel* for defence construction. There is little in the way of camouflage in these barren islands, and digging is almost impossible because of the ground water level. For the same reason, vehicle movement is very difficult and, after rain, there are almost no tracks, except on the higher slopes. The locals use only cross-country vehicles and even these do not always manage to traverse the water-logged, yet rocky terrain, so communication is mostly by air, with coastal motor vessels operating inshore.

At the time of the Falklands Campaign, the Goose Green area was defended by the Argentinian 12th Infantry Regiment/3rd Infantry Brigade commanded by Lieutenant-Colonel Italo Pioggi. A two company task force, responsible for Darwin Boca House and its surrounding area, had one platoon on Darwin ridge in the north, with two supporting elements positioned above them on the hill. Two more units were located on the rear of this hill, around a line of gorse bushes – later to become an important feature in the fighting. One platoon of another company held Boca House, while two were in position behind the line of the gorse bushes, linking up with the men defending the Darwin ridge. A small reserve company-sized group was maintained near the regimental HQ at Goose Green. There was a battery of six 120mm mortars in support, south-west of HQ, and four 105mm mountain howitzers to the east. In addition, six twin-barrel 20mm anti-aircraft cannon and two radar-controlled 35mm guns were deployed around the airfield perimeter; these guns could also be used in a ground role, especially in guarding the access to Goose Green from the direction of Darwin. A marine infantry battalion was stationed at Port Stanley, available for use with helicopter. The Argentinians had fortified their defences as well as they were able, using mines, barbed wire and other equipment, but surprisingly both Camilla House and Port San Carlos were initially left virtually undefended.

In the British forces, part of the Royal Marines 3rd Commando Brigade under Brigadier Julian Thompson was the 2nd Parachute Battalion, a select outfit with a proud fighting history. It was commanded by Lieutenant-Colonel Herbert Jones, otherwise known as 'H'. Jones was an excellent commander and was to prove in the forthcoming battle that he was also a combat leader in the finest traditions of the regiment, just as the fight for Goose Green was to go into the books as a classic infantry battle.

2 Para was organized into three rifle companies, 'A', 'B' and 'D', with about a hundred men in each, and a patrol company, 'C', consisting of a recce platoon, a specially trained patrol platoon and an assault pioneer platoon. The battalion had in its ranks a substantial number of trained observers/snipers.

Having landed at Bonner Bay/San Carlos on 21 May 1982, the battalion deployed on the eastern ridge of Sussex Mountain, astride the route for Camilla House, with 'C' Company manning the forward observation points. Their task was severely hampered by lack of co-ordination with the patrolling SAS teams, which operated up front but reported directly to the task force, leaving the para battalion out of the communications chain. This lack of real-time intelligence was to become a serious restriction later. Colonel Jones, desperate for information, spent most of his time forward trying to get a glimpse of the fog-shrouded countryside, and his absence meant that important matters went undecided. Luckily his very able second in command, Major Chris Keeble, saw to it that staff at battalion headquarters were soon performing like veterans.

On 23 May, Brigade sent an order to 2 Para to mount a raid on Darwin and Goose Green to get things moving while the main force continued reorganizing in the bridgehead. The information garnered by SAS patrols on the Argentinian forces was all right as far as it went: they were usually quite correct with regard to numerical strength but their estimates on disposition and fighting morale was superficial and sometimes rather wide of the mark, practically useless for detailed planning. Luckily, there was an officer present who was acquainted with the local terrain and he helped to overcome the inaccuracies of the available maps. In fact, the raid was called off at the last moment – the vanguard was already moving out – and the battalion was now ordered to mount a full–sized attack on the following day.

As Jones was briefing some of his officers, a report came through from one of the patrols that they had captured an Argentinian officer, with his disposition maps. Rushed to headquarters, they were found to be a tremendous help in planning the attack, which projected a night attack on the forward positions of the enemy, to be followed by a daylight assault on Goose Green. The operation, which was to be in six phases, aimed at making as much headway as possible during the hours of darkness, exploiting the element of surprise and the better training of the British troops. In his briefing the CO emphasized the difficulties of navigating over the rough ground, the bad visibility and the limited support available; this support included a three-gun 105mm howitzer battery and a 4.5in gun from HMS *Arrow* which was standing offshore within range, which would be directed by an officer from the Royal Navy attached to the battalion's support company commander. Due to lack of transport, they had to leave behind their 2in mortars, and only two 81mm mortars went with them, but air support was promised to be on hand from dawn, weather permitting.

The operation started at 2300 hours when the support company moved out to set up a base of machine-guns and Milan anti-tank missiles. The naval officer took up a position west of Camilla Creek. At 0230 HMS *Arrow* opened fire on Argentinian artillery positions, directed by muzzle flash, and at the same time 'C' Company moved its scouts to locate and secure the start-lines for the two assault companies. Guides were sent back to bring 'A' Company and they, too, set off, moving cautiously over the difficult ground in the direction of Burnside House to the east. In the total darkness it was extremely difficult to locate objectives, but by 0545 gunfire from *Arrow* was landing on the house, although the men on the ground really felt the lack of their 2-inch mortars. With the shells bursting around them, the lead platoons stormed the house. They were unsuccessful in firing the 84mm Carl Gustav, but 60mm rockets helped the men get within hand-grenade range against sporadic counter-fire, and the house was cleared by 0700.

'B' Company's mission was to capture the forward Argentinian outposts on the land bridge. They set off three hours before dawn, guided by scouts from 'C' Company, who reported that the neck of the isthmus, surprisingly, was clear of mines. The Argentinians' position was surrounded by trenches, but when 'B' Company stormed across, using phosphorus and M79 grenade-launchers, they encountered little resistance. The assault platoons swept forward, the other units following behind, exploiting full surprise, but as they continued they met increased opposition. In the darkness some of the men became disoriented and the company became dispersed. Flares had to be lit to show the men where they were, and they reassembled only with difficulty, wandering in from every direction – a very good illustration of the problems involved in directing an attack over difficult terrain on a dark night.

But the men had no time to consider such theoretical notions – things were hotting up; the Argentinian artillery was firing with great accuracy; luckily for the British, many of the shells that came at them were duds, and also the damp ground absorbed many of the splinters, or casualties would have been much higher. The British artillery base back at Camilla House returned fire, but because of their limited ammunition the counterfire was not really effective.

'D' Company, in reserve behind battalion HQ, now edged forward. Although it advanced along a marked track, navigation was extremely difficult and the company scouts missed their rendezvous with 'C' Company's runners. Colonel Jones was unwilling to wait, as he wanted to make the most of the remaining hours of darkness when, he thought, his men had the edge

GOOSE GREEN, MAY 1982

BRENTON LOCH

Camilla Creek House

Boca House

Burntside House

Coronation Point

Airstrip

Darwin Hill

DARWIN

Schoolhouse

Carcass Bay

GOOSE GREEN

DARWIN HARBOUR

2 PARA
'D' Coy
'B' Coy
'C' Coy
'A' Coy

over the enemy. 'D' Company therefore pushed forward, but came too close to 'B' Company, with a resulting danger of the two forces firing at each other by mistake.

The 'D' Company commander, using flares to keep his men together, began to push through the enemy trench section, leaving the fighting to his section leaders, who fought extremely well against resistance. Once through, they turned round and went back, combing the trenches to clear out any last pockets of opposition.

At 0850 'B' and 'C' Companies joined up, meeting the pioneer platoon ammunition carriers en route. Having reorganized, 'B' Company was told to advance towards the Boca House ridge, while 'A' Company was ordered to advance on Darwin Hill, via Coronation Point overlooking the bay. With still about two hours before first light, 'A' Company set off, making for the high ground. At first light they found themselves in a gully filled with gorse bushes, below the enemy position which opened up with accurate fire, causing immediate casualties. Unable to pinpoint the enemy positions, the British company commander made repeated attempts to outflank the enemy but to no avail; his force was hopelessly pinned down.

2 Para had fought well during the night; its junior commanders had proved their worth, in view of the fact that this was their first combat action. But this did not prevent the commanders from realizing that the Argentinians were still in full control of the ground they held, and full of fight. In order to keep the initiative, Colonel Jones moved his tactical HQ forward behind 'A' Company, which was the most dangerously exposed, to see what was going on. He was far from pleased with what he saw: By now HMS *Arrow*, their main support station, had been forced to leave its location, as its main gun had malfunctioned, while his own 105mm battery was short of ammunition; it was now up to the Paras to carry the fight.

'B' Company began an assault on Boca House under heavy fire, but was forced back with heavy casualties. 'C' Company and the support group, who overlooked the battle from the high ground, wanted to go and help, but they were turned down by the Colonel, who preferred to keep his reserves intact. Proposals to outflank the enemy positions over some seemingly undefended ground near the eastern shoreline were also rejected, as the Darwin Hill situation was given precedence. 'A' Company was indeed in urgent need of help, and called for a Harrier airstrike, only to be informed by Brigade HQ that weather conditions had forced the suspension of all air operations in the area. Ironically, just as this information came through over the radio, Argentinian Pucara fighters flew over the battlefield! They came over to attack the British artillery positions near Camilla Creek, but one of them was shot down by a Blowpipe missile.

Meanwhile, still reluctant to commit his reserves because of the long battle he knew lay ahead, Jones urged 'A' Company to make another attempt at gaining the high ground and, doggedly, the Paras tried once more. With the company commander and his staff in the lead, the men stormed uphill, only to be beaten back by heavy fire, and several officers, among them the second in command, were killed or wounded. Seeing 'A' Company's predicament, Colonel Jones and a small party worked their way up on the Argentinians' flank and Jones assaulted the enemy, regardless of his own safety. As he stormed the position, he was struck by a bullet and fatally wounded, in full view of his troops. Shocked into immediate action, 'A' Company rallied and rampaged up the hill – this time the Argentinians broke and ran.

When word of Colonel Jones' death reached battalion HQ at Camilla House, Major Keeble collected some ammunition carriers and quickly moved forward to take command, receiving a radioed update from the company commanders en route. Keeble decided on his own plan for continuation of the battle: 'A' Company was to reorganize and hold Darwin Hill, won at such cost, while 'B' and 'D' Companies would mount a unified attack to capture Boca House; a reinforced 'C' Company was to capture the high ground overlooking Goose Green airfield.

'D' Company's commander had a good eye for terrain, and suggested outflanking Boca House by going around by the seashore. Keeble accepted the plan and 'D' Company was soon on its way, unobserved by the enemy who were pinned down by 'B' Company, as well as by fire coming from the support company in position up on the gorse ridge. The Milan battery also went into action and proved extremely effective.

Thus, well supported and covered, 'D' Company reached its destination undetected and stormed the Argentinian position in an attack well-coordinated with 'B' Company. The Boca House position fell quickly, enabling the Paras to push through and gain access to the high ground overlooking the airfield, but there they came under heavy fire from mortars, 35mm anti-aircraft guns, and even from the guns of a damaged Pucara which someone had resourcefully mounted on a wagon!

'D' Company had to skirt a minefield and was temporarily delayed. In trying to bypass it, the men came within the range of fire from a school building above, which was actually 'C' Company's objective. The resulting confusion was exploited by the defenders, who increased their fire, but the junior commanders on the British side worked together, and the schoolhouse was soon cleared with phosphorus grenades and set on fire.

Just before nightfall two Argentinian Skyhawks screamed over at low level, and strafed both companies; one of the Skyhawks was destroyed by a Sidewinder missile fired from a Harrier, one of a few of them which providentially arrived on the scene at exactly that moment. Then a lone Pucara came in from over the hills, dropping napalm, which fortunately missed its target, but a Blowpipe missile fired by a Marine did not, and the Pucara crashed on to the airfield, barely missing some of the advancing Paras.

About one kilometre to the south an Argentinian Chinook helicopter and six Hueys landed, disembarking a reinforced marine infantry company previously based in Stanley. These came under accurate fire from British artillery, which had now arrived within range, and the choppers flew off quickly, some of them still with troops on board. Some more Harriers then came in and dropped cluster bombs on the Argentinian positions on Goose Green.

By nightfall, Major Keeble was in full control of the area around Goose Green. The Paras, together with a company of a Royal Marines, who had been brought in during the night, then went into Goose Green, forcing the Argentinians to surrender on the following morning.

In all, more than 1,100 prisoners were taken, over twice the number the British had expected to be in the place! But 2 Para suffered heavy losses: fifteen men were dead, including the commanding officer, and thirty wounded. Argentinian losses were 250 killed and about the same number wounded.

28. 3 COMMANDO IN THE FALKLANDS

While the battle for Goose Green was still in full swing, 3rd Commando Brigade with its attached units were on the move to Port Stanley, where the Argentinians had concentrated a considerable force.

The terrain around here is also extremely tough going, even on foot. Three mountain ranges rise concentrically in the Stanley area. The closest, overlooking the town, port and airfield, comprises from north to south: Wireless Ridge, Tumbledown Mountain, Mount William and Sapper Hill. Tumbledown dominates the region and controls the two access roads to Port Stanley.

The second mountain range is 1,000 metres to the west and incorporates from north to south: Mount Longdon, Two Sisters and Mount Harriet. Of this group, Two Sisters looms largest, also overlooking the entire area.

Five kilometres farther west is the third chain, including Mount Estancia, the 458-metre-high Mount Kent, and Mount Challenger, which joins up with Mount Kent along a 30-kilometre-long ridge.

These features form part of an excellent defensive geography, enhanced by bare, rock- and boulder-strewn countryside and narrow tracks, which in any case are usually flooded. The weather conditions in this semi-arctic tundra are dreadful, and low-flying aircraft find that visibility is often reduced to near zero.

On 27 May 1982 3 Commando Brigade started its long and arduous march east. Helicopter capability had been reduced drastically following the sinking of the *Atlantic Surveyor*: only one Chinook, twenty Sea King and seventeen Wessex choppers were available and, even of these, only a small number would be working with 3 Commando, mainly for the purpose of ferrying artillery and heavy equipment. This meant that all personal gear, including weapons and ammunition, had to be carried by the troops; the load sometimes topped 65 kilograms per man. In spite of the difficulties, the brigade's 45 Commando Battalion reached Teal Inlet, about halfway to Port

Stanley, in good time, covering nearly 80 miles along the northern road in less than two days of forced march. In view of the appalling weather at the time, this demonstrated how well-trained and motivated the troops were. 3 Para, moving east from San Carlos on the southern route, made Teal almost simultaneously.

They were soon joined by 'B' Squadron of the Blues and Royals medium recce troops with their Scorpions and Scimitar armoured fighting vehicles and Samson armoured recovery vehicles. Delayed by a snowstorm, the brigade's 42 Commando was finally heliported at night to a landing site below Mount Kent; there the battalion made ready to assault the Argentinian position above.

Reports had come in that Malo Hill, a 200-metre-high feature overlooking Teal Inlet, was occupied by an Argentinian special observation force, which would endanger the Commando build-up, so the Royal Marine Arctic Warfare Cadre, an élite within an élite, was brought in to eliminate the OP. The assault team was landed by units of 846 Naval Helicopter Squadron, flying through terrible weather, and the cadre moved undetected towards its objective. They positioned a team to fire support for them, so they were covered as they closed in. On signal, six 66mm rockets slammed into the building which comprised the observation point. Huge explosions were observed, and snipers picked off Argentinian sentries seen at the windows, allowing the assault team to charge. The Argentinians fled, but some of them rallied in a nearby gully and started a fire fight, causing a number of casualties. After half an hour, however, the objective was deemed secure and the men withdrew, taking prisoners with them.

The plan of battle for the troops assembled in Teal Inlet was to capture the ring of mountains which formed the outside of the horseshoe, with 3 Para attacking Mount Longdon, 45 Commando going for Two Sisters, and 42 Commando moving on Mount Harriet.

All this high ground was strongly defended by the Argentinians: 4th and 7th Infantry Regiment and Unit 601 of the Special Forces were firmly established up there, supported by mortars, artillery and many well-concealed machine-guns, while extensive minefields protected them from below. They had excellent night vision equipment, far superior to that of the Commandos. They also had the advantage of terrain, the craggy mountain tops offering superb cover while the bare slopes made an approach upwards almost suicidal.

Furthermore, the gale force winds and freezing rains caused the British troops continuous suffering which only their training helped them endure. After several hours of marching in these conditions, almost 75 per cent of the men had varying degrees of trench foot, mainly due to their inadequate footwear which had been getting more and more soaked since they had landed at San Carlos weeks before.

The only good thing about the weather was that it kept the skies clear of attacking Argentinian jets, although even short spells of good weather brought Skyhawks screaming in, which strafed the British logistical bases and forward HQ at low level but inflicted little damage. Even without the jets, though, the British were taking punishment from long-range artillery shells, since every movement was detected by well-concealed forward observation posts.

Since they lacked updated aerial photos and accurate maps, the British Commandos had to carry out patrolling operations just to get some information on enemy defences – before they could even begin to plan the attack. There was almost no reliable intelligence available as to the exact strength of the opposing force, never mind where they actually were. Several nights were spent, therefore, by Commandos and Paras in probing the minefields, pinpointing positions and looking for the best approach routes. All this was co-ordinated by a specially created 'master patroller' at Brigade HQ who controlled outgoing patrols, debriefed them on their return, and collated their intelligence.

One patrol of the Arctic Cadre actually spent an entire 24-hour period hiding in the midst of an Argentinian position on Mount Harriet. This feat probably saved many lives later on, since these men located not only most of the enemy machine-gun positions but also a long tripwire connected to a demolition charge on Two Sisters.

The battle opened with 3 Para climbing Mount Longdon; the first units crossed the start line in darkness led by guides from 'D' Company, but an exploding land mine raised the alert and the Argentinians began to rain down heavy fire; the flashes illuminated the sky, almost turning night into day. Casualties began to mount, but the Paras went on, doggedly ignoring the fire.

Sergeant McKay, whose platoon commander was hit, took over for the assault on a heavy-gun emplacement which seemed to be the key position on the mountain top. Throwing grenades as they ran, they knocked out the enemy gun, but not before the sergeant and one of his men were killed. McKay earned a posthumous Victoria Cross for his heroism.

Realizing the situation, battalion HQ called for artillery and naval gun support; this came in quickly and accurately, falling in some cases, as close as 50 metres from the advancing troops. After a ten-hour-long battle, Mount Longdon was finally captured, although 3 Para suffered almost 80 casualties in that blood-drenched night.

To the right, 45 Commando attacked the well-defended 300-metre-high Two Sisters rock ridges. Carrying Milan missiles in addition to their personal equipment, the overloaded Marines stumbled up the slopes, several of them being knocked unconscious when they stumbled over rocks and boulders. These climbing casualties delayed the men's advance but they carried on, led through the minefields by recce guides, who had been waiting for them there.

Suddenly, just as they were getting ready to stand and assault, Argentinian artillery came crashing down on the start-line; fortunately, the fact that they were still lying low kept casualties to a minimum. Now, according to plan, the British artillery started to thunder as the rifle companies attacked, firing machine-guns, 84mm MAWs and 66mm LAWs. Zulu Company stormed the Argentinian positions with enemy flares bouncing and fizzing around them, machine-gun fire whistling over their heads. At 0430 their commander, Colonel Whitehead, was able to radio brigade HQ that Two Sisters was secure, but realistically organized the defence in expectation of the counter-attack which would inevitably come at dawn – two hours away.

Mount Harriet, the southernmost of the three objectives, is a steep, craggy hill, some 300 metres high, protected to the north by a rocky outcrop and Goat Ridge, which is near Two Sisters Mountain. The 4th Argentinian Infantry Regiment had established itself extremely well on the mountain and its environs. Extensive minefields had hampered the recce patrols sent out by 42 Commando, although they also restricted the defenders from forward movement. The British patrols probing the enemy positions had eventually, after long, hard hours of work, succeeded in mapping most of the enemy locations and what emerged was the picture of a formidable complex of well-positioned defences which would be far from easy to overcome.

The main Argentinian defences on Mount Harriet consisted of four company-sized all-round positions, well concealed among the craggy boulders. Forward outposts were placed at vantage points, with strong, platoon-sized forces holding positions on Goat Ridge.

Colonel Vaux, commanding the 42 Commando, after examining the terrain and the defences, chose a rather complicated right flanking man-oeuvre for the attack. He decided against either a frontal or left hook, partly because if they chose the latter alternative, they might run up against the right flank of 45 Commando, which was attacking Two Sisters at the same time. A complex night attack is one of the most difficult military operations to control and it was only natural that Vaux preferred to keep as far away as possible from friendly forces. The bad visibility caused by the notorious Falklands weather made close-proximity operations even more dangerous, and Vaux did not want to have his hands tied by having to watch out for friendly forces coming too close.

42 Commando's excellent night patrols had already prepared the ground for attack and its scouts led the assault companies forward to their start positions. Vaux had selected Mount Wall for his tactical HQ instead of joining up with main assault, so that he could sustain overall control from his vantage point. Mount Wall enabled the command group to follow every stage of the night battle, including the activities of brigade and naval units. It was a magnificent, yet terrifying experience, seeing the black night suddenly erupt into what the Colonel later described as a 'space age fantasy'. At one moment, the awestruck command group followed with their eyes the trajectory of an Argentinian Exocet missile: It zoomed across the sky like shooting-star, then fell to the sea and exploded in a ball of fire, with the blackness of HMS *Glamorgan* silhouetted against it.

The battle was now joined. Infantry companies stormed the outer defences, while the tracer bullets crisscrossed the night sky in both directions, accompanied by the crumps and flashes of mortar explosions. Milan anti-tank missiles streaked with fiery tails towards the machine-gun positions and every impact was followed by vivid flashes and heavy explosions. The battle continued at close quarters and Carl Gustavs and LAWs began to wreak havoc among the enemy positions.

The Argentinians fought back with surprising fervour, the close proximity of their regimental headquarters on the mountain being a motivating factor. But, although their fire was mostly accurate and effective, the soft ground and good combat deployment of the British Commandos diminished the damage, so that casualties remained bearable and did not affect fighting morale.

British company commanders directed the battle while junior officers performed with great personal courage and initiative, the result both of their arduous training and of their strong motivation. It was these junior leaders, commanding sections and platoons, who bore the brunt of the night battle and of the inevitable casualties.

The Argentinian resistance broke just before dawn and the Commandos had firmly established themselves on the mountain just before an Argentinian airstrike came in at first light. By now, however, with most of the dominating positions in British hands, Port Stanley was in sight – ready to be taken. One final push, during which 3 Commando and 5th Infantry Brigade attacked simultaneously to take Mount Tumbledown and Wireless Ridge, ended with the recapture of the Falklands.

29. GRENADA – INTO A HOT DROP ZONE

The tiny island of Grenada is one of the Windward Islands, situated in the Caribbean, almost on the back doorstep of the USA. Formerly a colony of the United Kingdom, it had attained independence in 1974, but as the years went by many Cuban soldiers were sent to the island, and unrest grew. In October 1983 this culminated in riots, during which the Prime Minister, Maurice Bishop, was first kidnapped and then murdered by rebel forces which, according to the CIA, were backed by Cuba. In order to avert the takeover by Cuba of the whole island, and also to prevent harm to the many Americans who were living – some of them studying – in Grenada at that time, the USA decided to mount a military action to return the legal government to power.

On the afternoon of 21 October Lieutenant Colonel Ralph Hagler, commanding the 2nd Battalion of the 75th Rangers stationed in Fort Lewis, Washington, was ordered by the senior officer at JSOC Fort Bragg to get his battalion ready for immediate combat. Hagler, a veteran from the Vietnam war, was no newcomer to such alerts and flew immediately to North Carolina, where he met other officers who were already studying maps and aerial photographs of Grenada. Among them was Lieutenant Colonel Wesley Taylor, commanding Hagler's sister battalion, the 1st Rangers.

The US invasion of Grenada, code-named 'Urgent Fury', was to be the large-scale use of special forces, each with their own mission. It was also a rush job: it had to be carried out at short notice, with not much time for detailed planning, so the lights burned through the night at Fort Bragg as Major General Richard Scholtes discussed tactics with his staff officers. Their plan was for Task Force 123 – as it was called – to comprise two Ranger battalions, Navy SEAL teams and an Air Force combat control group, as well as a contingent from Delta Force, all of them well-trained, highly motivated soldiers.

General Scholtes briefed the officers personally, assigning Hagler to drop his battalion on the northern part of the island at Pearl Airport, while Taylor's men were to jump on Point Salinas airfield in the south – one of the main objectives of the entire mission. Initially, the plan seemed fairly simple, but when the officers went into detail they discovered that their real information was minimal. The only maps they had were hopelessly outdated British tourist ones – and even these were only photocopies. Moreover, Hagler and Taylor found that they would be able to use only half their men, as there were not enough Air Force crews trained for night operations in C-130 transports.

The Rangers themselves – wearers of the coveted black berets – were a source of great pride to their commanders. The men had received extremely good training in night jumps; some of them even had experience in free-falling, and were able to steer their parachutes for many kilometres while in the air.

As he arrived back in his office at Fort Lewis, Hagler received a fax which completely changed his plans. According to the new instructions, his battalion was to follow Taylor's into Point Salinas, assist in securing the airfield, and then go on to attack Camp Calvigny, releasing some American students who were being held hostage. This was the camp of the People's Revolutionary Army, the Cuban-backed local militia which defended the island.

There was very little intelligence available on the deployment of these defenders, their armaments, or their combat motivation. At that time there were many Americans on the island who could easily have provided this information, but US Army intelligence had virtually ignored the little island – surprisingly, since it was so near the southern coast of the USA – and it was now much too late to obtain the badly needed data. The most worrying thing for Hagler and his staff was the reported deployment of anti-aircraft guns on and near Point Salinas airfield which, according to the very vague maps, seemed to have hills looming above it.

While the Rangers were dropping and mustering, 1st Special Operations Wing USAF was to fly close support from four AC-130 Spectre gunships, armed with two 20mm Vulcan cannon, a pair of six-barrel Gatling guns, a 40mm door gun and a 105mm anti-tank gun. This 'battleship' would become a familiar feature in Grenada's skies as it flew air cover for any ground commander who was in trouble.

At dawn, then, on 25 October 1983, 18 C-130s escorted by the AC-130E Spectres swooped down on Grenada. Leading the formation in his green Hercules was Lieutenant Colonel Hugh Hunter, commanding 8 Special Operations Squadron. On the flight deck was Wes Taylor, whose 300 men were grouped in the transports, while following on were Hagler's 250 Rangers. As they flew, information came in of heavy anti-aircraft defences on the airstrip, as well as on one of the hills which overlooked it.

After examining the available aerial maps, Hagler and Taylor decided that the enemy guns would be ineffective below 500 feet altitude, so they ordered the men to drop well below the normal drop height, thus cutting down their exposure time in the air to less than fifteen seconds. Before the drop, the Rangers helped each other load heavy gear into manpacks, on the assumption that the airstrip would probably not be open for follow-up cargo landings, and they would have to carry their own gear. Priority was given to weapons and ammunition so that they would not need a supply line for 48 hours. According to Sergeant 1st Class Larry Rodriguez: 'We were told that the aircraft planned to come in after the jump would not be able to land with the rest of our equipment, so we took everything to sustain us for the entire operation, and most people jumped with excessive loads.' The sergeant's load, for example, consisted of his M60 machine-gun, rifle and a .45 pistol, 1,000 rounds of ammunition and some grenades: 'It was the heaviest rucksack I ever carried!' he commented later.

About a hundred miles east of Grenada, the Hercules went down to wavetop level to evade possible detection by radar and the Rangers prepared for the drop. The aircraft roared over the airfield at 500 feet while the first formation, 'A' Company, 1st Ranger Battalion, began to drop, using the fast 'Shotgun' technique, jumping from both sides of the aircraft. They encountered, however, extremely heavy, concentrated fire from the ground and, although it did not hit the aircraft, it was bad enough to make them interrupt the drop and call for the Spectres. These came in and made a pass over the airfield; on their way they spotted several 23mm gun positions on the adjoining hillside, which they attacked with some of their own deadly weapons, suppressing most of the air defence guns and enabling the drop to continue.

As the 250 Rangers from 2nd Battalion began to jump, small calibre fire was still persisting and, as he looked out just before he jumped, Colonel Hagler saw some mortar fire west of the airfield. The first man out of the aircraft, Hagler heard some sniper fire on his way down but, within 21 seconds, all the men were in the air, and the first men touched the ground 9 seconds later.

Two Rangers had some trouble with their parachutes, and were left dangling by the lines, 20 feet below the Hercules. Sergeant Tisby and Master Sergeant Quinines, the jump masters, managed to pull the men back inside and they landed later, with their equipment, joining the rest of the force. In spite of the low jump and 20-knot ground winds, only one paratrooper was injured in the jump, breaking his leg; the remainder landed safely.

The Rangers quickly regrouped on the small landing areas and then charged the enemy, supported from above by the gunships, which flew close cover with Navy fighters. The enemy, totally taken by surprise, retreated to the beach, some of them surrendering. There was a Cuban battalion defending the airstrip, but only one platoon was guarding the actual base; the other two were on the beach, waiting for what they had thought would be an amphibious attack from the west; all their guns were facing that way too, making their defensive effectiveness minimal against aircraft coming from the other direction.

On the north-east of the island, the Marines were attempting to secure the coastal town of Grenville with adjacent Pearl Airport, Grenada's main international airfield until the opening of the new one at Port Salinas, scheduled for April 1984. Navy SEAL teams in fast assault boats had been landing since before dawn at several points around the airport and its beachhead. One of these teams, however, was detected by an enemy patrol and pinned down throughout the night by fire from an APC, against which the lightly armed SEALS had no answer.

The main assault was carried out by 22 Marines who had come over in USS *Guam*. Brought to the shore at dawn by Marine helicopters, they landed at the airport without meeting much opposition, supported by Cobra attack helicopters and Spectre gunships. Taking the airfield was fairly easy – but other Marine operations were not. Several of their attack helicopters were lost, two Cobra pilots being killed when their choppers were downed by Cuban SU-23 guns. Another CH-46 was lost at sea. Earlier, tragedy struck when a force of SEALs and a USAF Special Forces control team jumped in darkness to join up with whaler boats waiting near the USS *Clifton Sprague*, some 30 kilometres away from the island. This type of jump requires very accurate timing in unbuckling the parachute harness in order not to drown. In the dark, however, this was far from easy and four of the sixteen-man team were lost at sea. The others, assembling aboard their waiting whaler, made for the coast to find a suitable beach for landing. As they neared the shore, however, the men spotted a Grenadian patrol boat and, to avoid discovery, shut down the engine. As a result, the choppy sea flooded the boat's engine and the team leader decided to return to the warship, so as not to endanger the entire operation if they were discovered at that early stage.

Back at Salinas airfield, by now in US hands, the Rangers discovered that the Cubans had hammered stakes into the concrete runway to prevent landings there and, as the Rangers were starting to clear the runway for the incoming cargo aircraft, which were already en route, the Cubans mounted two counter-attacks, rushing down the slopes of the abutting hill. One Cuban force ran straight into the 1st Battalion and was soon defeated in the course of a short firefight. Another attack came down on the eastern side of the airstrip, supported by two BTR-60 troop carriers. The Cubans, however, were immediately detected by Rangers from 2nd Battalion before they could even dismount, and every Ranger in the area fired at them with everything they could: small arms, LAW and recoilless guns. Both armoured carriers were hit, making them a death trap for the unfortunate soldiers inside; another carrier coming up behind turned round in an attempt to escape, but was caught by crossfire between the Rangers and the gunships above.

By 1100 hours the airfield was declared 'secure' and MAC C-130, operating from air bases throughout the USA and using Grantley airport, Barbados as a staging base, began landing medics, evacuating wounded and lifting in supplies. Men and *matériel* were flown in on C-141 and C-130 transports. However, some of the aircraft still came under fire as they circled the airfield, waiting to land; others had to wait until the sources of the shooting were suppressed. Sometimes as many as five aircraft were circling above Salinas during the early days of the invasion and, as only one C-141 and two C-130s could be parked on the ground simultaneously, the Starlifter would pull to the end of the runway and turn round, while the Hercules landed behind, right off the busy tarmac. With only one all-terrain downloader, unloading the C-141 was a lengthy process.

Although the airfield had been declared secure, it was still under fire from sniper and mortar positions in the surrounding woods, and it took a full three days to finish the job and secure the entire area against the determined Cuban soldiers, who must have known by then that it was all over for them, but went on fighting anyway. The supply aircraft were now coming in thick and fast, together with troops of 82 Airborne Division from Fort Bragg, who started to land on 25 October. This show of force finally demoralized the defenders, and soon they began coming down the hill to surrender, although some of the more courageous escaped inland to set up guerrilla operations from the jungle-covered hills.

The main mission of the 82nd was to relieve the Rangers from holding the airfield so that they would be free to release the American hostages taken by the Cubans and the Grenadian FRA. Students caught during the *coup d'état* had been rounded up and were in a dangerous situation. Fears that their plight might come to resemble that of the Khomeini-held diplomats in Teheran a few years earlier made an immediate rescue operation necessary – in fact, that was one of the main reasons for mounting 'Urgent Fury'. The students were concentrated in two campuses – one, the True Blue medical school, near the eastern end of Point Salinas, and the other farther north near the town of St. George. Each group was guarded by about one hundred armed men, Cubans and FRA.

At 3.30 p.m. on 26 October, Colonel Hagler's Rangers assaulted the guards in a classic twin-pronged operation, taking them completely by surprise with the use of Marine Sea Knight helicopters which flew in low towards the beach. Spectre gunships suppressed Cuban counterfire as the Rangers jumped from their helicopters at ten feet, stormed the campuses and had the hostages free within minutes. Only one helicopter was hit by ground fire and crashed into the sea. The Rangers inside opened the ramp and scrambled down it to safety, sheltering from Cuban fire behind the nearby sea wall.

On 27 October, tired but happy, the Rangers were quite ready to go home when, suddenly, they received orders to carry out another mission: it was to take the Edgmont military barracks, where Soviet, Cuban and Grenadian FRA soldiers were believed to have created a fortress with anti-aircraft guns and mortars galore. Again Navy A-7s and Air Force C-130 Spectres were called upon for support and the Rangers decided to use the 82nd Airborne's Blackhawk helicopters as well.

Staging near the target, the Rangers used four UH-60s for a surprise attack to get over the high barbed wire fence which surrounded the site. Sadly, in the last wave, one of the helicopters was hit while landing inside the camp and its pilot was wounded in the arm and leg; he lost control of the helicopter, which crashed into another aircraft already on the ground. All the Rangers who remained inside remained unhurt, but five who jumped clear, or who attempted to do so, were killed or badly wounded by enemy fire. Another Black Hawk then started to land but the pilot, probably shocked by the sight below him, came in too fast and also collided with the wrecked helicopters, its whirling rotors hitting more Rangers. This was a heavy price to pay and, with sad irony, when the Rangers took the camp they found there only twelve Cubans, all dead. If there had been any more, they had all escaped. The next day, considerably more sober, the Rangers went home.

One more operation, however, was mounted before the invasion was over: the taking of Richmond Hill where, in a nearby prison, several political prisoners were being held. In order to capture the objective, the high ground overlooking the town of St. George had to be taken. The assault met almost no opposition. 'Urgent Fury' was over.

When they assessed 'Urgent Fury' in retrospect, the US Army top brass were not displeased with the results: they had used two under-strength Ranger battalions, with six paratroop battalions which had been used mostly for mopping-up, and they had succeeded everywhere. As the first major American combat deployment since Vietnam, it could be counted a success, particularly when compared with the fiasco of Desert One, the abortive rescue operation to Teheran.

30. OPERATION 'JUST CAUSE', PANAMA

P anama is only a small strip of land with a population of less than 2.3 million, but it is of vital strategic importance to the United States: it stretches on both sides of the Panama Canal, which connects the Atlantic and Pacific Oceans and is the only channel through which shipping can pass.

The previously good relations between the two countries began to deteriorate in 1988 when Panama's military chief, General Manuel Antonio Noriega, was indicted by two Florida-based grand juries on charges of drug trafficking. Noriega, who was the *de facto* leader of the state, ruling it with an iron hand, laughed at the charges and began to topple the political institutions, finally seizing power by ousting the elected president.

His next move was to take revenge on the United States itself, by declaring a state of war in December 1989. That evening a US Marine officer was murdered in Panama City and another naval officer and his wife were brutally beaten. These actions could not remain unanswered, and President George Bush placed his armed forces on high alert status to prepare for an intervention in Panama with the aim of capturing Noriega and bringing him to justice.

Two senior American commanders were ordered to update plans for such an operation – General Maxwell Thurman, commanding the 13,000 US troops presently stationed in Panama itself, some of whom were there undergoing jungle training, and Lieutenant Carl Stiner, commander of the US 18th Airborne Corps at Fort Bragg. Six task forces were to mount the strike which was to be carried out with maximum surprise in order to avoid heavy casualties from the Panamanian Defence Force, which numbered some 5,000 men, some of them highly motivated and loyal to Noriega. Nearly 23,000 American troops would simultaneously assault twenty-seven objectives in or near Panama City and along the important Canal installations. The plan, code-named 'Just Cause', called for the operation to be concluded within twenty-four hours, so that all the strategic objectives would be under US control by 20 December 1989.

First into action were a team of US SEALs, who set off from an American naval base on Panama shortly before midnight on 19 December to neutralize a Panamanian patrol boat, *President Porras* which the planners thought might interfere with the American operations. Clad in tight-fitting black spandex diving suits, the naval Commandos boarded two fast raiding craft and silently slipped out to sea. Having crossed the channel leading to the Panamanian docks, the boats sailed along the shore lined with mangrove trees. Reaching their destination some 50 metres from the objective, which was fully lit, the divers took a compass bearing and then slipped silently into the water, navigating by compass board and depth-gauge which were fitted in front of their equipment, visible in the dark with the aid of special glow lamps. Each swimmer carried explosive charges in waterproof packs. After a short underwater swim, the SEALs reached the *President Porras* undetected; one team fitted their demolition charges on the propeller shaft, while the others attached their charges under the boat. Suddenly, the boat's engines started and the divers swam off to seek cover. The boat's crew had woken up by now and started to toss hand-grenades into the water, but the swimmers were already too far away to suffer any casualties. As they waited, four loud explosions shattered the still night. Shots began to come from some nearby vessels, but they were wildly inaccurate, and the divers were already well on their way back.

Just after midnight on 20 December, the first US paratroops started to drop on to Torrijos International Airport. Seven hundred men of the 1st US Ranger Battalion made their combat drop from a low 500 feet into the darkness from several C-130 Hercules transports which had flown straight over from the USA. Their mission was to secure the airfield for a bigger drop to follow.

Lieutenant James Johnson, son of the commander of the 82nd Airborne Division, was among the first men out of his C-141 Starlifter. The young officer carried a heavy load, including his personal weapon, Claymore mine and radio – the whole totalling 35 kilograms. It was 0212 as he stepped out of the door into the tropical night. Below he could see coloured tracer bullets whizzing in all directions, but he had no time for aesthetic appreciation, since he realized that he was heading for a sharp drop on some thick overgrowth. His parachute caught on a large tree but when he untangled his harness he fell quite smoothly to the ground.

Many of his team were not so fortunate: some of them dropped in a nearby marsh and had to be drawn out very carefully, as their heavy load could have dragged them under. Others dropped heavily and sprained ankles or broke legs. The supply drop which followed was a catastrophe. Some Sheridan tanks of 73rd Armoured Battalion were dropped on the airfield, but, of the first eight, one became mired in the swamp and another smashed into the ground as its parachutes did not open. Another important piece of equipment, a fire control truck, landed upside down. Assembling the troops and supplies took much longer than had been expected, and the officers had great difficulty in getting their men together, as some of them had to hack their way through head-high elephant grass using their combat knives.

By 0430, however, Lieutenant Johnson was able to radio his commander that he had most of his men assembled. At this time they were supposed to be boarding the Black Hawk helicopters, but these did not arrive until three hours later. Johnson and his men boarded quickly, but by then the sun was up, which obviously would make things more difficult.

The plan was for the Black Hawks to fly in formations of six aircraft, each carrying sixty paratroopers. The flight would be guided in by scout helicopters and AH-64 Apaches, whose first mission this would be. After a landing zone had been secured, some AH-1 Cobra gunships would hover nearby to cover and support if needed.

The first task for the 82nd Ready Brigade was the capture of Panama Viejo, which overlooked the bay at the eastern end of Panama City. US intelligence had gained information that 250 of Noriega's most loyal troops, the notorious UESAT, were stationed there. Johnson's platoon was assigned to capture three observation posts near the fort. As they touched down on the adjacent beach, the men were covered by a hail of automatic fire from a barracks located on some nearby high ground. While Johnson and his men started to move out, another wave of helicopters came in to land, but the paratroopers jumped out into deep mud which had been stirred up by the previous landings. Some of them sank up to their armpits and had to be pulled up by their landing gear, hooked to choppers hovering overhead. Others formed a human chain to pull each other out, while all the time bullets whizzed over their heads. They were free from the quagmire within minutes, but valuable time had been lost.

Now the supporting Cobras went into action, attacking the barracks and a nearby anti-aircraft gun, which was knocked out before it had even opened fire. Johnson and his men then stormed the barracks, where resistance stopped as soon as the Americans set foot in the compound.

Things did not go so easily, however, in the city: Panamanian Defence Force (PDF) troops ran through the streets, firing automatic weapons and lobbing grenades through the windows of houses, and, as they wore jeans, it was impossible to distinguish them from the ordinary Panamanian citizens, making it very difficult to fight them. Also hiding in the crowds which thronged the streets were men of Noriega's so-called 'Dignity Battalions' or Dinbats, actually no better than street gangs out for personal gain but dangerous for all that: they were known to have brutally murdered some opponents of Noriega in earlier times.

As the fighting escalated, the Hotel Marriott in downtown Panama City became the focus of attention. Some American civilians who had been staying there were rounded up by masked men of Noriega's forces, were brutally abused and in fear of their lives. An airline pilot managed to get away in the confusion and phoned the White House in Washington for help. The message got through to General Stiner at For Bragg, who in turn radioed Lieutenant Colonel Harry Axson, commanding the paratroop battalion which was just entering the city from the direction of Fort Viejo. The colonel immediately ordered one of his companies to the hotel – but they had to get there first.

Advancing through heavy fire, hugging the sides of the buildings, the troopers ran from cover to cover, dodging the bullets which pinged around them. Just as the first men reached the doorway of the hotel, a large truck rounded the corner of the street at high speed, brakes squealing, and from it some UESAT men wearing protective vests blazed away with machine-guns. The truck zigzaged between the American paratroopers, who frantically raced for cover, but not before two of them had been wounded. Some paratroopers returned the fire and even managed to set light to the truck's cabin, but the shooting continued. Then one paratroopr, Specialist James Smith, went and stood directly in the path of the truck; aiming his grenade-launcher, he let go and scored a direct hit; the truck shuddered to a halt and, reloading quickly, he followed it up with another shot which sent the truck swerving into a building. Their way clear, the company raced into the Hotel Marriott and rescued the frightened civilians.

Another task force, which had set out at daybreak to capture a hill fortress on top of Tinajitas hill, was undergoing a terrible ordeal. Intelligence elements had estimated that a battalion of Noriega's best PDF forces were defending the fort. The landing zone designated for the US task force was on a low ridge about one kilometre south-west of the fort; as the Black Hawks came in to land soon after eight in the morning, they drew fire from the defence forces above them, and mortar fire fell near the landing zone, hitting two of the choppers. The paratroopers assembled, however, and set out to climb to the summit. It turned out to be an arduous climb: drenched in sweat in the hot tropical sun, the men soon became exhausted as they climbed through the elephant grass which reached high above their heads. It was only 700 metres to the top, but, at a crawling pace, in those conditions and under constant fire, it seemed a lot further. The PDF mortar men, from their position on top of the hill, had time to correct their range, and coolly pick off the advancing Americans, 22 of whom were wounded and two killed during the climb and the assault which followed. By that afternoon, however, the fort had been captured and the PDF fled to a nearby village.

Several kilometres from Tinajitas stood Fort Cimmaron where Noriega's most loyal units were stationed. US intelligence officers had feared that the nearby electricity plant which controlled the power for the entire city might be destroyed and a *coup de main* strike was planned to secure the fort as quickly as possible. The force assigned to capture the fort was supported by two Sheridan tanks and gun-mounted Humvees, but they had set off late, having had to wait until the vehicles could be manhandled from the marshlands where they had been dropped earlier. When the motor column came near the fort and the men were preparing to strike, it emerged that most of the PDF battalion guarding it had melted away during the night. The few men who had stayed behind fought back, but were quickly subdued by superior firepower.

As special Commando forces secured all the strategic sites along the canal zone, there still remained one more very important objective, in fact the main point of the exercise: the capture of the dictator himself. General Noriega had been in the officers' mess at the airfield when the first Ranger battalion dropped shortly after midnight, but as they began to assemble on the ground he jumped into his limousine and headed for the city, dodging the roadblocks which were just being set up along the route. Throughout the day US agents had been searching for him all over the city; finally they came to believe that he had taken refuge in his headquarters, the Comandancia, and this was to become the scene of the last violent battle.

The Comandancia was a complex of several concrete buildings, sited in the southern part of the city not far from the seashore; it was well defended, with thick walls, capable of withstanding a powerful attack. In order to assault such a target General Stiner had assigned a lot of firepower to reduce the expected strong resistance. Two AC-130 Spectre gunships were detailed to support Apache gunships and several Sheridan tanks. Since its impressive performance in Vietnam the Spectre had been modified to carry, apart from many rapid-firing automatic cannon, a powerful 105mm howitzer which could accurately hurl forty-pound projectiles. The Apaches could launch Hellfire anti-tank missiles, able to penetrate even the thickest walls.

This was all very well in theory, but as the convoy of vehicles, including the Sheridan tanks, approached the buildings, it came under heavy RPG fire which knocked out two APCs, one of which exploded, killing two and wounding eighteen of its passengers. The burning vehicles blocked the street, but the two Sheridans manoeuvred round them and fired point-blank at the compound, while the wounded men were dragged out of the blazing hulks.

Now it was time for the infantry, who dashed forward. The tanks stepped up their fire and from above the Spectre and Apaches destroyed the upper floor. Within minutes the whole compound was ablaze but snipers still continued to fire from the ruins. General Stiner therefore detached a Ranger company to reduce the target and they, together with the paratroopers, overcame any remaining resistance.

Noriega, however, if he had been in the Comandancia, was not to be found. It was to be another two weeks before he gave himself up; he had been hiding in a private apartment.

Operation 'Just Cause' was the largest US intervention since the World War involving airborne troops. Twenty-three US soldiers had died and more than 300 were wounded, while the civilian toll, never finally established, was probably several hundred. Many of the US special forces who were engaged in Panama would use the skills they had learned there two years later – and halfway round the world – in Operation 'Desert Storm'.

31. THE SECRET WARRIORS OF 'DESERT STORM'

D uring the planning stages of Operation 'Desert Storm' in mid-January 1991, General Norman Schwarzkopf, overall commander of the coalition forces against Iraq in the Persian Gulf, faced one special problem. Information garnered by satellites and high-flying spy planes on the Iraqi air defence system had found it to be virtually impregnable. But in order to get his massive ground forces into action and rout the half-million Iraqi troops dug-in on the Kuwait-Saudi border, an air strike of unprecedented proportions had to be mounted to knock out Saddam Hussein's communications infrastructure. The US staff officers estimated that hundreds of aircraft might be lost to the Iraqi air defence if it were not first neutralized.

However, Colonel George Gray, commander of the USAF Air Commando Unit, came up with a plan, in which he was supported by Peter de la Billiere, the British General who acted as Schwarzkopf's deputy. Joining the SAS in 1954 while in the Far East, the then Captain de la Billiere had hunted guerrillas under the most difficult conditions, operating for weeks at a time in the swamps of Selangor near the Malacca Straits. As a major he had led countless patrols through the jungles of Malaya and Borneo, the desert in Oman and, much later, in the Falklands. He was, therefore, a very experienced soldier and a good man to have on one's side.

As the two men faced Schwarzkopf, the sandy haired Colonel Gray proposed an amazing plan to neutralize the Iraqi air defence system just before the first formations of attack aircraft were to fly to their targets. The burly Schwarzkopf, himself a veteran fighter in many campaigns, listened carefully. Like most ground soldiers, he tended to the conventional view of things and was somewhat sceptical of these special operators, always looking for unconventional ways to deal with military problems. He also remembered the awful débâcle at 'Desert One', just ten years before. A fiasco like that could ruin his own carefully worked out battle plan. General de la Billiere, however, was very persuasive; he could not agree to his special forces remaining idle in such a large-scale operation; in fact he thought, and said, that the conditions here were ideal for special operations and that, given enough leeway, his men could play havoc with the enemy defences. Schwarzkopf in any case had no alternative and, reluctantly, gave in.

As he walked to his own headquarters, Colonel Gray was extremely pleased to have been given the green light, but he knew that he faced tremendous odds. His plan was excellent: every detail had been taken into consideration; his equipment was first-class, and his men confident.

Major Bob Leonik, lead pilot of the Pave-Low helicopter squadron – the Green Hornets – was far from positive. Although the Pave-Low choppers could fly anywhere in the worst possible weather and were crammed with the most exotic electronic equipment, including devices to blind enemy radar and missiles, the adverse weather in the Gulf desert could play havoc with the sensitive electronics, as they had learned to their cost when four of the expensive helicopters had been lost in training flights.

At precisely 0020 on 17 January 1991 Major Leonik lifted his Pave-Low helicopter from the airbase in Saudi Arabia and headed for the Iraqi border which he crossed at 0220. His task force was divided into two teams, each consisting of Pave-Low and AH-64 gunships. This time, in order to prevent another fiasco like 'Desert One', they had brought spares of everything. To evade the Iraqi radar the formation flew at less than fifty feet, ducking into wadis and circling Bedouin encampments. The night was as black as pitch but their sophisticated night goggles enabled the chopper pilots to see relatively well ahead; anyway, they were flying with the aid of computers and sensors – more reliable than human eyes.

At about fifteen kilometres from their target – an Iraqi radar installation – the Pave-Low pilots dropped glowing chemical light sticks to mark the targets for the Apaches following behind them. An Iraqi ground controller suddenly spotted the approaching choppers and began to run towards the underground bunker which housed the control centre. But he never made it: as he reached the front entrance a Hellfire missile exploded and ripped the entire bunker apart. Five seconds later the second radar station which was located nearby vanished in a ball of flame.

The way was clear and as Leonik's party turned round to fly home he could already see the first formations of attack aircraft streaming in to their targets. The first airstrike was devastating, but losses were negligible, perhaps the lowest ever encountered in any war of the air.

Because of its geography and the way the Iraqi forces were deployed in 1991, Iraq was a perfect setting for covert and special forces warfare. Western Iraq, being the area from which SCUD missiles were being launched at Israel, was a primary target in view of the importance of keeping Israel out of the war in order to hold the precarious coalition together. The western part of Iraq is mostly desert, cut off from the river basin of the Euphrates and Tigris, where most of the country's population centres are located. With only a few bridges over the Euphrates, the most westerly of the two rivers, it is extremely difficult to move large contingents of troops, especially armour, to the western desert. A single multi-lane highway connects Baghdad with Amman in Jordan to the south and Syria in the north.

Rutbah, a large military base near the Jordanian frontier, is located in a bare, rocky and trackless expanse of desert, providing excellent sites in which to hide mobile SCUD missile-launchers. It also, however, made a wonderful place to operate special forces, who could move under cover for long periods without being detected. Even if they were seen, the coalition forces had air supremacy and could head off any Iraqi troops before they had time to hurt the Commandos. The reasoning was that, since the western Iraqi desert is quite small as deserts go, special forces could operate covertly, using helicopters and fast desert buggies to and from bases which they established in remote areas.

As soon as Iraq invaded Kuwait in August 1990, members of the SAS were flown from RAF Lyneham in Wiltshire to the Persian Gulf. Some of them were infiltrated in special helicopters or by parachute, gliding into their target areas, sometimes more than a hundred kilometres away. This was the first time in modern war that special forces (known as SF) were included in all combat scenarios, and this was thanks to General de la Billiere, who searched for, and found, suitable missions for this type of warfare. Using sophisticated space satellite communications equipment and global positioning to guide them in the featureless desert, these SF teams were able to roam at will, undetected, to pinpoint high-value targets such as SCUD launchers or their underground shelters, which were difficult to identify from fast, high-flying aircraft. The special forces were able to watch the Iraqi missile teams moving their mobile launchers from the hideouts and start preparing them for launching.

By the way, it turned out during the war that the Iraqi missile teams were very highly trained and took much less time in the launching process than had been estimated. Still, the delicate refuelling process allowed the special forces team enough time to do their job. Remaining undetected in the dark, and using laser target illuminators, they would strike the target with an invisible beam, which marked it clearly for the coalition fighter-bombers flying in to strike at the target before the SCUDs could be fired. In this way, combing the suspected areas for targets, SF teams including American Delta and British SAS destroyed a substantial number of ground targets which could not have been located merely by air even with the aid of the most sophisticated satellite photography. It was the men of the special forces who, with daring and skill, did most of the damage and once again proved their worth.

'Desert Storm' was the first campaign to test in battle much of the sophisticated equipment in the inventory; this included dune buggies, built on tubular frames with enormous tyres enabling them to cross even the worse terrain. Heavy machine-guns provided massive firepower, while battery-powered laser designators pinpointed targets from covert positions. Small satellite navigation systems and advanced night vision equipment enabled the SF teams to operate round the clock, while high-tech radios with frequency-hopping channels eluded enemy jamming and were able to transmit signals by short bursts over long distances. The British SAS and American SEAL and Delta teams who operated in the Gulf were a gigantic leap ahead of their forerunners of the Second World War or even after.

As Operation 'Desert Storm' was about to start its ground attack phase towards the end of February 1991, some 17,000 US Marines were waiting in their landing ships to hit the beaches of Kuwait, in what was believed would be the biggest amphibious landing since Korea. But the ground war really started on the night of 23 February when six SEALs landed under the command of Navy Lieutenant Tom Dietz. From Ras-el-Mishab in Saudi Arabia, they zoomed at 80 kilometres an hour in their fountain speedboats up the Kuwaiti coastline. At 2200 the boats stopped some 30 kilometres offshore and, untying their Zodiac rubber boats, they headed slowly for the beach, stopping every now and then to listen for suspicious noises from the Iraqi shore defences, but all seemed quiet. Close inshore, beyond the breakers, the SEAL team slipped overboard and swam towards the beaches, each man carrying a haversack filled with plastic explosives with delayed action fuzes. They hit the beach completely unobserved by the defenders. Lieutenant Dietz, pulling out his pocket night vision scanner, found all clear and signalled his men to set the timers, which were planned to go off exactly two hours later, when the mine breaching operations would start – at 0100, 24 February. The timing was critical if the ruse were to work and thus keep the Iraqis guessing as to when the amphibious landing would start. Explosives in place, the SEALs slid back into the water and made contact with the waiting speedboats. Once they were aboard, gunners started firing heavy machine-guns at the shoreline to wake up the defenders in their bunkers. Then, precisely at 0100, the charges went off, rocking the Kuwaiti coast. The Iraqis counter-attacked – at the empty sea.

Once the ground operations proper had started, SF came into their own, providing vital combat information unobtainable through air reconnaissance. One example was that of Master Sergeant Jeffery Sims and a small team of Green Berets. Inching up their periscope from the hideout they had dug in the ground deep inside Iraq, and using a long distance radio, the sergeant started transmitting vital information to his headquarters in Saudi Arabia on the movements of the crack Iraqi Republican Guards, known to be the greatest threat to the coalition forces. Sims and his team had been heliported into Iraq with a dozen other groups but of them all Sims was the deepest in, only 200 kilometres from Baghdad, close to the River Euphrates. The Green Berets had perfected the Vietcong's hide-site technique and could live in their underground holes for long periods undetected. Suddenly, however, as he was transmitting, a small Iraqi girl approached the hideout and curiously lifted the lid. First she gazed wide-eyed at the troopers crouching there, but then she ran away, screaming in terror. Her father also came and looked at them and ran off to alert the Iraqi soldiers. The Americans were soon surrounded by about a hundred Iraqi infantrymen who, however, kept their distance, reluctant to close in. This gave Sims a chance to signal for air support, and a team of F-16s came zooming in, guns blazing, forcing the Iraqis to keep their distance. Chief Warrant Officer James Crisafulli, a senior Black Hawk helicopter pilot of the special Aviation Regiment, was given the mission of flying the team out of Iraq. Flying into enemy territory in broad daylight and evacuating a special team in the middle of a fire fight is no easy matter and, just before he took off from base, a couple of Green Berets hopped on to help if need be. When Sims saw the Black Hawk approaching he fired a pen flare to pinpoint their position. Crisafulli had come at exactly the right moment: Sims and his men were on the point of being overrun, with more and more Iraqis gathering. While Sims and his men raced for the helicopter, the Green Berets blazing away from inside the chopper, three rounds struck the rotor blades and another whistled by the pilot's head, but they all managed to scramble on board, the chopper lifted off in a cloud of dust, leaving several enemy dead on the ground. It had been touch and go, but the Green Berets took it all in their stride.

Many of the clandestine operations carried out by SAS and American special forces in the Gulf War remain top secret, despite the many wild rumours which circulated in the media. However, one thing is sure: when all the stories are told, they will make fictional thrillers pale by comparison. Still, these operations are not without their price. Fourteen men were killed when an AC-130 gunship in which they were flying crashed after being hit by ground fire. The first casualty of the war was a British SAS corporal, killed in a battle with an Iraqi patrol as his team was returning to base, while another member of the SAS was wounded and captured, but returned safely after the war. Seven SAS men in all were taken prisoner during the war and, as some of them were wearing Arab disguise, they could well have been shot as spies, but no definite information was ever released by the British authorities. Special operations would remain part of the secret war.

PART THREE
Raiders from the Sky

32. THE LOW-LEVEL GAME

I t was on 18 December 1939 that the Royal Air Force had their first taste, and it was a disturbing one, of the capability of German radar. It happened when Wing Commander Richard Kellett, leading twenty-four Vickers Wellingtons, took off from King's Lynn at approximately 0930 and set course at 10,000 feet for the German Shillig roads and Wilhelmshaven. The RAF had carried out daylight operations previously – twice, and had been convinced that a tightly disciplined bomber formation could hold its own against fighter attacks. Events, however, were to prove otherwise.

At 1350 a German Freya radar station which was located on the island of Wangerooge, covering the approaches to the German coast, picked up the signals of the British bombers while they were still more than one hundred kilometres away. The German officer on duty alerted the Luftwaffe fighter base at Jever and six Me-109s led by Lieutenant Johannes Steinhoff were rapidly scrambled, while the RAF bombers flew steadily on, in perfect diamond formation, totally unaware of what was about to hit them.

The German fighters sighted the British formation from high above, and immediately pounced on them, scoring two kills before the British bomber pilots even knew what was happening, as Steinhoff and his wingman, attacking with cannon fire from above, quickly shot down a Wellington apiece. But that was only the beginning of the slaughter.

The Wellingtons, still in perfect formation, slowly turned over Wilhelmshaven towards the north-west, while Steinhoff's formation was joined by twin-engined Me-110 destroyers. In the running fight which followed ten Wellingtons were shot down, almost 50 per cent of the force. Those who did manage to return to base told their harrowing tale to their debriefing officers and, as a result, this – the first radar interception of the war – was also the last British daylight operation with heavy bombers for several years to come.

From then on the RAF converted to night bomber sorties, which became their standard *modus operandi*, and eventually succeeded in turning many German cities into smouldering rubble over the next six years. However, while the heavy bomber groups of Bomber Command paid their visits to Hitler's cities only by night, the fast light bombers still operated by daylight and, after a costly trial and error period, managed to perfect precision raids on point targets in occupied Europe.

One of the first of these low-level attacks was carried out by Bristol Blenheim twin-engined bombers of No. 2 Group, which was to specialize in those tactics during the war. There had been a previous, abortive, attack on Bremen, and it was decided to try again. Leading the crews of two squadrons of Blenheim bombers was Wing Commander Hughie Edwards, an athletically built Australian pilot who had already won the DFC for a mast-high anti-shipping strike off the Dutch coast. Before dawn on 4 July 1941 Edwards lifted off his light bomber from RAF Swanton Morley, together with eight Blenheims from No. 105 Squadron. Six more from its sister squadron, No. 107, joined the formation as they circled above the Norfolk coast.

Once over the Channel, the formation dropped to wavetop height, flying in two loose vics towards Heligoland. Visibility was excellent, and they made landfall at zero feet east of Bremerhaven, aiming straight for their target, Bremen. Dropping still lower, Edwards led his formation under the German defence balloons which hovered menacingly 2,000 feet above. In anticipation of exactly this hazard, the Blenheims had been fitted with special metal-cutting devices fitted to the wing edges, but their effects were in doubt, as they had never been tested in combat so Edwards cautiously tried to guide his force around the cables.

As they roared over the outskirts of the great city at rooftop level, Edwards signalled the formation to spread out, and he himself led the attack towards the harbour, so low that they had to twist and turn to avoid cranes, warehouse rooftops and high-tension pylons. Flak began to come up at them and the Blenheims, several of them hit, raced for the docks, some of them collecting yards of telephone cable as they passed. One aircraft, flown by Sergeant Pilot MacKillop, crashed into a warehouse, exploding in flames; another, trailing smoke, made a forced landing and, as the formation turned out to sea trying to evade the flak, the deputy formation leader was seen crashing into the sea. The rest got home safely.

In contrast to the unfortunate débâcle with the Wellingtons, the Bremen raid was a success: it achieved complete surprise and managed to penetrate a heavily defended prime target through the front door. Wing Commander Edwards was awarded a well-earned Victoria Cross for leading the attack; he finished the war as a Group Captain and as one of the most highly decorated RAF airmen, with the VC, DSO and DFC, later joined in this gallery of distinction by only two other pilots, Guy Gibson and Leonard Cheshire.

Following the successful Bremen operation, No. 2 Group mounted another audacious daylight mission, code-named 'Sunrise', targeting two power stations near Cologne. Eighteen Blenheims of 21 and 82 Squadrons made for the Quadrath generator station, while thirty-six aircraft from four other squadrons attacked the large steam generator station south of the city. Leading the Quadrath force was Wing Commander Kercher, who had already won a DSO leading a low-level raid on Rotterdam earlier in the war.

The fifty-four Blenheim bombers scraped the wavetops, then turned into the Scheldt Estuary, skimming sand dunes, trees and windmills, scattering grazing cattle. They crossed the German border and soon the tall chimneys of the power station could be seen looming out of the ground. Banking into a sharp turn, the leader attacked, zooming over the high-tension cables of the Brauweiler grid system, the spire of Cologne's cathdral visible just over the horizon. Jets of flak began to come at them from both sides as they flew over the target, now covered with smoke, and Messerschmitts, hastily scrambled from a nearby airfield, came up into the sky. The bombers went on with their mission, however, and explosions below could be felt up in the aircraft as the power station was engulfed in fire.

Their job over, several of the pilots swerved into the surrounding countryside, evading the now heavy flak by diving into a nearby gravel pit. The bombers flew so low over the ground that one of them nearly hit a German gun emplacement, scattering the soldiers, on whom the bomber's rear-gunner fired. One Blenheim hit a telegraph pole and chipped a propellar in the process but went on flying as if nothing had happened. Another, its engine spewing oil over the windscreen, nearly hit the spire of a village church but the pilot managed to veer sharply, missing it by inches.

As soon as the bombers were clear of the immediate danger area, they turned westward, making for the Dutch border. At one point, jolting through a severe summer storm, they crossed a Dutch town at street level. Passing over a Luftwaffe fighter base near Peer, some of the crew noted fighters taking off, and rear-gunners fired some quick bursts in an effort to delay them, then the Blenheims raced for cover behind sand dunes and woods until they could make for the coast, where an escort of Spitfires was waiting for them to arrive.

Daylight operations continued; one of the more remarkable – and ambitious – ones was 'Oyster'. The project was the destruction of the Dutch Philips radio and valve works at Eindhoven. Naturally an undertaking of such magnitude required high-precision bombing, not only to prevent casualties to the Dutch population but also to destroy the target completely. The uniqueness of this particular raid lies in the fact that four different types of aircraft were to be used, each with entirely different operational characteristics. Speed, range and manoeuvrability were characteristics possessed to a high degree by the Mosquito IV, while the American-made Lockheed Ventura, like the Coastal Command Hudson, did not have them at all. The wooden Mosquito's qualities were already a legend, its speed and manoeuvrability making it everybody's first choice for all difficult combat missions, its survivability giving crews their best chance to survive compared to other aircraft in which the mortality rate was becoming prohibitive. The North American Mitchell twin-engined bombers and the Boston III were also scheduled for the operation. The Mitchell proved an excellent aircraft to fly, well-suited for daylight operations, but the slow, short-ranged Ventura, with its poor manoeuvrability, was just the opposite. The Boston III, however, was a lovely machine, very much liked by its crews, as it was very comfortable, a great rarity in military aircraft of that period, and its low-slung engines allowed a good forward view from the flight deck.

A precise operational plan was thus worked out taking into account all the widely varying characteristics of the aircraft involved, and allowing for different approach routes to the target, while a wide range of aircraft would fly against various targets to divert German fighters from the high-priority objectives.

On 6 December 1942, as planned, the Bostons and Venturas took off from their base at Feltwell in Norfolk. Wing Commander Young, commanding 464 Squadron, roared low over the airfield, boxing in his sections in an impressive display of formation flying, rarely seen during wartime Britain in daylight. The Wingco's Ventura was painted bright yellow and the tail light flashed on for recognition. Bostons in flights of six formed up over the Essex coast and headed out to sea at wavetop level. The two Mosquito squadrons led by Wing Commander Edwards took a more northerly course and, with cloud base at 200 feet, they soon dropped as low as possible. Having crossed the water, both groups were soon heading inland over the Dutch salt marshes where hundreds of ducks and other birds wheeled upwards, disturbed by the thunder of the fast-flying aircraft. Many of these birds bumped into the aircraft, causing serious damage; in fact, as it turned out later at debriefing, most of the damage on that particular raid was caused by bird strike.

Meanwhile, leading aircraft navigators were reading the course with specially prepared strip-maps; pilots did their best to avoid slipstreams which kept jolting and bumping them. Over Woensdrecht, an FW 190 came up to attack them, but was soon left behind by the speeding aircraft. Just after midday, the leading Boston took the prearranged turning over Turnhout and set course for the target, seven minutes flying time away. Recognizing the landmark on the outskirts of Eindhoven, Wing Commander Pelly-Fry turned into the attack, climbing to 2,000 feet just below cloud level, the rest of his formation following him. The Emassinger valve factory, their target, was clearly identified, and the 11-second delay bombs were hurled through windows of the building.

Simultaneously, the other formation hit the Stryp plant. Several aircraft were seen crashing into buildings; this was probably caused by the heavy smoke which probably blinded the pilots; others claimed it was due to flak.

On their way back to base, German fighters pounced on them relentlessly, and the aircraft had great difficulty in forming up. Losses were heavy: four Bostons, nine Venturas and one Mosquito failed to return. Although the results were impressive, the losses sustained at Eindhoven once again shook the confidence of Bomber Command in mounting large-scale daylight missions, and for the time being No. 2 group concentrated on low-level precision bombing runs on prime targets.

33. DAYLIGHT RAID TO AUGSBURG

In April 1941 No. 5 Group, Bomber Command was chosen to mount another daylight operation, deep inside Germany, involving a round trip of some 2,000 kilometres, mostly over enemy territory. The target was Augsburg in southern Germany, where the MAN diesel engine works was located. As it was so far away, completely out of range of fighter cover, the only hope of success was in complete surprise. There seems to have been a marked clash of views between squadron commanders and Group regarding the chances of success for this mission, as No. 5 Group's experience was all in night bombing, but it was finally decided to go ahead.

No. 44 (Rhodesia) Squadron and No. 92 Squadron were chosen to fly the mission. No. 44 was the first Bomber Command unit to convert to the new four-engined Lancasters, having previously flown Hampden twin-engined bombers, and the crews were very pleased with the change from the cramped Hampdens. Leading the squadron was Wing Commander Roderick Learoyd, VC, who had gained his decoration in a low-level raid on the Dortmund-Ems Canal, the very man to train and lead the present mission.

No. 92 Squadron, based at Conningsby, also began to receive their Lancasters just after No. 44. Here the squadron was even more pleased to convert, as their twin-engined Avro Manchesters were not very popular. 92 Squadron was one of the Group's best units, containing many veteran aircrew. One of these was a fair-haired squadron leader named John Sherwood. Only twenty-two, he had already gained vast experience as a bomber pilot and had a well-earned DFC. He had received the nickname 'Flap', denoting his almost fanatical keenness.

However, the man chosen to lead the raid was Squadron Leader John Nettleton of 44 Squadron. Although two years older than Sherwood, he had far less operational experience and was, in fact, on his first tour. There were persistent rumours that Wing Commander Learoyd had actually refused to lead the raid, regarding it as wasteful and potentially suicidal, which might explain the fact that Group's final choice fell on Nettleton who, despite his superb leadership qualities, lacked the experience.

The fact was that light bombers would have been much more suitable for the raid and their crews were veterans at this sort of work. Unfortunately, however, the MAN works were out of range of light bombers, and the target was believed to be top priority, as it was of great value to the U-boat industry during the Battle of the Atlantic which was raging at that time. Therefore the newly appointed commander of Bomber Command, Air Marshal Arthur Harris, not only authorized the mission, but also emphasised how vital it was to the war effort.

It was planned to fly at extremely low level to the target to evade the enemy's early warning system, which was still very bad at detecting low-flying aircraft. It was believed that, by using a low-level approach route, some protection could be achieved against fighters and flak and so, to obtain some low-flying experience, both squadron crews chosen for the mission were given orders to practise long-range, low-level formation flying in daylight; the target, however, was not disclosed to them until briefing on 17 April 1941, the day of the raid.

They were told to cross the French coast at Dives-sur-Mer in Normandy and, circling the River Seine and the Vosges Mountains, reach the target over the northern tip of Lake Constance. Taking off late in the afternoon, the attacking force was to reach the target before darkness and return in the evening. A very complicated diversionary plan was drawn up, involving almost eight hundred aircraft, which aimed to allow the low-flying Lancasters maximum security by drawing off the Luftwaffe fighters defending the inner coastline. Once over this hurdle, it was thought that the attackers would have little trouble in reaching their objective.

At 1455 Squadron Leader Sherwood advanced the four throttles of his Lancaster L 7572 OF-K and released the brakes. The heavily loaded bomber, its great propeller blades spinning and engines pulsing with the strain, surged forward along the centre line of the Coningsby runway, then with speed built up, lifted off. As Sherwood circled, taking in the new sensation of flying in the afternoon sky after so many night missions, six other Lancasters formed up.

Seventeen minutes later, Squadron Leader Nettleton took off from Waddington followed closely by his two wingmen and two minutes later Flight Lieutenant Sandford took off, leading the other section, and joined up with the first vic. The two squadrons met over Selsey Bill, Sussex. Dropping down to wavetop height over the Channel, Nettleton's formation pulled ahead and shifted to a northerly direction away from the planned course, while Sherwood stuck strictly to the planned route. Nettleton's formation crossed the French coast at Houlgate, the pilots rising over the cliffs, while Sherwood's formation thundered at zero feet over the flat estuary as planned.

Inland, the two formations flew at 20 feet, roaring over the countryside in beautiful spring weather. A thousand kilometres of enemy territory, with all the dangers entailed, awaited them. Nettleton, leading the 44 Squadron's formation, was just north of Bernay — four kilometres off course — when he flew across an airfield. His navigator, standing nearby on the flight deck, pointed the Beaumont woods out to him and, as they cleared the last trees, there was Roger le Beaumont airfield, home of the famous JG 2 Richthofen Wing, one of the best divisions in the Luftwaffe, commanded at that time by Major Walter Oesau, a veteran fighter leader, who had already racked up his hundredth kill and had been decorated with his country's highest awards. The airfield, although excellently camouflaged, was well known to RAF intelligence, and the original flight plan had made adequate provisions to avoid it. Indeed, Sherwood's formation, now flying south of Bernay, was undetected and continued on course. Nettleton, however, due to the original deviation, was now to lose two-thirds of his formation to the Richthofen Wing.

As the British bomber formation appeared, flying low over the wooded boundary of Roger le Beaumont, Major Oesau's pilots were landing their Messerschmitts in sequence after having engaged the British diversionary

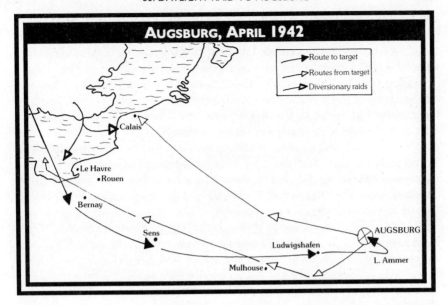

AUGSBURG, APRIL 1942

Route to target
Routes from target
Diversionary raids

Calais
Le Havre
Rouen
Bernay
Sens
Ludwigshafen
Mulhouse
AUGSBURG
L. Ammer

sorties in the Cherbourg peninsula. Suddenly, noticing the four-engined monsters looming into view, Otto Happel, the duty controller, shouted to the pilots to take off again. It is worthy of note that, at this stage of the war, the Lancaster was virtually unknown to Luftwaffe pilots and, if they were unrecognizable in daylight, they would certainly have had things even easier by night.

Oesau raced to his machine which was standing near the control tower and, slamming the canopy shut, shot into the sky in hot pursuit of the Englishmen, who had just disappeared over the airfield boundary. The first Messerschmitts, some of which had still been up in the air, waiting to land, were already in action, lining up on the Lancasters' tails.

First to be hit was Warrant Officer Beckett, flying in the rear vic, whose Lancaster was struck by a hail of cannon fire from Hauptmann Greisert. Immediately afterwards another Lanc, piloted by the veteran Rhodesian Flight Lieutenant Nick Sandford, was shot down by Feldwebel Brosseckert, who managed to set fire to all four engines at once. Then the plane of a third member of the rear formation, Warrant Officer Crum, was severely hit but Crum managed to execute a perfect crash-landing near Barc, saving himself and his crew.

Nettleton's vic by now had cleared the main danger area but was frantically trying to evade the German pursuers by ducking even lower, searching for cover behind the Barquet woods. This tactic, however, came too late to save them. Major Oesau in his Me-109 was already coming into position behind Warrant Officer Rhodes. Closing in fast, he fired his cannon and soon the bomber was on fire. Rhodes probably lost control, as the heavy bomber reared up sharply, stalled and – diving between the two remaining Lancasters and by some miracle missing them – crashed into a clump of trees.

That left the Lancasters of Nettleton and Flying Officer Garwell as the only survivors of 44 Squadron. As the victorious Germans, almost out of fuel, turned for home, the two British bombers grimly flew on towards their target, which was still a long way off. A few kilometres to the south-west, Sherwood's formation flew on unscathed, unaware of what had happened to their companions. Some of the crew members did notice smoke and reported it to their pilots, but as they were under strict radio silence, they were unable to find out what had happened to the sister formation.

Nettleton and Garwell reached Augsburg without further incident and began their run-up to the target, but over the factory buildings Garwell's Lanc was repeatedly hit by flak and crashed. Squadron Leader Nettleton, the sole survivor of the formation which had left Waddington, returned to base safely.

Minutes later, Sherwood's formation identified the target area and started their run towards the MAN factory buildings, exactly as briefed. Their landmark was a canal which forked away from the River Lech. They were greeted by light flak, since their target was now fully alerted by Nettleton's attack. Sherwood, in the lead, was aiming for the centre of the diesel engine shop, with his wingmen in perfect formation beside him, gunners firing away at the enemy flak positions below. The bomb aimers released their loads exactly on target and the pilots slammed the bomb doors shut as soon as their lethal cargoes were clear.

Now Sherwood pulled his aircraft even lower, right down to street level, with Flying Officers Hallow and Rodley following close behind. As they reached the outskirts of Augsburg, Rodley suddenly noticed smoke billowing out of Sherwood's Lancaster. He watched, horrified, as the smoke thickened and turned black as a fire began to blaze near the cockpit. Still Sherwood hung on doggedly; the two wingmen stayed with him as he started losing altitude. Sherwood's navigator could be clearly seen, standing next to his pilot, almost engulfed in the flames which had burned the top of the cockpit roof right away. Then the blazing Lanc hit the ground and exploded in a ball of white heat.

Flight Lieutenant Penman took command and assembled the formation for its long journey home. En route to the Dutch border another aircraft was lost, but the rest of the formation reached Coningsby safely, the last aircraft landing at 2315. Of the twelve aircraft which had taken off, only five returned. Forty-nine crew members were missing — most of them dead. Nettleton, the sole survivor of 44 Squadron, was awarded the Victoria Cross and took over command of the squadron from Learoyd, but was lost only three months later on a bombing raid on Turin in a much smaller operation than the daylight one which he had survived.

The gallant Sherwood miraculously survived; strapped into his seat, he was catapulted out of the cockpit on impact and, barely scratched, picked up by surprised German soldiers, who had not expected any survivors from the blazing wreck which had crashed in their area. He spent the rest of the war in a POW camp, returning home in 1945, to spend several years in the peacetime Air Force, becoming a wing commander. He died in the early eighties, a sad man, denied any recognition for the brilliant job he had done for his people. In fact, Sherwood never received any decoration for his exemplary leadership, outstanding skill and personal courage, so clearly demonstrated throughout the mission. It was Sherwood's discipline which saved the mission; he got all his formation on target, whereas Nettleton arrived with ony two aircraft surviving: his minor error in going off course at the beginning of the operation snowballed and resulted in the elimination of almost his entire force within a matter of minutes.

Although the Augsburg raid had been practically a disaster, No. 5 Group decided to go ahead with another daylight raid! They dispatched forty-four Lancasters to attack the submarine building yards near Danzig; the mission involved some 3,000 kilometres' flying, one of the farthest ever attempted by Bomber Command. On 11 July 1942 the formation set out at low level. Skirting the Danish coast, they ran into dense cloud cover, which made target recognition extremely difficult, and the raid was abandoned.

Three months later, however, the group undertook an even more daring target: the French Schneider armament arsenal at Le Creusot. To avoid a repetition of the clash with the Luftwaffe which had taken place during the Augsburg raid, they planned to fly wide over the sea, crossing the French Atlantic coast south of the Ile d'Yeu and flying another 650 kilometres from there to the target. It was known that there was a Freya radar installaion on the coastline, but it still had limited effectiveness against low-flying aircraft; accordingly the British pilots were trained in special low-flying formation work – a difficult task, as no less than ninety-four bombers – the largest formation ever flown in daylight attack – were scheduled to take part in the mission.

Formation commander on the raid was Wing Commander L. C. Slee, commanding 49 Squadron at Scampton. Among the other crews taking part were some from both 44 and 97 Squadrons. 106 Squadron was commanded by Wing Commander Guy Gibson, later to gain fame as the leader of the Dam Busters.

After forming up over Upper Heyford, the force flew over Land's End, keeping well below 1,000 feet, while Coastal Command Whitleys flew anti-submarine sweeps to keep any German spotter submarines below the surface. Losing height over the water, the Lancasters flew far out over the Bay of Biscay, then turned east towards the coast of Brittany in as close a formation as the pilots dared to fly. Crossing the French coast some fifty kilometres south of St-Nazaire, the formation kept below 100 feet and roared into the Loire valley for its 700-kilometre flight over some of France's most beautiful scenery, brightly lit by the afternoon sun. Although the rear-gunners, normally in the most boring position in the bomber, enjoyed the view immensely as the famous castles, villages and rivers swept by beneath them, the pilots and navigators found the flight trying and exhausting, with no co-pilot to assist. The tall trees, church spires and high-tension lines over which they raced became occupational hazards calling for quick reactions, and bird strike was also a constant menace.

The actual attack on Le Creusot was made from a higher level, to avoid congestion over the target and enable smaller delayed-action bombs to be used. This time the attack was a complete surprise and little opposition was encountered. Only one aircraft was lost in the entire operation, and results were good. Nevertheless, after Le Creusot, No. 5 Group stopped daylight raids for some time, reverting to its primary role as a night bomber group.

34. THE DAMBUSTERS

No. 617 Squadron, Royal Air Force was formed during the hectic days of March 1943 with a specific mission in mind: to destroy the Ruhr dams in a single strike and thus incapacitate Germany's military industry in the Ruhr. RAF Bomber Command had been attacking this region since the beginning of the war, with only marginal results to date, since it was very heavily defended. A special bomb had now been developed by the famous aircraft designer Sir Barnes Wallis; it was the 'bouncing bomb' – a revolving depth-charge which, it was hoped, would blow the 40-metre-high, 650-metre-long and 34-metre-wide wall of the Moehne Dam – the main target for the night attack; it held large masses of water in an artificial lake and, if blown, it would inundate the entire region, which housed vital industrial complexes for the German military machine.

Such a feat had never before been carried out by bomber aircraft and, to ensure success, pinpoint target acquisition would be required which, in turn, demanded crews with both discipline and great flying skill. Chosen to form such a squadron, train it, and lead it into action was Wing Commander Guy Gibson, then commanding No. 106 Squadron. The 25-year-old pilot had already proved himself in combat; he had flown many missions over enemy territory, becoming one of the best captains in Bomber Command, with 73 bomber and 99 night fighter sorties to his credit. He had been decorated with two DSOs and two DFCs, and was one of the very few men with both the experience and the personality to form and lead an élite squadron.

On 21 March 1943, therefore, 'X' Squadron (thus temporarily designated for maximum security) came into being at RAF Scampton in Lincolnshire, setting up in a disused hangar on the windblown airfield – a modest beginning to the long and brilliant career to follow. The ground crews arrived first; a colourful group, selected for skill and integrity from several squadrons, they were quickly shaped into a working unit by 'Chiefy' Powell, an excellent administrator who would become an outstanding figure in the squadron. Gibson had been given complete freedom in selecting his aircrew from Bomber Command and on 24 March they gathered at Scampton – a very well-decorated lot; so many 'gongs' had probably never before been seen on any one station!

Gibson wasted no time in niceties and, although he was not allowed to divulge the actual mission, immediately set up a strict training programme involving a great deal of low-flying and precision target practice bomb runs, which kept the aircrews – all veterans – guessing. The technique developed by Barnes Wallis for the attack involved a cylindrical, barrel-shaped bomb which was to be sent spinning backwards, bouncing towards the dam wall where it would sink into the water and explode below the waterline, creating sufficient force to blow the dam. This required modifications to the Lancaster's bomb bay, resulting in the Lancaster BIII which underwent the conversion process at AVRO in Manchester; the first aircraft arrived at Scampton, already modified, on 18 April. Other modifications included the removal of the mid-upper gun turret and the fitting of two lights under nose and belly, which were synchronized so that their beams would mesh at exactly 18.3 metres – this being the required flying altitude, computed by Wallis, to ensure the effective launching of the bomb.

At 2110 on 16 May 1943, Gibson ordered a red Very light to be fired from his cockpit, signalling Squadron Leader Joseph McCarty's five aircraft to start rolling for take-off. McCarty, an American serving with the RAF, was to lead five aircraft in a second attack wave. They were to fly over the longer, northern route by turning north at Texel, Holland, then rejoin the main route at the island of Vlieland in the Zuider Zee and make for the Rhine at Kleve.

Gibson himself, with the first wave of bombers, took off from Scampton at 2139, flying over Southwold where he dropped to less than fifty feet over a calm sea. The night was bright and warm, and the pilot flew in his shirtsleeves, opening his side window to let in some fresh air. Flying next to him on his right was Flight Lieutenant John Hopgood's Lancaster, on his left that flown by Flight Lieutenant 'Micky' Martin, an Australian. The 'Dambuster' formation crossed the Dutch coast at ground level at 2300 hours, using three different crossing points. But the German radars had already found them some distance out at sea.

As the Lancasters rumbled over the offshore flak ships, they were able to evade their fire, but the air defence centre at Glize-Rijen was fully operative, although still unaware of the target at which the bombers were aiming. The low-flying bombers now took their first losses. Over Texel, Sergeant Pilot Byers was hit by a 105mm anti-aircraft gun firing pointblank; the aircraft crashed into the Waddensee, while the bomb he was carrying exploded four weeks later – four weeks of terror for the local population.

Farther south, Gibson's formation sped over the dikes north of Antwerp. Making for the Rhine, they jumped over high-tension wires, warned by the bomb-aimer in the nose. Navigating by landmarks such as visible canals or road and rail junctions, the formation reached the German border near Venlo, and headed north-east to the IP south of Münster, just beyond the River Rhine. Near Haldern Flight Lieutenant Barlow had been blinded by searchlights and crashed. A little later, near Marbeck, Flight Lieutenant Bill Astell crashed into a high-tension pylon and a ball of flame could be seen spreading in the black sky.

Gibson's formation had by this time passed into the Ruhr valley, where the outer defences poured light flak into the weaving, jinking bombers, still flying in close formation. Passing over some trees, however, they came to a Luftwaffe airfield which had not been marked on RAF intelligence charts. Searchlights opened up on the leading aircraft, blinding the pilots, but as they passed low over the runway, the three rear-gunners exchanged fire with the German flak towers, before the bombers plunged once again into the darkness.

The pilots were getting very tired, sweating profusely both from nerves and from the fatigue of flying low, which required the exertion of considerable force. The lack of co-pilot, always a problem with the Lancasters, now made things extremely difficult, as one pilot had to handle the controls by himself, all the way there and, hopefully, back. In some of the more experienced crews, the flight engineer stood near the pilot, to assist if necessary in working the heavy controls. Every man had his job, though: navigators peered at their charts, while bomb-aimers tried their best to penetrate the darkness and warn their pilots of approaching obstacles. Every bridge, hamlet and hill was a potential menace as it appeared, to be left behind with a sigh of relief.

The formation was just passing Dortmund and Hamm, a well known target to veteran bomber pilots, when it reached the little town of Soest. They traversed a low, wooden-covered hill and there, below them, saw the dark waters of the great Moehne lake shimmering in the bright moonlight; and there, squat and sinister, was the dam itself, looming up like a great battleship at sea.

At ten minutes past midnight on 17 May 1943, Gibson's Lancaster was still ten minutes away from the target. John Pulford, the flight engineer, had just set the Wallis bomb revolving as briefed, and the navigator, Pilot Officer Torger Taerum, was making his final adjustments ready to operate the special spotlights which had been fitted to acquire the exact altitude for the bomb run.

On the ground, the silence was still unbroken; the guards inside the watchtowers over the dam were trying hard not to doze off, lulled by the monotonous sounds made by the pacing lookout on the gun position above. The villagers, ignorant of the fate which awaited them, had been asleep for hours as Wing Commander Gibson's Lancasters roared low over their final stretch.

At twenty-five minutes past midnight, the German gunners heard the noise of the approaching engines and saw the bombers coming in low over the water. Several things started to happen at once: The telephone at the 20mm anti-aircraft gun position rang. It was the duty officer at Schwansbell Castle near Luenen, the sector air defence headquarters, alerting all defence forces on the dam. While he was speaking, the German guard yelled back over the roar of the planes that the bombers were already overhead and attacking. He slammed down the receiver and raced for cover as his position came under fire from the Browing guns of Sergeant Deering's Lancaster. The German gunners fired in the general direction of the engine noise but the low-flying bombers were still invisible, merging with the dark waters of the lake. The only illumination was that of the tracers from the Lancasters' guns.

Suddenly two bright beams pierced the surface of the lake as Gibson's navigator got ready to drop the bomb at its exact destination. Gibson, sweating in his seat but completely composed, guided the heavy bomber towards the dam wall which grew menacingly as he thundered in at water level. The German gunners started to pump bullets at the bomber, some of which could be heard to 'ping' as they struck home. The pilot controlled the bomber, checking height and speed, until the Pilot Officer John Spafford, his face glued to the bomb sight squeezed the release button and announced 'Mine gone!'. The German gunners ducked as the four-engined monster, spitting fire, roared on, almost scraping the dam's parapet. As it passed over, Flight Lieutenant Hutchinson, the radio operator, fired red Very lights, blinding the gunners below.

As Gibson hurled his aircraft into a tight right turn, the rear-gunner opened fire with his four machine-guns on the German gun positions. Then they had reached the safety of darkness, clear of danger. Gibson's mine, rotating at 500 rpm and bouncing three times over the water as designed, hit the dam wall near the waterline and sank. An eerie silence followed, then seconds later a terrific detonation could be heard. The blast sucked the wind out of the German gunners' lungs, while a 300-metre-high column of water rose into the air, white foam covering the dam and hiding it from view. Gibson and his crew, cruising above, watched eagerly but, when the water subsided, the dam was still intact.

Gibson called in the next aircraft in line to attack. Its pilot was Flight Lieutenant John Hopgood, a 21-year-old Englishman, with two DFCs already to his credit. With his usual determination the young pilot slammed his heavy bomber into a tight turn and, dropping low over the lake, aimed for the dam wall, which seemed to come at him with terrifying speed. But the Germans had by now recovered from their initial shock and were ready for him. Hopgood lined his aircraft up over the far side of the lake and raced towards the dam wall, a sitting target as his bomb-aimer lined up his sight trajectory. Gibson, who was circling above, flicked on his navigation lights in an attempt to draw the enemy fire, but the Germans concentrated on the approaching aircraft. Although Hopgood's front gunner fired furiously, 20mm shells whipped into the British bomber, and a flame appeared, coming from the port inboard engine. Hopgood calmly went on with the bomb run, ordering his flight engineer to feather the burning engine. The fire subsided for a moment, but soon rekindled, sweeping the whole of the port wing as the stricken bomber, relieved of its load, lurched upwards. The bomb fell, but, bouncing once too often, dropped over the dam wall on to the power station behind and, as the Lancaster, now blazing from end to end, flew over, the bomb exploded with a blinding flash, completely destroying the power station. Hopgood, having fought a losing battle with the controls of his ship, yelled to his crew to bail out. Two men succeeded in getting out at the very last minute before the giant aircraft, blazing like a huge torch, crashed into the ground near the village of Ostronnen, a few kilometres from the dam, killing all those left on board. But the dam had withstood Hopgood's attack.

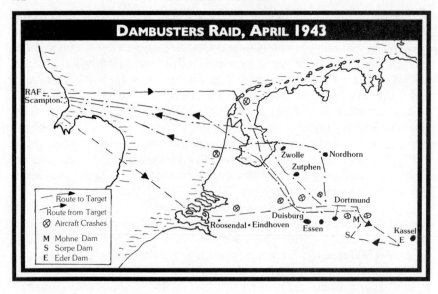

Gibson, watching the tragedy unfolding below, had to swallow hard, but, knowing the work had to go on, ordered the next man, Flight Lieutenant Micky Martin, to start his bomb run. Martin, an Australian veteran with 36 operations to his credit, had no illusions as to what he was facing, especially as he was coming in from the same direction as Gibson and Hopgood, so that the Germans had had time to fix the precise range. As he came in, they let fly with all their guns and the bomber was hit repeatedly, but his experienced bomb-aimer, Bob Hay, guided the pilot calmly towards the target. Once again the bomb dropped and the lake seemed to shake with the gigantic explosions, cascades of water and foam rising high into the night, but incredibly the wall still stood, defying its attackers.

Two men were crouched in the undergrowth up on the hill, watching with total fascination as the drama took place only a few hundred metres away from them. One was Flying Officer Tony Burcher, a member of Hopgood's crew, who had managed to bail out of the burning plane. Stunned by his fall, he was leaning against a tree while he watched. Also taking cover was the foreman of the German power station, who had made his escape only seconds before the building was destroyed. They were now privileged to watch one of the greatest bombing actions of the war.

To Gibson, although less than ten minutes had passed since he dropped his own bomb, it seemed like an eternity. Chafing with frustration and impatience, he called in Squadron Leader Melvyn Young, an American-born flight commander, who unhesitatingly dropped down towards the lake, while Gibson and Martin circled round firing at the defences to divert their attention. At precisely 0040 Young dropped his bomb, but once again it failed to breach the dam. The situation was now getting very dangerous: the attack had been going on for too long and Luftwaffe night fighters were on their way to the area, scrambled urgently from nearby airfields. Luckily, though, local telephone lines had been disrupted by the bombing, so the Germans had very little idea of what was really going on.

But now it was Flight Lieutenant David Maltby's turn to attack. As he raced for the dam, determined to breach it this time, his aircraft roared low over the wall, dropping dangerously low behind it. A huge wave cascaded over and then, suddenly, as the Germans watched in awe and terror, a crack became visible in the thick wall. It widened rapidly, water starting to come through. The fleeing defenders saw a great column of water rushing through the beach, cascading downwards like a giant waterfall into the valley, the air full of foam and spray. The Moehne Dam was breached! Gibson and the other crews watched in fascination, even diving down and circling around to get a better view. Tony Burcher saw it too, from his hiding-place.

At precisely 0056 Gibson ordered his radio operator to send out the message of success. On the ground millions of tons of water rushed through the valley, spreading ever more widely. Complete villages disappeared in minutes; cars, mostly military transport from nearby bases, were flooded and overturned, their headlights flickering dimly through the water until they went out.

Their work at the Moehne completed, Gibson led his remaining aircraft to the second objective of the night – the Eder dams.

But there was a third target. Twenty kilometres to the south of the Moehne dam was the Sorpe, a concrete dam containing some seventy million cubic metres of water. Originally the Sorpe dam had been designated to the second attack formation led by Squadron Leader Joe McCarty with four aircraft. However, McCarty reached the target quite alone, the rest of his formation either lost or having had to abort. McCarty found the Sorpe dam with some difficulty, as there was a morning mist creeping into the valley. He made his run in across the lake without encountering any opposition, but realizing that he was alone, he took no chances and made ten trial runs before releasing his bomb. It hit home precisely as planned, and crumbled the dam first time, allowing McCarty to return home without further ado.

Seventy kilometres south of Kassel, Gibson led his four remaining Lancasters, of which three still had bombs, straight to the Eder dam. Four hundred metres long and almost fifty high, it acted as a regulating reservoir for a strategic waterway, the Mittelland Canal, which connected the Ruhr valley and Berlin. At about 0130, as Gibson's force arrived over the dam, the morning mist was settling over the target, which was located in a deep river gorge surrounded by wooded hills. The plan was to attack over the lake, which was the only direction allowing sufficient space for the bomb run. Gibson first called in the Australian Flight Lieutenant David Shannon, the youngest member of the squadron but one of its best pilots, to begin the attack.

There were only a few people awake at the time, but coincidentally, only a few hours before, during a routine meeting the local civil defence warden had raised the matter of a possible attack on the dams, only to be told by the authorities that this was highly unlikely. Now he was awakened by the noise of the Lancasters and, looking out of his window, could even see one of the air crew also looking out! Starting his dive over the 300-metre-high Waldecke Castle, Shannon flew his bomber in and, aiming for the wall, levelled out after a steep dive from 350 to 20 metres – an extremely difficult manoeuvre with a heavily laden bomber, demanding both physical and flying skill.

The first run failed and Shannon pulled the bomber, engines roaring into a steep turn and tried again. In all he made five runs, until Gibson ordered him to stop and take a break, calling Squadron Leader Henry Maudsley to try his luck. Maudsley flung the great Lancaster into the valley as if it were a model aeroplane, and ran straight for the dam. He too failed the first time, and had to have two more tries. Gibson and Shannon both watched as he fired a red Very light, signalling that he had dropped the bomb . . . but it bounced and overshot, hitting the parapet and detonating precisely as Maudsley's bomber passed overhead. The aircraft, although badly hit, managed to gain height and flew off but misfortune struck once again when, near Emmerich, close to the Dutch border, a lucky shot by light flak caused the aircraft to crash.

Just before two o'clock, Dave Shannon tried again and flying back into the valley, dropped his bomb, resulting in an enormous pillar of water. A gap could be seen in the dam, but in order to make sure Gibson ordered Flight Lieutenant Les Knight, the last man with a bomb, to attack. After one dummy run with Gibson flying beside him, Knight let his bomb go. It hit the wall exactly in place, exploded, and made a large breach, causing a huge tidal wave to gush down into the valley below.

On the road leading to the Eder Valley, a convoy of military vehicles, their blue black-out headlamps wavering in the morning fog, was passing through a village as a dispatch-rider caught up with them, screaming for an immediate evacuation. All the population, military and civilian, rushed out of their houses and made for the high ground as water engulfed the valley and houses and vehicles vanished in the flood. Gibson and his remaining crews watched the awesome sight. Then, their work completed, those Dambusters who had survived the night set out for home.

35. AT GROUND LEVEL TO PLOESTI

During the Second World War the US Air Force was officially in favour of high-level bombardment of German war resources and, following the arrival of the Eighth Air Force in Great Britain, 'boxes' of high-flying B-17 Flying Fortresses became a common sight in the skies of Central Europe. Although the American planners had been impressed by the courage and daring of the RAF Lancaster raids on Augsburg and the Ruhr dams, they felt that the cost of such raids in men and aircraft was not justified by the borderline results. There are exceptions, however, to every rule; some Americans, both airmen and officers, differed with their top brass as to the effectiveness of low-level attack on certain targets. Ploesti was one of those exceptions.

Ploesti in Roumania was one of the largest oil production complexes in Europe, its vital facilities the best defended, with hundreds of German anti-aircraft guns surrounding the entire region. The V-shaped valley in which the main oil installations were located was formed by two sloping ridges of the Buzau Mountains which also provided excellent defensive positions overlook-ing the area. The facility was also within range of many Luftwaffe fighter bases. The main one at Mizil housed JG-4 Squadron's Messerschmitt Bf-109s, commanded by a well-known fighter ace, Hans 'Asi' Hahn. The NG-6 Squadron with its black-painted Me-110 twin engined fighter destroy-ers was posted at Zilistea, a few miles to the east, while on the outskirts of Bucharest, several fighter bases fielded locally-built low-wing IAR-80 fighters. As if this were not enough, Italian, Roumanian and German fighter units were also stationed around the area.

As Ploesti was out of the range of RAF aircraft operating from the Middle East, high-flying Soviet bombers usually had the job of attacking it, but unfortunately they had scored most of their hits on decoy targets placed some distance away from the genuine installations. However, RAF reconnaissance aircraft had by now identified these decoys and co-operative Roumanians and some Americans who had worked there before the war also gave more information on location of the real Ploesti installations.

The first American attack on Ploesti was a high-level mission flown on 11 June 1942 by a force led by Colonel Harry Halverson. Briefed by British intelligence, the American pilots took off from RAF Fayid in the Suez Canal zone and, after an uneventful flight of 1,300 kilometres, all in darkness, they hit the proper target, completely surprising the defenders, but, as only thirteen Liberators had taken part in the raid, the results were negligible.

This attack taught the USAAF planners that they could reach Ploesti but that in order to do some real damage, a massive airstrike would be necessary. But the element of surprise was essential: a way had to be found to evade the well-placed German radar stations in the Aegean islands, Greece and the Balkans. As the discussions continued, it became apparent that the only chance lay in a carefully planned low-level mission, flown by expert crews. The first airman to plump for a zero-altitude attack was Colonel Jacob E. Smart, one of the pick of the bomber commanders, who was chosen to plan the mission.

In order to prove the validity of low-level tactics, Smart and a friend, Colonel Keith Compton, commander of the 376 Bombardment Group, decided on an experiment: a ground-level attack on a heavily defended target near Messina in southern Italy, to be carried out by three B-24 Liberators, led by a top-notch pilot named Major Norman Appold. Taking off at midnight from Luqa airfield in Malta, Appold's three aircraft flew at wavetop height, the bombardiers who sat in the nose getting soaked with spray. At dawn the pilots encountered heavy mist over the Straits of Messina and decided to head for the Italian mainland. Appold and his companions flew contour over the cloud-covered Calabrian Mountains, shaving the ridges and plunging into ravines, then storming across a Luftwaffe airfield and slamming their bombs into a factory at Crotone. This raid was followed almost at once by another, flown by a Major Favelle. Favelle, too, knocked out his target, but on turning away he ran straight into a German formation of Ju-52 transports taking off from a nearby airbase. Their forward guns blazing, the Liberators headed east for home, leaving two of the Junkers on the ground in flames. Colonel Smart's low-level tactics had been vindicated. The Ploesti raid was on.

On 1 August 1943 178 Liberators rumbled over the North African desert at Benghazi, their 712 Pratt & Whitney engines whipping up a sandstorm as they took off. The ground crews, their eyes watering from the dust, waited at the take-off station to top up the fuel tanks, ensuring that the aircraft would have enough fuel for the long ride ahead. One by one the heavily laden bombers took off. Operation 'Tidal Wave' had begun. Suddenly disaster struck when one bomber crashed soon after take-off and the contents exploded, killing all the crew.

Once up in the clear air, each bomber took its assigned place in the formation; they flew low over the sea, heading north towards the first assembly point. Unknown to them, the Luftwaffe's radio monitoring station in Greece had already become aware that there was a mission, although they did not yet know where the Liberators were heading. Nearing Corfu, there was another accident when the lead aircraft of 376 BG, with Flavelle at the controls, suddenly began to veer wildly, dipping up and down in wild gyrations, until it finally fell into the sea, taking with it the navigator for the entire group, probably the most important man on the mission, since he was the only one who could identify all the markers on the route and pinpoint the targets. This loss was to have serious repercussions.

Over the mainland, the aircraft climbed to 10,000 feet to cross the Greek mountain ridges, running into thick cloud as they rose. The pilots scattered to prevent collisions as they were flying blind on instrument control, but the clouds lifted before they arrived in Roumanian airspace, and they reassembled into their formations.

Quickly dropping to treetop height, the bombers flew over the lovely plains of Roumania. They were watched by open-mouthed peasants, some of them in their Sunday best, out making the most of the sunshine. Some of the Americans waved to them, smiling at their astonishment. But their smiles were soon gone.

The loss of the group lead navigator now began to have its inevitable effect on the mission. As the lead group, Keith Compton's 376, the Liberados, approached Targoviste, the ancient capital of Roumania, the colonel mistook it for the turning-point, and took a right turn, flying parallel to the railway line below.

He should have flown on farther, to Floresti, and then turned right. Now the lead group was twenty miles short of the Initial Point leading to Ploesti and the present heading would take them straight into the centre of the German defences at Bucharest! The group followed its leader, however, although

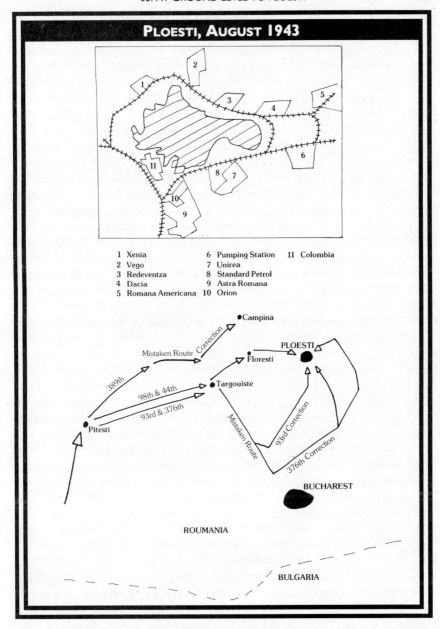

PLOESTI, AUGUST 1943

1 Xenia	6 Pumping Station	11 Colombia
2 Vego	7 Unirea	
3 Redeventza	8 Standard Petrol	
4 Dacia	9 Astra Romana	
5 Romana Americana	10 Orion	

many of the pilots broke radio silence to warn of the wrong turning. Lieutenant Colonel Addison Baker's 93rd Group also followed Compton.

On the ground the Germans were ready for the attackers. In the defence centre at Bucharest a young Prussian officer with the unlikely name of Douglas Pitcairn of Perthshire pressed the alarm button in front of him. Pitcairn was the descendant of a Scottish clan which had emigrated to East Prussia a hundred years before. He had fought as a fighter pilot in Spain and, following crash injuries, now served as a ground controller in one of the tightest spots in Europe.

Colonel Baker almost immediately realized that he had led his group into the wrong turn; he could see the smoke of the Ploesti refinery from his window and decided to turn left – a decision which would have disastrous consequences if he was wrong. But he stuck with his decision and turned left, halfway to Bucharest, while Compton's group carried on. Baker's co-pilot John Jerstad, the youngest major on the mission, who had been in on the plan from its inception, fully agreed with his boss. Baker's group roared fast over the ground to make up for the time they had lost.

Three different forces were now making for three different targets and the German ground controllers became quite confused. Baker's group went for Ploesti across strips of tall green corn and, as they went even lower to form up, some of the bombers later found stalks of Roumanian corn stuck in their bomb bays! As Baker led his aircraft into the attack, they had to evade balloon cables which were festooned with explosives and they were also attacking from an unfamiliar direction, due to taking the wrong turning at Targoviste, so that all the weeks of briefings and rehearsals were in vain. But they stuck to the attack.

The battle over Ploesti began in earnest when guns began to fire from point-blank range at the approaching bombers, Co-pilots did their best to point out the sources of fire to their gunners. Some gunners were hit, moved aside from their guns, while other men took control. The pilots attempted to duck even lower to avoid the guns, flying between smokestacks. Baker and Jerstad held their course, although to their left and right aircraft were hit, some crashing in flames. Suddenly Baker's was seen to be hit by a balloon cable which snapped, and the balloon went straight up. Then the flagship was hit by an 88mm shell which smashed the front nose. Smoke was streaming from the aircraft, but the pilot carried on steadfastly. Just before reaching the target, Baker's plane took yet another hit; it was burning from end to end, but he led them right up to the refinery stacks at the large Vega works. Once over, the aircraft finally died. Tipping right wing over, it nearly hit the bomber piloted by Colonel Brown, who took evasive action, before Baker's ship, engulfed in flames, crashed into a field. Not one man managed to jump.

Meanwhile, bombers were attacking everywhere. Colonel Kane's 98th Group attacked the Astra Romano plant, with devastating effect, while Keith Compton's 376th had finally made its escape from the Bucharest defence perimeter and reached Ploesti from the south-east, attacking the Romana Americana works, formerly owned by Americans. Soon the entire valley was engulfed in thick smoke and flames. Some pilots, trying to escape the fire, flew so low that, in certain cases, the anti-aircraft gunners were higher than their targets, and some shot at each other! Their bombs away, the bombers raced back through the refineries, releasing their delayed-action bombs, while the pilots struggled with their controls to avoid the blazing buildings. Not all made it, though: One Liberator slid along a macadamed street and exploded at the end of it, another slammed right into a four-storey building which crumbled upon impact. One very skilled pilot managed to crash-land his blazing bomber in a field, saving all his crew, but some of the aircraft collided with others in the air, and exploded.

Then the German fighters came into battle, disregarding the thick flak. Some of them were hit by their own defenders, but they carried on grimly, attacking the bombers almost at ground level. One American bomber slid into a cornfield, flaps down, hitting the ground in a cartwheel which threw several of the crewmen out of the plane. Some walked away, others died.

Once they had put their bombs in the targets, the survivors set out for home, hotly pursued by Asi Hahn's fighter pilots. Low on fuel and constantly harassed, some of the Americans preferred to try for alternative landing strips in Cyprus, Malta and even Turkey, but the Germans alerted their fighter bases in Greece and some of the bombers were caught in an ambush, the unsuspecting pilots having thought that they were out of danger.

Of the 178 bombers which had taken off from Benghazi, 45 were lost over the target; only 88 returned to base, most of them badly damaged. Twenty-three landed at alternative airfields, all damaged. Almost a third of the airmen taking part were killed or wounded. From the point of view of results, however the mission could be accounted a success. Oil production at Ploesti was severely curtailed and in some cases disrupted for several months.

36. LIGHTNING STRIKE TO BAGHDAD

I n 1981 the Iraq-Iran War was in full swing; ceaseless bombardments ploughed the fields into marshland on the borders of both countries; thousands of men died. It was reminiscent of some of the bloody ground battles fought over Flanders during the First World War. But while all this was going on, Iraq's dictator was already preparing his next war. His aim was nothing less than the complete devastation of the State of Israel by weapons of mass destruction. Saddam Hussein knew that his forces, although massive numerically, could not beat Israel: they had experienced total defeat during the 1973 Yom Kippur War, but he had determined to destroy the 'infidel' by using doomsday weapons, doing away with the Israelis once and for all.

Israeli leaders were, naturally, concerned with this new threat, against which there was little or no defence. The nuclear option in the hands of this ruthless dictator had to be prevented by any means possible before it could mature into a destructive weapon. As more and more hard evidence of Iraqi nuclear capability emerged, the Israeli government unanimously voted to go in and destroy the nuclear reactor near Baghdad before it could become active. This decision initiated one of the most daring air operations ever attempted, an operation which required precise planning, since it was understood that failure would bring with it extremely negative political consequences.

In charge of planning on the IAF staff was a very bright young colonel named Aviem Sela, head of the Operations Department, himself a veteran fighter pilot with scores of combat missions to his credit. At that time the Israel Air Force still flew older types of aircraft which had been delivered during the early seventies. These included the American A-4 Skyhawk and F-4 Phantom, both of which had performed superbly during the savage air battles of the Yom Kippur War. While both were excellent combat aircraft, however, their range was limited. This meant that in order to reach a distant target like Baghdad and hava a reasonable chance of returning to base, mid-flight refuelling would have to be carried out over enemy territory – an extremely dangerous operation.

Planning for this mission had begun as early as November 1979 when, during a staff meeting at the IDF GHQ in Tel Aviv, the air force chief of staff, Major General David Ivry, declared that his forces were capable of carrying out the mission, and presented several options. Ezer Weizman, who had once commanded the Air Force himself, and was now Defence Minister in Menahem Begin's government, was somewhat sceptical as he listened to the options. The first involved Skyhawk and Phantom fighter-bombers refuelling in flight with heavy support; the other two were variants, only the flight route there and back being slightly different. Many of the officers were concerned about the refuelling process over hostile territory, considering that high losses and/or captured airmen might result, with all the political problems entailed in those scenarios.

Then Israel had a stroke of luck which altered the entire picture. The Shah of Persia had ordered large numbers of modern fighter planes from the USA, but following the Khomeini revolution in 1979, all exports had been stopped. Thus the first batch of F-16 fighters, which Israel had been expecting only in the eighties, were delivered immediately. General Ivry, familiar with the characteristics of this super-modern fighter, was convinced that the F-16 could fly the mission without refuelling en route, attack the designated target, and also defend itself once clear of the reactor so that almost no support would be needed to and from the reactor.

The F-16 Fighting Falcons arrived and were quickly integrated into the Israel Air Force. Lieutenant-Colonel Razi, a veteran fighter pilot who had logged a large number of F-4 Phantom sorties, and who commanded the first F-16 squadron to arrive, had spent several months training with the USAF, becoming highly proficient on the aircraft and its flight profile, and wishing nothing better than to test its superb capabilities as soon as possible. However, when he and his navigation officer were briefed about the mission by Colonel Sela, Razi was astounded. He left the briefing room at GHQ, in his own words, with his 'ears ringing like church bells'. His responsibility was tremendous: not only did he have to fly a 2,500-kilometre mission unsupported, but also he had flown the new F-16 for only a relatively short time and had a lot to learn, as did the younger pilots in the group. But the challenge was something that no fighter pilot in the world could refuse.

Razi and his navigator, therefore, sat down to some meticulous planning sessions in order to hammer out the technical details for this tricky operation. Two major problems had to be resolved: first, whether they could fly unrefuelled; if the weather turned bad in mid-flight, they would be in trouble and it was impossible to predict the weather so far ahead of time. Razi was convinced that he could do it, if he could fit sufficient drop tanks on the aircraft. His instructors in the USA had warned him against dropping empty fuel tanks while flying with external hardware loads, as it could be dangerous, but after long deliberations with technical experts, Razi and Sela decided to take a chance and ignore the warning. In any case, there was no alternative if the tricky and dangerous option of in-flight refuelling were ruled out.

The second, and more difficult decision, was the actual destruction of the reactor. It was decided to attack with 1,000kg bombs aimed from an attack angle of 45 degrees, with delayed-action fuzes to facilitate penetration into the reactor core after smashing its outer concrete walls. It was thought that eight F-16s would be the ideal number. They would attack in two flights, one after another in quick succession – five-second intervals between each aircraft. F-15 Eagles would provide top cover, while electronic aircraft would jam hostile radars and missile sites, and in-place Medevac helicopters would be on stand-by to pick up aircrews who had to bail out. Two additional F-16s and four pilots would also be available to step in at the last moment if necessary.

The date for the attack was provisionally set for 10 May 1981, and Razi, the F-16 wing commander, after much badgering of the Chief of Staff, had stepped down in rank so as to be accepted as an ordinary line pilot on the mission. The first four-aircraft formation would be led by him, the second by Major Hami, the other F-16 squadron leader. Most of the pilots selected were quite high-ranking officers, normally formation leaders, who had willingly agreed to fly as line pilots just to be in on the show.

After a last-minute briefing by Chief of Staff Lieutenant-General Rafael Eitan and David Ivry at the Etzion airbase in Sinai, the pilots were just ready to climb into their cockpits when an urgent telephone message from Prime Minister Begin called off the mission at the very last moment. It transpired that Defence Minister Ezer Weizman had had second thoughts and persuaded his boss to postpone the mission. But not for long. Actually, it was extremely lucky that things turned out that way because, when he checked the time-delay fuze settings, Colonel Razi found to his amazement that the technical officer had set them wrong, much shorter than was required to penetrate into the reactor core.

The next date was set for 7 June, the eve of an important Jewish holiday. Three days before, Ivry and several of his senior officers had flown to Naples in Italy to participate in a ceremony marking the changing over of commanders of the US 6th Fleet. No one outside their closed circle had any inkling that something was brewing back in Israel.

On Sunday 7 June the weather was clear in the southern Negev and Sinai as the aircrews assembled for yet another briefing before setting off on their formidable assignment. The briefing went well and every pilot was sure that he knew his own task thoroughly. The first formation was to blast the reactor's outer walls and smash the cupola by penetrating with delayed-action bombs into the interior, where the explosion would create a chain reaction. The second formation would act as back-up to make sure that, no matter what, the reactor would be totally destroyed. The Met people reported that a sandstorm was blowing inside Saudi Arabia and Iraq, with visibility up to 500 metres, but the latest Baghdad weather was clear, with high clouds and visibility of more than 10 kilometres. They also predicted that the sandstorms would subside during the afternoon, a good omen for the return flight.

While preparations were being made at the Etzion air base, Hawkeye early warning aircraft were already on station, their long-range radars combing the sky for enemy activity. Electronic aircraft activated their sensors, looking deep inside enemy territory for suspected aircraft. All was ready for the big show. Shortly before 1400, the fighter pilots were already strapped into their seats, with ground crews scrambling to make final adjustments. The aircraft were heavily loaded with bombs and drop tanks. Colonel Razi had double checked with the technical officers that the fuzes were set right this time.

The fighting Falcons lined up and taxied to their check-points at the end of the runway, where everyone did their last pre-flight checks once again, just to make sure. At 1457 Razi, nodding his head, signalled straight ahead with his forefinger. Ground crews, wearing ear mufflers, topped up the fuel tanks, so that they would be full to the brim on take-off – every drop of fuel would count on this mission. Razi pushed his throttle and afterburner to full power and, as the engine started to wind up, he began to thunder down the runway, his wingman lined up with him. Soon the whole formation was airborne, each aircraft in place. The other formation took off soon after and, gaining altitude fast, the jets disappeared from view at four thousand feet.

Here fate, and the weather, took a hand. In order to evade the Jordanian radars along the Aqaba coast, it had originally been planned to fly round it from the south. Shortly before take-off, however, the wind changed, forcing the jet-fighters to take off in a north-westerly direction, instead of the planned south-easterly one. This new direction took them slap over Aqaba, where they crossed at low level straight over King Hussein's royal yacht. The king, himself a pilot who often flew jets, immediately recognized the Israeli jets and, judging by their direction, knew that they presented no danger to his own kingdom. But as a close friend and ally of Saddam Hussein, he telephoned his headquarters in Amman and ordered the duty officer to warn Baghdad. Whether or not his call was answered is not known, but it so happened that Saddam Hussein was absent at the time, visiting his troops along the Iranian front.

As his formation crossed the Gulf of Aqaba, Razi could see the many ships at anchor, unloading vital supplies to bolster Iraq against the Iranians; then they were over the Saudi coastline heading for the rugged mountains which they crossed at 300 feet, flying in the valleys between the mountains to escape detection by Saudi radars at Tabouk airbase. Ninety minutes of flying time lay ahead. All radio and electronic systems on board were shut down, to avoid detection by the sensors, which continually swept the area.

To prevent boredom, which could lead to attention lapses during a monotonous flight, Razi ordered a climb after one hour and, signalling this, he took the formation up to five hundred feet to rest the pilots' eyes. Then it was time to drop the first fuel tanks and, finding a remote place within the mountains, he ordered the crews to jettison. Once the tanks were clear the speed increased to 450 knots.

Soon afterwards the formations entered Iraqi airspace and the scenery changed as they approached the Euphrates and Tigris river basin with all its greenery, a complete – and welcome – change from the boring desert wastes over which they had been flying for hours. Breaking electronic silence, Razi ordered the Halon pressure on, a measure which could save lives if fuel tanks were hit by enemy fire. Thundering at 'beer bottle' height over the green pastures, the pilots could see peasants craning their necks.

Now they were crossing the Euphrates, a large tract of water covering vast areas of land. No enemy fire was encountered, and no MiGs were seen on the radar scopes. As they neared the target, hugging the ground, the sense of speed was tremendous. The outskirts of the great capital were already looming ahead when Razi, turning on his air-to-air button, searched for the navigational point, a small island in the great lake, but could not find it. However, the nuclear reactor dome could be seen clearly, shining in the afternoon sun. Still no enemy fire or fighters on the scopes. It seemed too good to be true!

Ordering a sharp climb to ten thousand feet, Razi took his formation straight into the target area and then, diving first with full afterburner, he went down at 600 knots, rolling upside down at 35 degrees until the computer's pixel started shrieking, as the bombs were released. The g pressure became tremendous as the colonel hauled his fighter out of its dive, pulling up and out and releasing IR chaff as he went, for good measure; but, apart from some light flak there was no enemy reaction. The eight fighter-bombers attacked, as briefed, at five-second intervals and, as Major Hami attacked, he could already see the cupola disintegrating in a fiery ball, smashing on to the outer walls. Utter devastation could be seen below as the last ship pulled up and left the target area. All reported in by radio to Razi, although one of the younger pilots gave them all some tense seconds until he came on. Over the River Euphrates the formation climbed to 42,000 feet and, clear of their weight load, increased their speed to 600 knots.

As they set course westward the pilots could see an airliner coming in to land at Baghdad International Airport, but no Iraqi fighters came up to intercept them. No missiles were fired, although Iraqi gunners kept on firing their anti-aircraft guns over the reactor site – at an empty sky.

The flight home was uneventful although, as they crossed the Jordanian border with Iraq, near H-3, the frontier airfield, some activity could be seen on the radar scopes; but no one came up to intercept the returning fighters, now in full flight for home. The landing was easy; no victory rolls were allowed and General Ivry personally broke in on the radio frequency, telling the pilots to land carefully so that no last-minute disasters would mar their success.

As Razi was driving home to his family to celebrate the holiday, he gave a lift to a soldier who was holding a transistor radio in his hand. Just as he started the engine the news came over the air, annoucing to an astonished world that the IAF had smashed the Osiris nuclear reactor near Baghdad. The great secret was finally out.

Now, nearly eleven years later, as more and more evidence comes to light of Saddam Hussein's nuclear and other mass-destruction capabilities, when almost every day the post-'Desert Storm' United Nations investigation teams stumble on new hideouts of yet more non-conventional weapons, one can understand better how much effort the dictator invested in bringing Iraq to the nuclear option. No one can know how ready he was to use it – but we can guess.

PART FOUR
Warriors of the Sea

37. SINKING THE TIRPITZ

T he German battleship *Tirpitz* had perhaps the most inglorious and tragic wartime career of all the Second World War warships. She never saw action against the British fleet, her activities being limited to a few furtive excursions from her hiding-place in the Norwegian fiords. Even so, she presented a constant threat to British shipping and it took large forces to keep her bottled-up until she was finally destroyed in the winter of 1944.

Tirpitz was, with her sister ship, *Bismark*, the most powerful ship in the world. With her deep-water displacement of more than 42,000 tons, she carried a large variety of guns, the biggest being 15-inchers in massive turrets, of which there were eight, twelve 5.9-inch and scores of smaller 37mm and 20mm anti-aircraft guns. The ship was heavily armoured, her sides being more than twelve inches thick and her deck a massive eight inches. In spite of this she could develop a speed of more than 30 knots and could outrun any fast destroyer at that time. The German warship completely outclassed any British battleship.

Tirpitz was launched in April 1939 at Wilhelmshaven docks in the presence of the Führer and many prominent Nazis who saw the occasion as a gesture of defiance against the Royal Navy, who had ruled the seas until then. Her sister ship, *Bismark*, gave the Royal Navy a nasty shock when she sailed out into the Atlantic Ocean in 1941 and demonstrated her powerful armament and high speed by striking at urgently required convoys headed for the British Isles. One can only imagine what would have happened if the two German battleships had acted in concert.

The fates decreed, however, that *Tirpitz* was not battle-ready until February 1941 and, a few months later, *Bismark* was sunk during a famous naval action in the Irish Sea. The loss of *Bismark* shocked German naval commanders, together with Hitler himself, who decided to guard *Tirpitz* from a similar fate by ordering her to leave for Trondheim in Norway, where he believed she would be safe from British attack.

The British Admiralty was very unhappy with the new deployment. At that time, the convoys to northern Russia were at their height and any danger to the shipping routes in northern waters might make a crucial difference to the war effort there; *Tirpitz*'s speed and armament presented a threat which had to be thwarted. Many bombing attacks were therefore flown against the Norwegian fiords, but without success.

On 6 March 1942 *Tirpitz*, with an escort of three destroyers, left her hideout at Trondheim and made for the open sea. The flotilla was quickly spotted by a British submarine. She alerted the Home Fleet which, taking no chances, set out with two battleships, a battle cruiser and an aircraft carrier, plus a large escort. As bad weather prevented aerial reconnaissance, the two fleets passed each other with 150 kilometres between them and no contact was made. Two days later, however, the weather cleared and an aircraft sighted *Tirpitz* which was immediately attacked by Fleet Air Arm Albacore torpedo aircraft. Although the British pilots attacked with determination, there were no hits. Breaking contact later that evening, the German battleship was soon safe in Narvik harbour and a few days later she ran the gauntlet of the British submarines and returned to Trondheim.

Hitler and the British Admiralty were both concerned about the short engagement, but for different reasons. The British feared that, if *Tirpitz* were let loose in the Atlantic, she could wreak havoc on the convoys which were already having enough trouble with the 'wolf packs' – groups of German submarines which hunted the shipping lanes incessantly. It was for this reason that the operation to destroy the docks at St-Nazaire in Normandy was initiated and its success wiped out the only dock big enough to give the great battleship refuge, but the British never forgot the need to kill *Tirpitz*.

The most powerful demonstration of the abilities of this giant ship came in the summer of 1942 when the Arctic convoy PQ-17 was nearly annihilated. At that time, the German Naval Command had assembled sufficient means to strike a severe blow at the convoys transporting reinforcements and supplies to Russia, and the warships based in the Norwegian fiords were ideal for the task. These included, apart from *Tirpitz*, the pocket battleship *Admiral Scheer*, the heavy cruiser *Hipper* and scores of destroyers as escorts, all of which assembled in Altenfiord on the northern coast of Norway. As the hapless convoy was pounding through the Barents Sea, however, it was slaughtered by submarines. The larger warships had no share at all in the action and *Tirpitz* was recalled to Trondheim before she had fired a single shot. The rough sea voyage, however, had caused enough damage to require a long-overdue refit and she settled, heavily guarded by mines and submarine nets, in the fiord.

The British decided to take advantage of this opportunity and to disable her by using new methods. On 26 October a fishing boat steered by the outstanding Norwegian resistance leader Leif Larson left the Shetlands and sailed for Norway, carrying six British frogmen and their Human Torpedo mounts, called Chariots. These were two-man craft which the Italians had developed and which had been used successfully in daring ventures against the British fleet in the Mediterranean. The craft carried a 350-kilogram explosive charge, and was powered by an electric motor which drove it at 3–4 knots. En route to their objective the party was hit by bad luck. Extremely rough weather developed as they came within striking distance and, during the violent storm which ensued, the Chariots, which were being towed underwater, broke adrift and were lost. There was nothing for it but to escape to neutral Sweden, which all but one man succeeded in doing. *Tirpitz* had escaped another attack.

Her refit completed in February 1943, the battleship was sent to join the battle cruiser *Scharnhorst* at Altenfiord, increasing considerably the threat to the Arctic convoys. But she was still not involved in any engagement until that September when for the first time *Tirpitz* used her armament in action – and even then, it was hardly a worthy opponent. Both warships were sent to destroy the weather station on Spitzbergen in a hit and run affair, after which *Tirpitz* hurried back to her safe hideout in Norway before the Home Fleet could manage to cut her off. Although the big guns had caused considerable damage, the weather station was back at work only a few days later, and *Tirpitz* had wasted valuable fuel for nothing.

The Royal Navy then decided to attack the battleship with their new X-craft; these midget submarines were crewed by four men, and could remain submerged for 23 hours, although under almost unbearable conditions, as there was almost no space for the crew. They packed a substantial punch, though. Two external, crescent-shaped charges carried two tons of explosives as well as limpet mines. The prototype of the midget submarine had been conceived by Commander Godfrey Herbert before the First World War, but turned down by the Admiralty. During the thirties working plans had been started on a two-man boat, which was later modified. Of the present type, six were delivered for trials in January 1943 when they carried out mock attacks on ships at Loch Cairnbawn, the base for the 12th Submarine Flotilla. The present plan was that six of the midgets would each be towed by a submarine to the entrance of Altenfiord where they would cast off, making their way separately, submerged, to *Tirpitz*.

On 11 September 1943 the X-craft towed by their parent submarines left Loch Cairnbawn and out to sea. Two of them were lost en route. On the evening of 20 September the remaining four were detached to make their way into the fiord, but two more ran into difficulties and were abandoned, leaving only two to carry out the mission. These were X-6 *Piker*, commanded by Lieutenant Donald Cameron, and X-7, whose skipper was Lieutenant Godfrey Place. During the planning stage the RAF had flown several Spitfire reconnaissance sorties over the fiord, the aircraft taking off from the Russian air base at Vaenga, so the midget submarine crews had fairly good information as to the exact position of the ship. The sea passage was very rough, with a gale force wind lashing the sea into huge waves. The small craft pitched and heeled and the crews were violently seasick as they struggled with their controls, trying to keep afloat behind the towing submarines. As they entered the fiord their first obstacle was the hazardous trip through the minefields, but these were cleared with surprising ease. It was bitterly cold and the crews were shivering, nine days of pitching in the stormy seas taking their toll. Lieutenant Cameron stood on a seat with his head out of the open hatch.

He was soaked to the skin and numb with cold, but in spite of the misery he was confident that he could carry out his mission. Now came another hurdle: the craft encountered technical problems, the periscope was flooded and an electric motor burned out, making submerged operation extremely difficult, but Cameron worked the periscope by hand and they approached the gate through the shore-to-shore barrier. By chance, *Tirpitz*'s ship-to-shore communication was malfunctioning, so the gate had been left open for passing boats, although on board the ship a constant hydrophone watch was kept.

Cameron brought his small craft to periscope depth, but could hardly see what was going on. Suddenly he could hear the noise of a ship's propellers passing across his bows so, raising his scope, he saw a patrol boat making straight for the boom which had been lifted to let it through. Taking advantage of this incredible luck, Cameron quickly submerged and followed her in. Once over, he surfaced and started his diesels for maximum speed.

Just at this moment a German petty officer who was leaning on the rail watching some crewmen washing the quarterdeck, saw a glimpse of light shimmerng in the water. At first he thought it was a big porpoise but he soon realized that it was a submarine – only twenty yards from the ship! He sounded the alarm but five precious minutes passed until action stations was sounded, time enough for Cameron to approach his target and attack. Just as he was nearing the gigantic battleship, X-6 fouled a rock and shot upwards towards the surface. Cameron managed to stop her before she broke surface. Through the scuttles he could see a cloud of mud rising up. The gyro compass went out of order and the controls were switched to magnetic. Cameron dived his craft to seventy feet, steadied her and went for *Tirpitz*, ordering the mines released a few yards from the warship's bottom. Then disaster – *Piker* hit the battleship's hull full tilt and was unable to move. There was nothing to do but surface and surrender before the craft was destroyed by the explosion.

It surfaced so near the grey hull of *Tirpitz* that Cameron could have touched it with his hand. Sub-Lieutenant Leine, who had been watching the scene, dashed down the gangway with two armed sailors, jumped into a launch and headed for the midget sub. Hurling grenades and firing submachine-guns, the Germans approached; then the man in the bow threw a grapnel which fell on its deck and hooked on to the hatch just as it opened, and Cameron and three other crew members, haggard and exhausted, came out with their hands up and jumped into the launch.

While Cameron and his crewmen were climbing up to *Tirpitz*'s deck, X-7 started its attack. Lieutenant Place laid his charges near those of X-6, remaining unobserved until he had finished, but when he attempted to make his getaway the boat got entangled with the enclosing net. The small craft was thrown clear by a violent explosion, which badly damaged the submarine and forced it to surface. By now Place's craft had come into full view of the capital ship. Captain Meyer and Commander Junge, who were both on the bridge, alerted by the first explosion, now directed heavy fire at the surfacing craft. Lieutenant Place just had time to run his craft alongside a floating gunnery target on to which he scrambled, waving his white sweater in an attempt to stop the fire. But his submarine sank, taking down with it his remaining three crew members. Astonishingly, one of them, Sub-Lieutenant Aitken, popped up to the surface three hours later, having used his Davis Escape apparatus. But the other two ran out of air and died.

On the ship, the British prisoners were being heavily guarded below deck by sailors carrying Schmeissers when, suddenly, a tremendous explosion rocked the ship, lifting the giant hull right out of the water. The cabin where the prisoners were held went dark and they remained there until a German officer shouted at them to get on deck, where there was much confusion. Men could be seen running wildly in all directions as the great ship began rapidly to list to port, steam gushing from broken pipes. No sight could have been more rewarding to the British sailors, even facing the prospect of a long stay in a German prison camp. But although she was heavily damaged *Tirpitz* did not sink.

Even though she could no longer be considered battle-worthy the British Admiralty would not rest until she was sent to the bottom. In the spring of 1944 the aircraft carriers of the British fleet assembled to mount an air attack on *Tirpitz* and finish her off once and for all. Although the raid achieved total surprise, most of the torpedo-carrying bombers reached their target, and several armour-piercing bombs hit home, the battleship still floated, defying them all, at her moorings.

In the end it took No. 617 Squadron, the Dambusters, led by Wing Commander Willy Tait, to send her to the bottom with blockbuster bombs in November 1944. The first two direct hits pierced the armoured deck, which peeled back like a tin of sardines. Then her magazines blew up in a tremendous explosion which rolled her over. As the Lancasters flew off, the crews could see the long black hull glinting in the water. *Tirpitz* had finally died.

Lieutenant Cameron and Place spent the rest of the war in German prison camps, and returned afterwards to collect the Victoria Cross which each of them had deservedly been awarded.

38. THE HUMAN TORPEDOES

During the Second World War the Italians had one very special, and very renowned, unit. It was the Underwater Division of the 10th MAS Flotilla; deployed in small combat teams, they used manned torpedoes as their principal weapon.

The Italians had always been pioneers in the use of manned torpedoes. As far back as May 1918 they had mounted some daring raids, using special attack craft, on the Austrian Fleet at Pola. In one of these raids, Lieutenant Commander Antonio Pellegrini had penetrated the harbour in an attempt to destroy the warship *Radetzky* which was moored there. Although the raid had failed, it nevertheless caused quite a stir at the time.

There were further developments during the thirties when the 10th Flotilla was raised at La Spezia, and by the outbreak of the war it was ready to begin offensive patrols.

Following the humiliating defeat of the Italian Navy at Taranto, in which several warships were sunk by Fleet Air Arm torpedo-bombers, the 10th swore revenge on the Royal Navy and struck several times at the British. One of these attacks was directed at the British naval base at Suda Bay in northern Crete. On 26 March 1941, just before dawn, an Explosive Motor Boat unit commanded by Lieutenant Luigi Faggioni slipped into the harbour undetected and approached the cruiser *York*, aboard which reveille was just being sounded. Heading for their prey at maximum speed, two MTM struck home and sent their deadly load into its side hull. The explosion caused the cruiser to list and founder almost immediately. The defenders had not anticipated a surface attack and believed that the attack came from low-flying aircraft. It was only after Faggioni was captured that the truth came out, to the amazement of the Royal Navy.

During the summer of 1941 several abortive attacks were made on the Grand Harbour of Valetta in Malta, which led to increased vigilance on the part of the British, who now expected a strike at either Gibraltar or Alexandria. It was, indeed, the latter target that the 10th MAS had in mind.

On 17 December 1941 the Italian submarine *Scire* left her base on the occupied island of Leros in the Dodecanese under her skipper, Captain Count Julion Borghese, a distinguished-looking nobleman, one of the leading submarine captains in the Italian Navy. *Scire* was no ordinary boat. On her deck three large containers were mounted, each containing a slow-running Human Torpedo, also known by their crews as 'Pigs'.

The submarine's skipper was aware that his departure had been observed by Greek agents who would transmit the information to British sources in Cairo, but he knew that the raid on Alexandria harbour, the most important British military port in the Middle East, had been planned very meticulously by the Italian underwater experts. They had been working closely with intelligence officers who received up-to-date information from Egyptian agents, and knew that two of the three major British warships, the battleships HMSS *Valiant* and *Queen Elizabeth*, were in port. The third, HMS *Barham*, was at sea and would be sunk before the raid by a German submarine.

Now Borghese and his 'Pigs' cut thorough the Mediterranean Sea at top speed in the silent darkness. The Italian captain managed to get his boat as close as possible to the Egyptian shore before dawn, dodging British anti-submarine patrols, and entered the shallows off the Nile Delta, which was flooding at this time, making the approach easier for the sub. At 2000 hours on 18 December, Borghese brought his boat to periscope depth, blew his ballast and, as the compressed air roared to the surface, eased the boat to surface in the dark waters. On the horizon, about ten kilometres away,

Alexandria could be seen, lit up by lightning. All was quiet, and Borghese thought they were still undetected.

He ordered the six frogmen to get ready, and they hurried down the conning tower and settled on their craft. The frogmen wore tight-fitting rubber diving suits and heavy goggles; their breathing apparatus was strapped to their
chests. Their craft, fully charged and ready to launch, electric motors humming, came into the water and slid silently off towards their objective.

The group leader was Lieutenant Luigi de la Penne, a young man of twenty-four, who had already gained considerable experience in underwater warfare, and was quite determined to sink a British battleship that night. As the craft parted from their parent boat, Borghese wished them luck, then slammed his tower hatch closed and submerged.

Linked together with cable which kept them in line, the attack craft drove slowly towards the harbour. The crew could hardly be seen: only their heads were above water. Captain de la Penne had been assigned the battleship *Valiant*, a 32,000-ton vessel, while her sister ship, *Queen Elizabeth*, would be attacked by Captain Antonio Maceglia. A third party would go for a loaded tanker and destroy it with incendiary bombs.

After two freezing hours in the icy winter sea, the team saw the beam from Alexandria's Ras-el Tin lighthouse, a welcome indicator, enabling the team leader to get his bearings. Soon the three attack craft approached the breakwater at the harbour entrance. So far they had still not been detected, but suddenly, as he was about to give the order for the three groups to split up, de la Penne saw a patrol boat coming directly at them. The crew was lobbing small depth-charges overboard as it went, a normal precaution against frogmen or small underwater craft. The British boat, although unaware of their presence, had nearly reached them when it abruptly turned away. As soon as it disappeared, the attack leader ordered his party to move towards the submarine nets which barred the port's entrance and search for gaps. None could be found, and attempts to break in failed. Then, as if by magic, the booms were floodlit and dragged open as three British destroyers steamed slowly through the opening. De la Penne, shouting for the other two craft to follow, nearly glued himself to one of the warships and entered through the gap. Once inside the group split up, each one going for his specified target.

De la Penne went straight for the large bulk of the battleship looming up one thousand metres away. It took him a full half-hour to get close enough, all the while hearing the sound of the pinging iron balls in the antisubmarine netting around the ship. As he manhandled the craft over the barrier his crewman, Seaman Emilio Bianchi, was already clear and diving for the bottom of the ship. Above surface, on the deck of the batleship, all was quiet; no one was aware of the danger only inches away from the hull. Submerging just a few metres from the ship, de la Penne brought his 'Pig' to a depth of five metres and hit the hull with a dull thud. Stiff with cold, he could not stop the electric motor, and the craft plunged to the bottom. Bianchi was already

ALEXANDRIA HARBOUR ATTACK, DECEMBER 1941

Arsenal Dock

Mahrussa Quay

Outer Breakwater

Floating Docks

Cruiser

Petroleum Wharf

Valiant

Queen Elizabeth

Timber Wharf

Parent Submarine *Sciré*
Penne and Bianchi
Merceglia and Schergat
Martelotta and Marino
Anti-Submarine netting
Main defence nets

attaching the magnetic charge as de la Penne started manoeuvring his craft so that he could free the torpedo tube beneath the battleship's hull. After a great effort he got it clear, set the fuze, and then struggled to the surface – where he was met by a stream of bullets fired at him by the British crew, now fully alert. Then a small boat came looking for him and he and Bianchi, who had been hugging a nearby buoy, were picked up.

The British officer who began to interrogate them was Commander Buster Crabbe, himself an underwater expert, who was to go missing after the war while inspecting a Russian warship in Portsmouth, creating a full-blown international incident. Both men stood their ground and refused to confess they had fixed their charges. Crabbe, to avoid wasting valuable time, sent them into a locked cabin aboard the battleship exactly over the spot where de la Penne had placed his explosives. Facing certain death, as he knew they would blow in a few minutes, he asked to be taken to the captain and informed him of the imminent explosion, but still adamantly refused to tell him where the charges were placed. The angry skipper sent him right back to his cabin and, within a very few minutes, there was a tremendous explosion which rocked the ship and blew in the locked cabin door. He and Bianchi, amazed that they were unhurt by the blast, raced up the ladders to the deck, which was in total confusion.

Queen Elizabeth was only a short distance away and as they looked at her she too suddenly erupted in a huge explosion, followed by a spurt of water. It looked as if Marceglia and his crewman, Schergat, had done their work well, but as they scrambled into the boats, trying to escape, they were picked up by a shore patrol. The third party also managed to set their charges on to the tanker they had been assigned and were arrested as they swam towards the harbour steps.

That night, offshore, the submarine *Topazio* waited in vain for any of the frogmen to make the rendezvous, but no one came. The prisoners were interrogated and later sent to a prison camp in Palestine, but they earned great respect from the British, who were much impressed by the Italian Commandos' courage and daring.

The Italians and their 'Pigs' had really done a lot of damage. *Valiant* was immobilized for more than a year, a very long period in wartime when warships are at a premium; *Queen Elizabeth* was even worse hit: she actually settled on the harbour bottom, where she remained until raised and sent to the United States for repairs. She saw no action until shortly before the end of the war. With three underwater craft and six men, the 10th Flotilla had, at a single stroke, reversed the balance of naval power in the Mediterranean.

39. ISRAEL'S NAVAL COMMANDOS IN ACTION

Early in the winter of 1940, about forty members of the *Hagana* (the Jewish defence organization in Palestine) who had undergone seamanship training were called to a meeting at Haifa, when volunteers were requested for a secret mission behind the enemy lines. A few days later a group of thirty men assembled at the fairgrounds in north Tel Aviv, where they met British Army experts who were to train them in the art of naval demolition work. Their top secret training lasted for several months.

Later, during the battle for Greece, where the Germans were pushing the British forces back towards the sea, a team of six *Hagana* trainees took part in a special Commando operation, blowing up part of the Corinth channel in order to delay the German advance, while two other teams participated in rescue operations off the island of Crete.

The British military wanted a team to blow up the Vichy French oil refineries at Tripoli in northern Syria. Detailed information on the objective had been supplied to the British by special agents who were operating in the area disguised as local Arabs. The target, located about one kilometre from the sea shore, was heavily guarded by Senegalese troops holding gun positions in the nearby hills.

This operation called for highly motivated troops, and the British decided to let the Jews, who had long been itching for action, have a go. In all, twenty-three men from the *Hagana* group were selected, commanded by Zvi Spector with a British officer, Major Anthony Palmer of the Middle East section of the SOE, attached as an observer. The group left Haifa port just after dawn on 18 May 1941 aboard the motor launch *Sea Lion*, a former Palestine Police harbour launch which had been commissioned by the Royal Navy. The group was divided into three sections that would operate independently in rubber boats launched from *Sea Lion* when it reached a certain point off the shore of Tripoli. Although the ship carried a special radio transmitter, strict wireless silence was to be observed during the passage.

Unknown to the group, RAF bombers had attacked Tripoli the previous night, with the result that the defenders were on high alert status. As *Sea Lion* disappeared over the horizon in Haifa Bay, a group of *Hagana* leaders stood silently watching. After several hours two short messages were received by radio giving position reports; then nothing. To this very day, despite exhaustive searches and countless investigations, nothing is known concerning the fate or whereabouts of *Sea Lion* or the men she carried. Their fate remains one of the war's unsolved mysteries. In fact, this mission has never been mentioned either in British reports of the time or in the history books. The only official document ever received from the British authorities was a short letter from GHQ Cairo dated 19 October 1941, addressed to Moshe Shertok, a prominent member of the Jewish Agency. In this letter GHQ advised that *Sea Lion* and its occupants were missing, presumed killed in action. Although the twenty-three men probably did not see any action, their endeavour became part of the tradition of Israel's naval Commandos.

After the war the *Palyam*, the naval section of the *Palmach* (the *Hagana*'s volunteer strike force) went into action against British shipping targets in retaliation for the Royal Navy's operations against Jewish immigrant ships bringing to Palestine survivors of the Holocaust. *Palmach* frogmen and underwater demolition experts blew up several harbour launches and damaged some of the larger transports that ferried the unfortunate immigrants (when the Royal Navy caught them) to detention camps in Cyprus.

During the 1948 War of Independence between Israel and the Arabs, the first IDF naval Commando operation was the blasting of the Syrian supply ship *Lino* in the port of Bari, Italy, shortly before she was due to set sail with a shipment of arms for Syria.

One of the most notable events of that war, however, was the sinking of the Egyptian Navy flagship *Emir Farouk* by IDF Commando teams employing ex-Italian Navy MTM-type explosive boats. These boats, which had seen action in the Mediterranean with the Italian 10th Light Flotilla, as mentioned in the previous chapter, were called 'Barchini'. Operated by a single man, the

5.20-metre, 1.5-ton MTM boat was powered by an Alfa Romeo 2500 95hp engine, giving a maximum speed of 63km/h. Its propeller and rudder were mounted as a single outboard unit which the pilot could lift in order to cross defensive netting guarding the harbours. The boat was armed with a 300kg bow-mounted explosive charge. MTM attacks had been carried out successfully by the Italian against British shipping in Suda Bay, Crete, Malta and, of course, Alexandria.

After the War of Independence, the naval Commandos were reconstituted and trained along the lines of the British SBS (Special Boat Service) with modern equipment and special training techniques to achieve the highest standards. The very best of the volunteers were subjected to rigorous selection tests so as to pick out the cream of this dedicated band. In some ways the criteria were even more stringent than those for the Israeli Air Force.

Over the years the Israeli naval Commandos became the aristocracy of the IDF, serving in many daring actions. But for many years their activities were a well-guarded secret. Although they operated behind enemy lines in several hit and run operations, especially in Lebanon and Syria, the first time they were mentioned in official reports was during the Six Day War of 1967, when a team of frogmen was launched into Alexandria harbour in Egypt from a submarine. Even though the mission failed and the team members were captured, it brought the naval Commandos into the headlines, although most of their exploits remained secret.

From 1968 to 1970, during the War of Attrition, the naval Commando came into its own, pulling off a number of astounding feats which are still talked about in professional circles. In the summer of 1969 the situation along the Suez Canal front had deteriorated considerably from the Israeli point of view: their positions were taking incessant Egyptian artillery fire, causing heavy losses to the Israeli soldiers manning the line. Egyptian Commando raids were also taking a toll at this time, and the IDF commanders decided that the initiative must be wrested from the Egyptians at once. One of the options was air attack along the Canal, but in order to achieve control over the operational area, some of the major Egyptian air defence systems had to be neutralized. One of these was Green Island, a fortified position situated three kilometres south of Port Ibrahim at the southern entrance to the Suez Canal.

The island had been built on a reef by the British early in the Second World War, to guard their strategic bases against the Axis in the Canal Zone. One hundred and forty-eight metres long and 40–70 metres wide, the island was surrounded by a concrete wall some 2.5 metres high. The fort consisted of a large courtyard surrounded by concrete buildings, with one square and five circular gun emplacements containing 85mm and 37mm anti-aircraft guns. For ground defence, fourteen fortified heavy machine-gun and 20mm automatic cannon emplacements had been constructed. On the northern side of the fort was a bridge built on ten pillars leading to a circular position on which a 5-metre-high building had been constructed to house an air defence radar with its antennae on the rooftop. More than 100 Egyptian troops, the majority gun crews, with Commandos acting as special backup, manned the fort, which was considered totally impregnable. This was the target assigned to a joint team of Commandos and naval Commandos. Just to ensure that they wouldn't have things too easy, the Egyptian Navy base of Ras Adabiya was only a few kilometres away, as were several Egyptian artillery positions on the western side of the Gulf of Suez, all within range.

Commanding the operation was a young naval officer, Lieutenant Colonel Zeev Almog, who at that time headed the naval Commandos; he would later become CO Israel Navy. The assault force of approximately twenty men, commanded by Captain Dov, was divided into two combat teams plus a third group which would set up a fire base on a small rock to the south of the target. There was also another force, commanded by Menahem Digli, which was in charge of the explosives, and Zeev Almog went along with them. Exhaustive training preceded the mission, a special model being constructed for briefing purposes, with all details of the fort updated as fast as real-time intelligence came in.

On the night of 19 July 1969, the assault force set off from the eastern shores of the Gulf of Suez in several rubber boats heading for their rendezvous point. The sea was calm with only a five-knot wind blowing; however, the rapid currents from the Suez Canal hampered the advance and caused some delay. The assault leader therefore decided to dive, but after fifteen minutes swimming under water, he found on surfacing for a position check that, instead of getting nearer to the objective, his men had been carried southwards by the heavy currents to a point some 600 metres from the island. Time was running short; the fire base team had already set up on the signal rock some 200 metres to the south. Changing course, the swimmers made up their time and reached the rock, which was just below the radar bunker position.

In complete silence the first combat team, six men in all with the commander leading, started to cut through the barbed wire defences surrounding the concrete wall at water level. The cutting took time, mainly due to the equipment being wet. While they worked, the men were hiding beneath the pillars of the bridge, up to their chests in water, and still undetected. On the bridge, only two metres above them, two Egyptian guards were pacing up and down, talking noisily. One of them lit a cigarette and threw the burning match down. It sizzled as it hit the water, while the attackers held their collective breath. Then the team leader, gripping one of the pillars tightly, ventured a look upwards. In the dim light he discerned a gap in the wire fence just to his right. Silently signalling his team, the leader and his cover mate aimed their automatic weapons at the two guards and squeezed, and the tense silence was broken by the sharp report of hot tracer bullets smashing into the hapless Egyptians. One of them fell to the ground; the other splashed into the water, his cigarette still burning.

The other members of the combat team were now in action, spraying the roof of the radar bunker with bullets, while from the south the fire base opened up, acting as a diversion and confusing the defenders, who, although fully alert, did not identify the direction of the attack and blasted away with all their weapons indiscriminately. Only seconds had passed, and the first combat team was climbing up the slippery, seaweed-covered wall; clinging like lizards to every niche and crevice, the men scrambled on to the concrete roof. Once on top, there was a momentary lull, and then the six-man team operated like clokwork: two men stormed the circular position, throwing grenades and quickly neutralizing it. The Egyptians were now intensifying their fire, although it still remained inaccurate. As he cleared the radar rooftop, the team leader came face to face with an Egyptian, who threw a hand-grenade in his direction, and a sliver of concrete from the explosion hit him on the head. He fell back, luckily into the arms of his men below. Made of stern stuff, he immediately got back on his feet; this time it was his turn to throw a grenade, blowing the Egyptian clear off the rooftop. Two others were later found dead at their machine-gun.

With the radar position secure, Captain Dov called in the demolition squad and they arrived at 0200. They had been delayed because of some trouble with their boats on the way. As they climbed up to the top of the fortress, there was some initial confusion because they had lost radio contact with Dov's force, and they were hit by enemy fire.

Meanwhile Digli ordered his team into action and they stormed the enemy positions, hitting an Egyptian ammunition dump with a lucky RPG hit and causing a tremendous ball of fire. Suddenly, out of the darkness came Captain Dov. He met Digli on the roof, where they also joined up with Almog, and the three of them started to get some order into the chaos.

The explosives squad, panting under their heavy load, clambered up the wall, helped by the men who were already there. From their positions they could see another battle in full swing, as the second assault team climbed up to the bridge, which was rather gruesomely lit up for them by a dead guard whose uniform was burning, and raced to their respective objectives.

The Egyptians were firing now at their maximum potential, tracer bullets tearing across the night sky, crossing and recrossing. Speed was essential, and the naval Commandos ducked and ran from cover to cover, firing short bursts of automatic fire against any source they detected. An officer clearing the square gun emplacement was hit in the neck and fell back. Just behind him was the captain leading the second combat team. Pausing momentarily to get his bearings before beginning the storming of the three outer positions, he was also hit by a burst of tracer coming from the courtyard below. Another man took over and urged the team forward, killing an Egyptian who emerged from a nearby hatch. Another, holding a live hand-grenade, was dispatched over the wall into the dark waters below, the grenade going off as he splashed.

Meanwhile the first team proceeded along the inner wall, mopping up the remaining positions; close to the southern tip of the fort, they had almost all the island under control, but as they descended a ladder leading down to the courtyard, one of them was shot dead. The others stormed into the Egyptians' quarters and the demolition experts placed their explosive charges as soon as the area was secured. Two more of the attackers were killed while storming the southern gun position.

The battle had now been going on for more than thirty minutes, and it was time to assemble the men for the withdrawal. Over the din of battle, orders were shouted calling them to assemble at the rendezvous point. The six dead and ten wounded were taken with them when they left the island at 0255. Seconds after they left there was a series of loud explosions as the demolition charges placed by the special squad went off. As soon as they had gone, the Egyptian artillery started to bombard the fort, pounding it for several hours after the Commandos had already reached the safety of the eastern shore. The Commando raid on Green Island was a complete success: the seemingly impregnable fortress was in ruins, never again to be used in its previous role.

Index